Adult Themes

GLOBAL EXPLOITATION CINEMAS

Series Editors
Johnny Walker, Northumbria University, UK
Austin Fisher, Bournemouth University, UK

Editorial Board
Tejaswini Ganti, New York University, USA
Joan Hawkins, Indiana University, USA
Kevin Heffernan, Southern Methodist University, USA
Ernest Mathijs, University of British Columbia, Canada
Constance Penley, University of California, Santa Barbara, USA
Eric Schaefer, Emerson College, USA
Dolores Tierney, University of Sussex, UK
Valerie Wee, National University of Singapore, Singapore

Adult Themes

British Cinema and the X Certificate in the Long 1960s

Edited by
Anne Etienne, Benjamin Halligan
and Christopher Weedman

BLOOMSBURY ACADEMIC
NEW YORK • LONDON • OXFORD • NEW DELHI • SYDNEY

BLOOMSBURY ACADEMIC
Bloomsbury Publishing Inc
1385 Broadway, New York, NY 10018, USA
50 Bedford Square, London, WC1B 3DP, UK
29 Earlsfort Terrace, Dublin 2, Ireland

BLOOMSBURY, BLOOMSBURY ACADEMIC and the Diana logo are
trademarks of Bloomsbury Publishing Plc

First published in the United States of America 2023

Cover design by Johnny Walker and Eleanor Rose
Cover image: The Amber Film Club on Frith Street in Soho, London, UK,
22nd May 1968. Photo © Maurice Kaye / Mirrorpix / Getty Images

A catalog record for this book is available from the Library of Congress.

ISBN: HB: 978-1-5013-7527-9
        ePDF: 978-1-5013-7526-2
        eBook: 978-1-5013-7528-6

Series: Global Exploitation Cinemas

Typeset by Integra Software Services Pvt. Ltd.
Printed and bound in Great Britain

To find out more about our authors and books visit www.bloomsbury.com
and sign up for our newsletters.

CONTENTS

PLATES

ACKNOWLEDGEMENTS

We collectively want to thank our contributors for their resilience as this book developed in challenging times. Thanks also to Sian Barber, James Chapman, Jane Giles, Sheldon Hall, Andrew Moor, Alison Peirse, Julian Petley, Vic Pratt, Laura Wilson and the staff of the British Board of Film Classification, the British Film Institute and the West Sussex Record Office for access to their archives, and permissions to reproduce some of the documents in this collection. A debt of gratitude must be extended to our editorial assistants Nicholas Krause and Ashley Quinn, who were instrumental in this book's promotional and indexing process. We are also grateful to our series editors Johnny Walker and Austin Fisher, as well as Katie Gallof and the staff at Bloomsbury for their support.

Ben would like to acknowledge the Centre for Film, Media, Discourse and Culture (and Fran Pheasant-Kelly), and colleagues in the Research Policy Unit and the Doctoral College, at the University of Wolverhampton. He would like to extend acknowledgements too to those people and organizations who have curated the kinds of films explored in this book: Abertoir (and Gaz Bailey), Aberystwyth Arts Centre (and Alan Hewson), the Bradford International Film Festival (and Tony Earnshaw), the Cardiff International Film Festival (and David Prothero), the Classic Film Society (Stonyhurst College), Eurotika! (and Pete Tombs and Andy Starke), the Flipside at BFI Southbank, Grimmfest (and Simeon Halligan), Home (and Jason Wood), the Leeds International Film Festival, the Manchester Film Festival, I Mille Occhi (and Sergio Grmek Germani and Olaf Möller), Moviedrome (and Alex Cox), the programmers at the Prince Charles Cinema and the Hampstead Everyman, and the 1980s staff and management of the Odeon Harrogate for their lax door policy. And he must acknowledge two late companions on his research travels in this area: Hilary Dwyer (1945–2020) and Tony Tenser (1920–2007).

Thankful nods from Anne to her fellow research members at LIBEX for their invaluable, ongoing foray into censorship and freedom of expression.

Christopher would like to acknowledge his wife, Eudora, and daughter, Elenore, as well as his colleagues in the Department of English at Middle Tennessee State University. He is also indebted to graduate students Christopher Anders, Brandon Black, Nicholas Krause and Ashley Quinn, whose questions, insights and enthusiasm in his seminar on British X certificate films informed his work on this volume.

Introduction:

'Passed As Only Suitable for Exhibition to Adult Audiences: X'

Anne Etienne, Benjamin Halligan and Christopher Weedman

On the eve of his appointment as secretary of the British Board of Film Censors (BBFC) in May 1958, John Trevelyan declared that the X certificate would facilitate a new mature era in British cinema: 'Now there is practically no adult subject which could not be considered for an "X" certificate if treated with sincerity and restraint' (cited in Aldgate 1995: 39). Trevelyan's pronouncement specifically aligned the X certificate with adult themes treated with artistic honesty.[1] Within a few short years, such vaunted filmmakers as Lindsay Anderson, Jack Clayton, Karel Reisz, Tony Richardson and John Schlesinger would embody this principled conception of X certificate cinema. Arguably being the first directors in British film history to provide the 'adults only' rating with a sheen of cultural prestige and respectability, their internationally acclaimed New Wave features 'were generally seen by critics of the time as a step forward for British cinema, a move towards a mature, intelligent engagement with contemporary British social life and a welcome breath of fresh air after the conformist entertainment provided by studio-bound British filmmakers in the first part of the 1950s' (Hutchings 2002: 146–7). However, studies like Peter Hutchings's *Hammer and Beyond: The British Horror Film* (1993), Leon Hunt's *British Low Culture: From*

Safari Suits to Sexploitation (1998) and Sian Barber's *Censoring the 1970s: The BBFC and the Decade that Taste Forgot* (2011) have shown that the X certificate continued to be routinely courted by exploitation filmmakers, who viewed it as 'a badge of honour' (Barber 2012: 26). The commerciality of the X certificate's risqué character may best be gauged by Hammer Films' eagerness to market their early sci-fi horror features as *The Quatermass Xperiment* (Val Guest 1955) and *X the Unknown* (Leslie Norman 1956), which, in the case of the former, was accompanied by publicity material encouraging cinema house managers to 'Xploit the Xcitement' of the film (Chibnall 2012: 47–8; Hearn 2011: 8). A contested terrain for gate-keepers and gate-pushers alike, British X certificate cinema was mired in controversy from its appearance in 1951.

Newspapers regularly boasted headlines with urgent pleas from conservative commentators, government officials and religious pressure groups to vanquish graphic images of sex, horror and violence from the nation's cinema screens. By the end of the 1950s, as the taboo excesses of Hammer horror and sexually provocative features like *The Flesh Is Weak* (Don Chaffey 1957), *Passport to Shame* (Alvin Rakoff 1958) and *Room at the Top* (Clayton 1959) were generating curiosity and ticket sales at the UK box office, the press condemned British filmmakers for their recent efforts to align the 'adults only' rating with sensationalist entertainment. For instance, *The Coventry Evening Telegraph* bemoaned the incessant

> wave of horror films involving things from under the earth, the sea, and from other planets, Draculas, Frankensteins and various other monsters. These, with a number of nudist films and the usual 'exposés' of low life, were and are a blot on the cinema, worms eating into the bud of a plant which thoughtful film makers and perceptive filmgoers are trying so hard to cultivate.
>
> ('The Best Pictures' 1959)

During the 1960s, thematically bold and adventurous British cinema grew to become largely synonymous with the X certificate, mirroring the sociocultural and moral transformations of the decade as discussed by Anthony Aldgate in *Censorship and the Permissive Society: British Cinema and Theatre 1955–1965* (1995: 33–62) as well as in Richard Farmer et al's *Transformation and Tradition in 1960s British Cinema* (2019: 1–7). Often based on the works of writers associated with kitchen sink realism, the British New Wave films of Anderson (*This Sporting Life*, 1963), Clayton (*Room at the Top*), Richardson (*Look Back in Anger*, 1959; *A Taste of Honey*, 1961; and *The Loneliness of the Long Distance Runner*, 1962) and Schlesinger (*A Kind of Loving*, 1962 and *Billy Liar*, 1963) offered cynical and unromanticized depictions of provincial life allied with a new frankness in tackling sexual mores, which reinvigorated and politicized British filmmaking. At the same time, the general liberalization that was afforded by the X certificate in the 1960s was also exploited by a parade of less idealistic filmmakers, studios and distributors intent on producing titillating and sensational entertainment rather than socially engaged art.

By the close of that decade, and following the heyday of the British New Wave, the Swinging Sixties had come to be mirrored by a 'swinging' (often London-centred) adult cinema that extended into the mid-1970s: X films by both native and foreign directors pushed back the boundaries of the representations of sex and violence; they seemed to relish breaking with societal norms, and so recalibrated cinema as an occasionally dangerous, potentially transgressive and often intellectual art form. Navigating between arthouse and exploitation cinema, directors such as Anderson (*if ...*, 1968 and *O Lucky Man!*, 1973), Michelangelo Antonioni (*Blow-Up*, 1966), Donald Cammell and Nicolas Roeg (*Performance*, 1970), Peter Collinson (*The Penthouse*, 1967; *Up the Junction*, 1968; *The Long Day's Dying*, 1968; *Fright*, 1971; *Straight on Till Morning*, 1972; and *Innocent Bystanders*, 1972), Lewis Gilbert (*Alfie*, 1966; *Friends*, 1971; and *Paul and Michelle*, 1974), Mike Hodges (*Get Carter*, 1971), Stanley Kubrick (*Lolita*, 1962 and *A Clockwork Orange*, 1971), Joseph Losey (*The Criminal*, 1960; *Eve*, 1962; *The Damned*, 1963; *The Servant*, 1963; *King & Country*, 1964; *Boom!*, 1968; and *Secret Ceremony*, 1968), Roman Polanski (*Repulsion*, 1965 and *Cul-de-Sac*, 1966), Michael Reeves (*Revenge of the Blood Beast*, 1966; *The Sorcerers*, 1967; and *Witchfinder General*, 1968), Schlesinger (*Darling*, 1965 and *Sunday Bloody Sunday*, 1971), Jerzy Skolimowski (*Deep End*, 1971) and Michael Winner (*West 11*, 1963; *The System*, 1964; *I'll Never Forget What's'isname*, 1967; and *The Nightcomers*, 1971) met in the X category, where they became odd bedfellows for the censors. In this sense, British X certificate cinema of this era may be characterized as one of adult themes. By the dawn of the 1970s, this category of films was well equipped to engage with the turbulence to come, as the dreams of the welfare state, and peace, love and harmony turned to strife, strikes and unrest – that new decade, since posited as a 'hangover from the sixties' and characterized by Andy Beckett as 'when the lights went out' (2010: 2). As a whole, X certificate films from the late 1950s through the mid-1970s seem to have taken on an essential role of tracking, exploring, exploiting and mythologizing an emergent society.[2]

For this reason, the volume focuses on the long 1960s rather than the lifetime of the X certificate (1951–82) to question to what extent, and how and why, X films can be understood as the outriders, agitators, nay-sayers and voyeurs of this emerging contemporary society. This periodization is roughly aligned to the historian Arthur Marwick's 'long 1960s', which he describes as spanning 'the late 1950s to the middle 1970s' (2005: 780), first postulated in his seminal study *The Sixties* (1998).[3] In this respect, our 'long 1960s' start in the immediate wake of the winding down of a post-war culture of austerity (with, for example, the televised coronation of Queen Elizabeth II in 1953, and the ending of food rationing in 1954), and the UK's grappling with its diminished, post-Empire position in Cold War-era geopolitics (acutely felt in the Suez Canal Crisis of 1956 and Prime Minister Harold Macmillan's 'Wind of Change' speech of 1960 recognizing decolonization). As contributors to this volume argue, this historical juncture is particularly marked in British cinema by an emphasis on a changing society – especially in terms of new youth cultures, variously presented as hedonistic, criminal, disenchanted and relatively affluent. When Trevelyan took up the position of Board secretary of the BBFC in 1958, he understood his role as that of a modernizer and so was able to manage this new, unruly British cinema, often via a resort to the X certificate ('John Trevelyan' 1958: 1; Trevelyan 1958: 8). The X was increasingly deployed not as a matter of quarantining a film, or warding off potential viewers, but of accepting and approving for distribution films exemplifying a freedom of artistic expression concomitant with the sense of an adult cultural medium. Since the spirit of the freedoms of the 1960s continued to resonate in British cinema well into the 1970s – and with Trevelyan's 1971 successor, Stephen Murphy, grappling with that legacy – we end our periodization in the years that are understood to have precipitated Murphy's departure from the BBFC in 1975 (see Plate 1).

Building upon a significant body of scholarship on British cinema between the 1950s and 1970s, as found in the pioneering criticism of Raymond Durgnat (1971) and John Hill (1986) to the more recent reappraisals of Duncan Petrie, Melanie Williams and Laura Mayne (2022) and Melvyn Stokes, Matthew Jones and Emma Pett (2022), this collection is the first to specifically chart X certificate British cinema across the long (and Swinging) Sixties.[4] A number of the films explored, from some of the most acclaimed filmmakers of this generation, are now deemed masterpieces. The X certificates awarded by the BBFC did little to deter audiences – and were even considered by the filmmakers to be a licence to go ever further, or a teasing promise (when seen in promotional advertising like the iconic yet highly controversial image of Sue Lyon wearing sunglasses and sucking a lollipop on the poster for *Lolita*) of the provocative and sometimes troubling content to come. Instead, the 'adults only' rating tended to attract the exact demographic it was originally designed to protect: underage teenagers, who often found 'forbidden fruit films' such as *Saturday Night and Sunday Morning* and *A Taste of Honey* to be, in the retrospective words of one patron, 'sexy, when puberty was approaching' (cited in Stokes, Jones, and Pett 2022: 105). Other lesser-known films, from often forgotten or disreputable filmmakers, are anything but masterpieces and, at times, could be found playing 'flea pit cinemas' with 'seedy reputations' (26).[5] Their X certificate ratings were a matter of punitive negotiation with the BBFC, and with the censor's sharp scissors in near-constant use, as discussed by Adrian Smith in relation to the Board's handling of the Compton Group's sexploitation film *Secrets of a Windmill Girl* (Arnold Louis Miller 1966). And yet such films remain as provocative cultural artefacts of their times, and deserving of critical attention, or even rediscovery.

'Please Receive the following Films for Censorship'

The X certificate was all the more contentious because, as chapters will highlight, it provoked tensions between the BBFC and local authorities. From its beginnings in 1912, the role of the BBFC was to 'protect the public from any risk of the production of objectionable pictures' (McKenna 1912), but its authority was not officially recognized by county councils (that dealt with cinema licences) before 1920. Since then, the certificate was a requirement in public cinema licences, the system of film submission became standardized and the classification categories were established (Trevelyan 1967: 126–7).[6]

The protection of children was given as the underlying principle of the certification system, which contained three categories marking the age division in the 1960s: U, for films suitable for all; A (for 'adult'), for films suitable for children under the age of sixteen if accompanied by a parent; X, for films with adult themes restricted to patrons above the age of sixteen (Hunnings 1967: 140–6; Trevelyan 1977: 82).[7] Pertinent to our study of the X as contested territory are the H and AA certificates. The H certificate (for 'horrific'), in use between 1932 and 1951, proved an apt category for horror films that contained disturbing and frightening scenes. In 1950, however, the Departmental Committee on Children and the Cinema (better known as the Wheare Committee) recommended that an X certificate be added for content 'unsuitable for children under sixteen, even accompanied by an adult' (Hunnings 1967: 143; 'Cert "X" is O.K.' 1950). For BBFC Board Secretary Arthur Watkins, the new X certificate would permit '"unquestionably adult" films to be passed instead of certificates being refused' (*The Yorkshire Evening Post,* 14 December 1950).

Despite Trevelyan's relaxed attitude, viewing the BBFC's role as 'a kind of barometer of public taste for the industry' as far as the X was concerned, his stance was still conservative compared to other countries which he described as immersed by the 'tidal wave of sex obsession spreading through Europe' (1970: 26–7). For instance, *The Keeler Affair* (Robert Spafford 1963), based on the Profumo scandal, had been banned in Britain while it was passed as 18 in France (Bier 2000: 16), and Julian Upton uses further examples to show that 'the existing ratings system seem[ed] untenable' (2017: 65). By the end of the decade, as a result of the increasing explicitness in the treatment of adult material, 219 films were awarded an X in 1969, more

than the other two certificates combined (Trevelyan 1970: 28). As debates
around permissiveness and pornography in the cinema signalled the need
for a solution that would satisfy gate-keepers without hampering the
industry – and possibly the expression of a daring cinéma d'auteurs – the
BBFC launched a new system. From 1970, the sixteen age boundary was
revisited, so that the AA certificate forbade access to spectators under
fourteen, while the viewing age of an X film was raised to eighteen – thereby
identifying them respectively as the teenage and the adult certificates (Phelps
1975: 49, 103; Trevelyan 1977: 62–3; Upton 2017). Until a new and
completely overhauled BBFC classification system eliminated both ratings
in 1982 (Barber 2011: 137), the X certificate became steadily less centred
around Trevelyan's conception of the 'adults only' rating as a framework
for auteurs to make adult-themed films with artistic honesty and, as Lucy
Brett explains, more often found itself largely the province of films desiring
to go beyond the pale of good taste (2017: 239), as discussed by Benjamin
Halligan in the final chapter.

Placing the focus on the long 1960s therefore enables the authors in this
collection to explore a key period in the evolution of the X certificate, which
became a useful tag for sexually charged films and films containing disturbing
and violent images that were destined for an adult audience. In addition, the
decade bears the stamp of Trevelyan for two reasons. First, Trevelyan was
the first secretary of the Board to be selected by the film trade associations
in 1958, rather than by the president of the Board (Trevelyan 1967: 127).
Since then, the responsibilities of the BBFC have been shared: the president
designing the broad general policy, and the secretary being in charge of
the executive. Second, his take on censorship not only responded to the
liberalizing mores of the Swinging Sixties but was also influenced by his desire
to encourage the bold influx of directors: artistic quality and the integrity
of the filmmakers proved a decisive aspect when awarding certificates. As
a result, Trevelyan's memoirs indicate that he favoured the work (and the
company) of British and international filmmakers such as Joseph Losey, for
whom he had 'admiration and affection' (1977: 209), Dušan Makavejev,
who 'has since acquired an international reputation' (116), Stanley Kubrick
and his 'brilliant analysis of violence in contemporary society' (128–9),
the 'outstanding film-maker' Roman Polanski (122), John Schlesinger, of
admirable 'creative talent' (208) and even filmmaking collaborators Andy
Warhol and Paul Morrissey.[8]

According to a memorandum submitted by the BBFC to the 1966 Joint
Select Committee on Censorship of the Theatre, 'the Board has no rules'
(Trevelyan 1967: 128). Such an admission may be interpreted as a refusal
to itemize forbidden topics or a way to avoid being caught in contradictory
decisions – as similar cases had befallen and publicly embarrassed Lords
Chamberlain since the turn of the century – and indeed it enabled the Board
to 'change policy without any announcement' (130). At a time when control

over the stage was foundering and Prime Minister Harold Wilson's Labour government was aware of the transfer of material across media and the discrepancies it created, the BBFC may also have wanted to dispel unhelpful comparisons with television. Since the passing of the 1964 Television Act, the Independent Television Authority was required to draw up a code in relation to violence in programme content and for the protection of children – a central concern for the BBFC, as evidenced by the evolution of the X certificate – thereby aligning standards with 'those to which the BBC must operate' (Le Cheminant 1967). Instead of a stringent and cumbersome protocol, the BBFC viewed their approach as 'a general working policy at any one time': the flexible and evolving process takes into account the examiners' 'divergent views' and the decision aims to reflect what 'would be the opinion of most reasonable and intelligent people' (Trevelyan 1967: 128, 129).

Trevelyan heralded a new era in terms of the films' assessment apparatus that earned him the epithet of 'the film censor with the diplomatic touch' in his *Times* obituary ('Obituary' 1986). At the core of most chapters in this volume, recourse to BBFC files of this period illustrates a multi-layered discursive and often informal process which would involve a variation of the following actions. The bulk of the examiners' work was to view and assess completed films, and each case file contains the formal submission of a film for certification, with a cover sheet emblazoned 'Please Receive the following Films for Censorship'. Sheaths of notes (sometimes unsigned) for internal use only would be produced on each film by any two of the five examiners: some were messily written (presumably scribbled in semi-dark and at speed, during BBFC screenings), while others clearly originate from later public screenings as they comment on audience composition (Aldgate 1995: 45–7). A summative response would then be drafted to filmmakers, listing cuts requested on an 'Exception Form' – evidence can be found there that Trevelyan's diplomatic skills were at work in conciliating with the more outraged examiners, as well as with the filmmakers when he engaged in a lengthy back-and-forth correspondence around requests. However, and though not compulsory this had been a practice since the first iteration of the Board in 1912, most British filmmakers would also send their scripts for pre-production advice.[9] This preliminary correspondence between Trevelyan and filmmakers (producers and directors) would often expand to discussions, the main points of which were also recorded in the files. Trevelyan was a particularly hands-on secretary as he also intervened during the production and editing phases, so that case files may contain comments on early assembly screenings of films. As noted in his memoirs, he 'used to see "rough-cuts" or "fine-cuts" of their films with them [Schlesinger and Losey], and we used to have long talks afterwards ... they regarded me more as an advisor or consultant than a censor' (1977: 209). Finally and on occasion, Trevelyan would pen a letter thanking the filmmaker for their troubles, lightly apologizing for BBFC interference, or suggesting that the film – now classified for general release – is all the better for the BBFC's intervention.

'The Less We Have of Groups of "Queers" in Bars, and Clubs and Elsewhere the Better'

Of all the subjects visible in British X certificate cinema of this period, it is striking that male homosexuality seems almost entirely absent as a main, formal focus. Across the long 1960s, X certificate films did not shy away from subtextual homosexual themes, but they depicted them with varying degrees of visibility and understanding. Homosexual characters and subcultures tended to be depicted as being subsumed into outwardly respectable modes of life such as Dirk Bogarde's married barrister Melville Farr in *Victim* (Basil Dearden 1961) and (arguably) the actor's dutiful manservant Barrett in *The Servant*; clear but unspoken 'types', as seen in Stephen Bourne's coded readings of Murray Melvin's 'lonely' textile design student Geoffrey Ingham in *A Taste of Honey*,[10] Brock Peters's 'warm' and 'gentle' jazz musician Johnny in *The L-Shaped Room* (Bryan Forbes 1962), and Dudley Sutton's 'kind and understanding' motorcyclist Pete in *The Leather Boys* (Sidney J. Furie 1964) ([1996] 2016: 148, 167 and 178); and over-the-top caricatures either safely quarantined through the casting of avowedly heterosexual actors such as Richard Burton and Rex Harrison's bickering hairdressers Harry and Charles in *Staircase* (Stanley Donen 1969) or employed as satirical embodiments of the transgressive sexual mores of the 'permissive society' such as Harry Andrews's ostentatious businessman Ed in *Entertaining Mr Sloane* (Douglas Hickox 1970). Likewise, homosexual concerns could be found in moments of general homosexual ambiences, as well as subplots involving supporting or briefly glimpsed minor characters in high-profile releases such as *Darling*, *Deadfall* (Forbes 1968), *if ...*, the two Ken Russell films *Women in Love* (1969) and *The Music Lovers* (1971), *Goodbye Gemini* (Alan Gibson 1970), *Villain* (Michael Tuchner 1971) and *Zee & Co.* (Brian G. Hutton 1972); or through quick asides, innuendos or intimations in films such as *Serious Charge* (Terence Young 1959), *No Love for Johnnie* (Ralph Thomas 1961), *The Family Way* (Roy Boulting 1966), *Two Gentlemen Sharing* (Ted Kotcheff 1969) and *Performance*. Two Oscar Wilde biopics unavoidably dealt with the subject too: *Oscar Wilde* (Gregory Ratoff 1960) and *The Trials of Oscar Wilde* (Ken Hughes 1960). BBFC responses to these films were variable, and predicated (as noted below) on their sense of artistic worth – but generally the BBFC enabled the films to be distributed in some form.

Darling captures casual homophobic comments via a vox pops scene, includes camp aristocrats seen taking advantage of 'boys' at a party (and where their predatory sexuality is racialized too), a then-daring visual repurposing of a portrait of the Queen, a gay photographer and scenes of casual gay pick-ups around a group of homosexual friends in Capri. However, the film is so predominantly heterosexual in its focus that all of these elements, groundbreaking in themselves, seem little more than fleeting details in its panorama of modern society. The homosexuality of *Villain* is bolder, and in this sense very notable for this period, but remains problematic: the sexual encounters include the same kind of violence that the protagonist Vic Dakin, Richard Burton's Ronnie Kray-like London gangster, visits on his victims, and are introduced with a sinister electronic score. His boyfriend, Wolfie (Ian McShane), is also depicted working as a pimp, procuring both males and females (including his own girlfriend, despite her protests) for swinging aristocratic parties. Trevelyan suggested that the homosexual element could be cut 'entirely' from *Villain*, so as to avoid 'stimulation': 'I have in mind these horrible cases that we get occasionally where naked young men are found dead, tied up and mutilated' (cited in Simkin 2012: 83). Moreover, Trevelyan's general guidance, drawing on his examiners' positions but echoing too the commentary on the decriminalization of homosexuality (see below), was: '[w]e feel that the more we can see of the characters going about their daily lives in association with other people who are not "queers", the less we have of groups of "queers" in bars, and clubs and elsewhere the better' (cited in Hargreaves 2012: 58). Simkin notes that *Goodbye Gemini* was cut for homosexual content as was, '[r]ather oddly, *Eskimo Nell* [Martin Campbell 1975, which] had a cut described thus: "Remove the word "Vaseline" on Scrabble Board & shot of homosexual's face as he looks at it"' (Simkin 2012: 83). One could assume that the subject matter of these two films (Swinging London youths and exploitation filmmaking, respectively), along with Trevelyan's serial killers, and 'bars, and clubs and elsewhere', was insufficiently exalted for a BBFC X acceptance of gay matters. Luchino Visconti's Italo-French co-production *Death in Venice* (1971), on the other hand, which obsessively concerned same-sex desire, received an AA certificate and a Royal premiere on 1 March 1971, with Queen Elizabeth II and Princess Anne meeting both Visconti and the film's star, Bogarde, prior to the screening.[11]

Historians of British cinema have tended to mount subtextual analyses or identified a 'queering' of 'norms' in order to identify often circumstantial or liminal evidence of cultures of male sexual difference.[12] Such readings seek to reorientate the deeper meanings of these films, aligned to wider debates about representation and identity in popular culture. However, in the light of work on sexual fluidity by Jane Ward (2015), they now seem somewhat deterministic in their binary categorizations. Sexual ambiguity could, after all, simply be taken as sexual ambiguity rather than palimpsest-like expediency on the part of sexual fugitives. Some films of the period embraced such ambiguity, albeit sometimes via elements of trans characterizations which are configured as gender-ambiguous, such as *Cul-de-Sac, Goodbye Gemini* and *Girl Stroke Boy* (Bob Kellett 1971). Others went farther by suggesting fluid sexual orientations such as Helmut Berger's bisexual portrayal of Dorian Gray in *Il dio chiamato Dorian* (*Das Bildnis des Dorian Gray/Dorian Gray*, Massimo Dallamano 1970). Set against the backdrop of Swinging London, and freely invoking Oscar Wilde to indicate scandalous sexual nonconformity, this Italo-West German-UK co-production from British exploitation producer Harry Alan Towers includes a dream-like sequence on a yacht where Dorian leaves the erotic embraces of two bisexual women before getting into a shower with aristocratic libertine Lord Henry Wotton (Herbert Lom), who lathers Dorian's shoulders with soap just before the camera zooms out through a porthole. This implied initiation into same-sex acts is immediately followed by another brief scene, where Dorian cruises the harbour docks for male sailors, including a young Black man with whom he later exchanges homoerotic glances in a public lavatory. Nevertheless, this absence of a formal focus on male homosexuality in the X film culture of the long 1960s is all the more surprising, since the 1957 Wolfenden Report's recommendation for the partial decriminalization of homosexuality had come into effect with the Sexual Offences Act of 1967 – albeit begrudgingly, on the part of the British state (Davies 1975: 120–4; Weeks [1981] 1992: 239–44).[13] There was, therefore, no legal basis for homophobic censorship beyond 1967. However, Trevelyan's urgings to effectively banish homosexual figures closely parallel the general establishment consensus on the matter at this point; even the reforming champion of the Sexual Offences Act of 1967, Arthur Gore, 8th Earl of Arran, would advise, in the House of Lords, that those 'for whom the prison doors are now open' should

> [...] show their thanks by comporting themselves quietly and with dignity. This is no occasion for jubilation; certainly not for celebration. Any form of ostentatious behaviour, now or in the future, any form of public flaunting, would be utterly distasteful and would, I believe, make the sponsors of the Bill regret that they have done what they have done. Homosexuals must continue to remember that while there may be nothing bad in being a homosexual, there is certainly nothing good.
>
> (Gore 1967)

Rare exceptions to the BBFC's position included *Sunday Bloody Sunday*, in the figure of a gay, middle-aged doctor played by Peter Finch, and with the filmmakers seemingly making up for homosexual invisibility through a relatively prolonged shot of two men kissing; and the semi-documentary *A Bigger Splash* (Jack Hazan 1973), which offered an immersion in the world of artist David Hockney, described as 'respond[ing] to his gay "stigma" by challenging social and aesthetic conventions in life and art' (Babuscio 1977: 42). In both a 1976 essay for *Gay Left* and the 1977 scholarly collection

Gays and Film, Richard Dyer finds rich material in European and North American cinemas, but barely anything from the UK.[14] He expresses frustration at the proliferation of homosexual stereotypes in films from both sides of the Atlantic, despite their limited progressive potential in a heteronormative mainstream, and the inadequacy of any counter movement towards 'rounded gay characters' – a category of inadequacy that seems to include *Sunday Bloody Sunday* for Dyer, whose homosexual protagonist he described as embodying 'mature resignation' (1977: 36). Instead, Dyer calls for 'the development of positively valued gay types' (1976: 11). Dyer's intervention would later be validated by research into the reception of 1960s gay British films by gay, and mostly young, cinemagoers; Stokes, Jones and Pett conclude that '[t]he 1960s may have witnessed the first stirrings of a movement to represent gayness more fairly and sympathetically in British films, but both the films themselves and many of those who watched them [often with some bafflement] still had a long way to go' (2022: 63).

The beginnings of a renaissance in gay visibility would not occur until the mid- to late-1970s, in terms of some serious grapplings with societal prejudices (as with Ron Peck's 1978 drama *Nighthawks*) and a full embrace of the 'otherness' of homosexual subcultures (most particularly in the work of Derek Jarman, notably 1976's *Sebastiane*, co-directed with Paul Humfress).[15] We speculate that producers, across the turn of the 1970s, simply remained unwilling to invest in pronounced gay subjects, fearing little to no audience and poor financial returns. Nevertheless, other cultural factors may have mitigated against, or stunted or delayed, the development of a gay British cinema during this period as well. These factors ranged on the spectrum from homophobic outrages from the tabloid press, coupled with the ascendency of British conservatism as a backlash to 1968 and the 'permissive society', to the consequences of such moralism in daily life. Of this time, Jarman recalled:

I was put up against the wall there many years ago by a violent gang who I thought were queerbashing. I was walking back home to Earl's Court from a showing of my film *Sebastiane*, nothing more exciting, when I was jumped on. Only the fact that I was middle-class, white and had a film on at The Gate [Cinema, Notting Hill] stopped a verbal assault – 'You fucking queer' – becoming physical. This gang were the police.
(Jarman and Christie 1993: 23)

The courts were seemingly equally lacking in sympathy: Mary Whitehouse successfully prosecuted the *Gay News* (and a contributing author, James Kirkup) in 1977 after their publication of a homoerotic poem about Jesus Christ, on the grounds of blasphemy (Nash 2017).

Consequently, there is a lack of material that would enable the inclusion of a chapter on male homosexuality, as identified as a main, formal focus of British filmmaking, within the historical scope of this study. Conversely, female homosexuality appears to have been a subject less troubling to the British establishment of the 1960s. Same-sex acts between women are present in films of this period – albeit reconfigured as a kink for heterosexual male titillation, particularly, as Claire Henry argues in a chapter within this volume, by Hammer Film Productions, once the popular horror film company began to financially flounder in the 1970s.

Exploring the X

The chapters in this collection engage with a body of X certificate films (lesser-known features or unexplored aspects of well-known films) to explore the limits of the permissive society from across arthouse and exploitation forms of British cinema, via mainstream studio films like *Alfie* and *Zee & Co*. In so doing, they illustrate the cultural, social and commercial value of both forms of production and the ways in which they sometimes merge due to fragile boundaries or the marketing strategies employed to promote them. In order to highlight the evolution of the culture of British X certificate cinema, and draw conclusions that will reframe this period of British cinema history, the volume adopts a chronological structure, alternating discourses on sexuality, violence and horror, or – in some cases – combining them. In their chapters, the contributors employ a variety of critical methodologies and exploit sources ranging from newly discovered archival material to personal interviews and promotional items. As an apt opener to the volume's chronological scope, Kim Newman's chapter traces the transgressive patterns of a cycle of sado-erotic thrillers and horror films that he dubs 'Green Penguin' cinema. An intriguing generic synthesis of gothic horror, crime and mystery conventions, Newman finds the imprint of Green Penguin cinema in a large number of 1960s and 1970s X certificate films, ranging from *Strip Tease Murder* (Ernest Morris 1961) to *Frightmare* (Pete Walker 1974). Green Penguin themes and styles sometimes trickled down to films granted lower age classifications, which can be seen in the A and AA certificates respectively awarded to *The Very Edge* (Cyril Frankel 1963) and *I Start Counting* (David Greene 1970). This provides some indication that an X sensibility permeated a wider group of British films during the permissive era.

This blurring of boundaries was also indicative of the films of Raymond Stross, as discussed by Christopher Weedman. An independent producer of self-consciously controversial dramas that straddled the line between arthouse and sensationalist cinema, Stross was among the first British filmmakers – apart from Hammer Films – to understand both the narrative freedoms and commercial possibilities that the X certificate afforded. After charting the evolution of the producer's career and persistent interest in exploring contentious social and sexual issues, Weedman traces the censorship history and reception of Stross's prostitution exposé *The Flesh Is Weak*, which was banned by the Watch Committee in the provincial seaside town of Worthing in September 1957. The desire of late 1950s British filmmakers to push the envelope in terms of sex and violence was not confined to subject matter alone. Sarah Street's analysis of Eastmancolor cinematography suggests that in *Horrors of the Black Museum* (Arthur Crabtree 1959) and *Peeping Tom* (Michael Powell 1960) the bold use of colour – and red in particular – foregrounds an artistic tension between the filmmakers' desire to both explore the aesthetic possibilities of colour and heighten the level of realistic graphic violence on screen. In the process, the films created a transgressive visual style that would become synonymous with the X certificate through much of its existence.

Looking at British New Wave cinema, Simon Lee reconsiders the seminal working-class drama *Saturday Night and Sunday Morning* with an emphasis on how the film's Czech-born director Karel Reisz acted as a mediator, who negotiated the occasionally conflicting objectives of the producers, writer Alan Sillitoe and the BBFC. Lee contends that while the film's producers were eager to capitalize on the film's daring sexual content, Sillitoe was instead intent on ensuring that neither the producers nor the BBFC would soften the subversive socialist rhetoric of the story's rebellious protagonist Arthur Seaton, who, like his narrative proxy Sillitoe, did not want to 'let the bastards grind you down'.

In his analysis of Stanley Kubrick's 1962 screen adaptation of *Lolita*, James Fenwick tackles the problematic sexual mores of the 1960s by offering a new perspective to previous studies. The chapter concerns itself with the correspondence between Kubrick and Canon L. J. Collins, the founder of the UK-based activist religious group Christian Action, who unequivocally objected to the director's intention of filming the novel's inflammatory story of a sexually exploitative relationship between an adult and a child. Drawing upon both archival evidence and recent allegations surrounding the making of the film, Fenwick demonstrates how the illicit depictions of sexuality afforded by the X certificate, in the case of *Lolita*, continue to reverberate more than half a century later. Kevin Flanagan addresses this theme of corrupted youths, this time in films that show them as moral and legal transgressors. He explores the cultural tension of bohemianism and paternalism found in a series of X certificate films about pre-Swinging London youth subcultures, including *Beat Girl* (Edmond T. Gréville 1960), *That Kind of Girl* (Gerry O'Hara 1963) and *London in the Raw* (Arnold Louis Miller 1964), but best exemplified by *The Party's Over*. Although made in 1963, *The Party's Over* was withheld from distribution until 1965 as the film's director, Guy Hamilton, endured a protracted dispute with Trevelyan and the BBFC over the film's look at bohemian youths imbibing in alcohol, jazz and sex, which culminates in both death and implied necrophilia. Assessing the censorship negotiations and press coverage surrounding *The Party's Over*, Flanagan argues that the film embodied the era's paternalistic cultural anxieties about American popular culture subverting the sensibilities of metropolitan youth.

Second-wave feminism burgeoned in the 1960s when the sexual revolution (aided by the access to oral contraception) was accompanied by reforms that would affect women's lives and rights (for instance, the revision of the Married Women's Property Act in 1964 or the 1967 Abortion Act). Three chapters discuss different aspects of the representation of women across arthouse, mainstream and exploitation cinema. Moya Luckett investigates the permissive attitudes towards female sexuality in a strain of mid- to late 1960s women-centred films such as *Darling, The Knack ... and How to Get It* (Richard Lester 1965), *The Pleasure Girls* (Gerry O'Hara 1965), *Her Private Hell* (Norman J. Warren 1968) and *Joanna* (Michael Sarne 1968), which highlight how the era's alluring depictions of young women's urban chic lifestyles and liberated sexuality were largely mediatized constructs. As Luckett contends, these films capitalized on the type of risqué content promised by the X certificate and, at the same time, were part of a larger cultural discourse surrounding issues of consumerism, femininity and modernity, which remain integral to the mythology of Swinging London. Adrian Smith guides us through the seedy world of British sexploitation cinema in his discussion of *Secrets of a Windmill Girl*. Consulting newly found archival materials related to the production, distribution and reception of the 1966 film and its retrospective portrayal of the nude showgirls that once headlined the Windmill Theatre, Smith reveals the sensationalist promotional and exhibition strategies utilized by independent distributors like Michael Klinger and Tony Tenser's Compton Group in the making and release of sexploitation films during the Swinging Sixties. Lucy Bolton examines the representation of middle-aged women's sexual desires from a wide chronological angle, the late 1950s through the early 1970s, in X certificate films such as *Room at the Top*, *The Roman Spring of Mrs Stone* (José Quintero 1961) and *Zee & Co*. Each film presents the lives of women subjected to social criticism, rejection and ridicule for expressing yearnings deemed, at the time, to be taboo for women of their age. These portraits are contrasted with Shelley Winters's trailblazing performance as Ruby in *Alfie*, where she garners respect for expressing and revelling in carnal desires that are off-limits to her female contemporaries. In order to understand the complexities surrounding the cultural reactions to middle-aged women's sexuality, Bolton turns to BBFC discussions, critical reviews and scholarship related to the star personas of Winters, Vivien Leigh, Simone Signoret and Elizabeth Taylor.

While Luckett and Bolton show the yearnings and challenges for women of all ages in the 1960s, Claire Henry's chapter suggests how female characters challenged (and rarely yearned for) male authority figures in Hammer's 'Karnstein trilogy' of lesbian vampire films *The Vampire Lovers*

(Roy Ward Baker 1970), *Lust for a Vampire* (Jimmy Sangster 1971) and *Twins of Evil* (John Hough 1971). She analyses how the studio took full advantage of the BBFC's new willingness to permit them to synthesize nudity and sexual content into their Gothic horror films. While much of the attention during this period was on the escalating number of X certificate films combining elements of sex and violence, Henry demonstrates how the sensationalistic scenes of lesbianism in the films raised the ire of the BBFC and, in the process, became instrumental in the emergence of the lesbian vampire subgenre. The BBFC's leniency can also be detected in *10 Rillington Place* (Richard Fleischer 1971). Tim Snelson explores how this dramatization of the gruesome exploits of London serial killer John Christie was made possible after a decade-long series of contentious negotiations with the BBFC, which resulted in the Board changing its long-standing policy about films drawing directly on real crime and court cases from the last fifty years. Snelson outlines the production histories of both *10 Rillington Place* and previous unmade films about the Christie murders, and contextualizes these projects within the discourse surrounding the death penalty and the notorious Moors murders in the 1960s. Benjamin Halligan's chapter closes the collection with an examination of the BBFC's transfer of power from Trevelyan to Stephen Murphy in 1971. This period saw the Board under intense scrutiny from both the Christian pressure group, the Festival of Light, and other conservative commentators due to the X certificates that were being granted to a number of controversial films boasting unprecedented levels of sex, violence and horror. Halligan argues that the BBFC's frequent interference with horror films during the pre-production, production, post-production and release stages was ultimately instrumental in changing the character of the films themselves.

As cinematically suggested in Kubrick's *Lolita* when Humbert Humbert holds the hands of both the frightened teenage Lolita and her middle-aged mother as they watch the monstrous Christopher Lee strangle Peter Cushing in Hammer's *The Curse of Frankenstein* (Terence Fisher 1957), the decade's fascination with British cinema depicting sex, violence and horror would cut across generational divides. As audiences matured in the long 1960s, the limits of the objectionable shifted as did the barometer indicated by the BBFC certification system. This collection of chapters is an attempt at assessing how the X certificate functioned and identified a cluster of films 'for adults only' ranging from – and at times blurring boundaries between – the socially acceptable to the perverse. The demand for X certificate entertainment, sometimes enabled, sometimes mitigated, sometimes fumbled, sometimes shirked, sometimes blocked by the BBFC, was to make for, and shape, a decisive, generative moment in British cinema history. We read the interplay of conflicting desires, fears and hopes for the future as a major element of the enduring allure, and richness, of British X cinema of the long 1960s – coalescing into, as the trailer for Antonioni's decade-defining *Blow-Up* puts it, 'a world where the beautiful and the bizarre take on new forms and hold new fascinations'.

Notes

1   In some respects, one could argue that Trevelyan re-aligned the X certificate to this type of filmmaking in the wake of both Hammer Films and Raymond Stross's production *The Flesh Is Weak*, which Christopher Weedman discusses in Chapter 2. Steve Chibnall discusses how the X certificate was originally envisioned as a mechanism to release reputable international films in cinemas in metropolitan cities: 'The certificate was conceived primarily as a means of allowing the metropolitan exhibition of a relatively small number of what we would now term "arthouse" films for specialist educated audiences, and eleven of the first dozen "X" certificates awarded were to continental films' (2012: 35).

2   The lack of films closely associated with Scotland, Wales and Northern Ireland (or even the West Country) in our focus on British cinema suggests that this emergent society was associated, by filmmakers and the film industry, with the English metropolitan regions and their immediate hinterlands. Folk Horror films of this period, fewer in quantity, and which did tend to look to areas beyond the metropolitan hinterlands and the English borders, embraced sometimes problematic notions of enclaves of society that were stubbornly refusing to emerge into the present, as most notably with the primitive culture of religious practices in *The Wicker Man* (Robin Hardy 1973). On Folk Horror, see Adam Scovell (2017).

3   A similar refusal to demarcate a period within the turns of decades, in favour of acknowledging the lived experience of that period, is apparent in Jonathon Green's pioneering project of curating the voices of the 'English Underground', which bleeds into 1971 (1988). Since then, numerous academic studies have identified 'the long 1960s' as a more appropriately expansive or discursive way of bookending their concerns. In terms of the elongation of the 1960s, in respect to the ongoing reverberations and legacies of the 1960s beyond the 1960s, we acknowledge Sarah Hill's model of cultural history too (2016), as well as Alain Badiou's critique of 'shutting down' a period, and so curtailing or defanging its meanings and importance, via a process of historicization: 'We are still the contemporaries of May '68' (2010: 41). Moreover, there is some evidence that cinemagoers of this period recognized the elongation of themes and concerns beyond just the turn of the decade, and so felt 'the sixties' could not be confined to a numerical definition (see Stokes, Jones, and Pett 2022: 175).

4   Additional relevant scholarship and popular criticism on British cinema from the late 1950s through the mid-1970s includes Terence Kelly, Graham Norton, and George Perry (1966); Ernest Betts (1973); Alexander Walker (1974 and 1985); Roy Armes (1978); Charles Barr (1986); Robert Murphy (1992); Brian McFarlane (1997); Anthony Aldgate, James Chapman, and

Arthur Marwick (2000); Justine Ashby and Andrew Higson (2000); Matthew Sweet (2005); B. F. Taylor (2006); Robert Shail (2008); Sue Harper and Justin Smith (2012); Sian Barber (2013); I. Q. Hunter (2013); and Paul Newland (2013). Scholarship on censorship and the British cinema during these years also includes studies from Neville March Hunnings (1967), Guy Phelps (1975), James C. Robertson (1993), Tom Dewe Mathews (1994), Aldgate and Robertson (2005) and Edward Lamberti (2012).

5 Interestingly, X certificate films were not the only films with scandalous reputations. According to a former cinema patron named 'Chester', there was a proscribed sexual subculture surrounding the screening of some A certificate films during this period. Chester recalls that '[i]n the days of "A" certificate films, it was quite commonplace for young boys to stand outside the cinema and ask a stranger going in if he would take them with him. For some men who fancied young boys, this was an ideal opportunity to sit alongside the boy in the darkness and grope him sexually ... it happened to me on a couple of occasions ... when I was 12 and 13 respectively' (cited in Stokes, Jones, and Pett 2022: 45).

6 Trevelyan further explains that any licensing authority maintains 'the legal right ... to reverse or vary any decision made by the Board. In practice local authority action affects only a very small number of films each year, the decisions of the Board being generally accepted' (1967: 127).

7 Historically, the BBFC also worked to 'protect' impressionable groups other than children, so that another principle also may have been in play – as with, as Robertson argues, the BBFC's moves to restrict access to Soviet films by British workers in the 1920s (1993: 27–31). This type of safeguarding is similarly evident in the BBFC's cutting of martial arts films due to the examiners' fears of juvenile copycat violence, as seen in their handling of the American-Hong Kong co-production *Enter the Dragon* (Robert Clouse 1973) (see Simkin 2012: 79–80).

8 Trevelyan, with wine and cigarette, is pictured between Warhol and Morrissey in the photo section between pp. 128–9. The caption reads 'a talk with [them] helped me to understand their approach to film-making'.

9 Famously, *Room at the Top*, discussed by Lucy Bolton in Chapter 9, reached the BBFC as a near completed film, carefully avoiding scrutiny of the script (see Aldgate 1995: 35, 43).

10 Geoffrey's homosexuality was disputed by Melvin (Griffiths 2006: 88, endnote 16), and indeed Geoffrey's persona and timbre does not seem so distant from Melvin's own, suggesting that he was not proactively performing a homosexual character. Weedman has argued that the critical distance that allowed Losey (an exiled American) to explore the subtle changes in British society in *The Servant* – both social and sexual – arose from Losey's unencumbered outsider status and so sharper perspective (2019: 93–9). On *Victim* and the BBFC, see Hargreaves (2012: 57–9).

11 *Death in Venice* concerns unrequited same-sex paedophilic desire, although was taken as a 'gay film' at the time; on this, and the film's problematic co-options and afterlife, see Halligan (2022: 257).

12 For representative scholarship, see Andy Medhurst (1991) on *Brief Encounter* (David Lean 1945), Keith Howes on Bogarde (2006) and Richard Griffiths on *This Sporting Life* (Anderson 1963) and, working with Colin MacCabe's analysis (1998), of '[t]he apparent queerness of *Performance*', Griffith (2006: 73). Playdon takes MacCabe to task further to this selective reading of *Performance*, as overlooking the film's ethnic diversity, which is seen as significant and innovative as well (2000: 1, 13).

13 Following the release of the Wolfenden Report, the Lord Chamberlain's office relaxed its ban on-stage representations of homosexuality in 1958, but it still maintained guidelines that would see plays heavily cut at best. For a comparative analysis of the censorial treatment of plays and their film adaptations, see Aldgate and Robertson (2005: 102–28).

14 *Gays and Film* even illustrates the timidity of its publisher on the subject matter. The verso side of page one (i.e. the back of the book's cover) suggests an institutional washing of hands: 'The opinions expressed in this book are those of the author and are not necessarily those of the British Film Institute. Neither do they represent official BFI policy' (Dyer 1977). The British Film Institute, further to Dyer's 'Images of Homosexuality' film season at the National Film Theatre, in July 1977, had been attacked in the House of Lords and by the Christian pressure group the Festival of Light. One programmed film, Tom Chomont's uncertified *Love Objects* of 1971, was withdrawn from the season (Davis 2021: 444).

15 The Campaign for Homosexual Equality (CHE) made the short educational film *David Is Homosexual* (Wilfred Avery 1978) for private screenings. The reach of this film, at the time, is unknown. However, echoing *Nighthawks*, it is predominantly pessimistic, and un-celebratory, in tone, despite its pathbreaking content.

References

Aldgate, A. (1995), *Censorship and the Permissive Society: British Cinema and Theatre 1955–1965*, Oxford: Clarendon Press.

Aldgate, A., J. Chapman, and A. Marwick (2000), *Windows on the Sixties: Exploring Key Texts of Media and Culture*, London: I.B. Tauris.

Aldgate, T. and J. C. Robertson (2005), *Censorship in Theatre and Cinema*, Edinburgh: Edinburgh University Press.

Armes, R. (1978), *A Critical History of the British Cinema*, New York: Oxford University Press.

Ashby, J. and A. Higson, eds. (2000), *British Cinema, Past and Present*, London: Routledge.

Babuscio, J. (1977), 'Camp and the Gay Sensibility', in R. Dyer (ed), *Gays and Film*, 40–57, London: British Film Institute.

Badiou, A. (2010), *The Communist Hypothesis*, trans. D. Macey and S. Corcoran, London: Verso.

Barber, S. (2011), *Censoring the 1970s: The BBFC and the Decade that Taste Forgot*, Newcastle upon Tyne: Cambridge Scholars Publishing.

Barber, S. (2012), 'British Film Censorship and the BBFC in the 1970s', in S. Harper and J. Smith (eds), *British Film Culture in the 1970s: The Boundaries of Pleasure*, 22–33, Edinburgh: Edinburgh University Press.

Barber, S. (2013), *The British Film Industry in the 1970s: Capital, Culture and Creativity*, Houndsmills, Basingstroke: Palgrave Macmillan.

Barr, C., ed. (1986), *All Our Yesterdays: 90 Years of British Cinema*, London: BFI Publishing.

Beckett, A. (2010), *When the Lights Went Out: What Really Happened to Britain in the Seventies*, London: Faber and Faber.

'The Best Pictures – and An Unwelcome Trend' (1959), *Coventry Evening Telegraph*, 3 January.

Betts, E. (1973), *The Film Business: A History of British Cinema 1896–1972*, New York: Pitman Publishing Corporation.

Bier, C. (2000), *Censure-moi*, Paris: L'esprit frappeur.

Bourne, S. ([1996] 2016), *Brief Encounters: Lesbians and Gays in British Cinema 1930–1971*, second edn, London: Bloomsbury Academic.

Brett, L. (2017), 'The BBFC and the Apparatus of Censorship', in I. Q. Hunter, L. Porter and J. Smith (eds), *The Routledge Companion to British Cinema History*, 231–41, Albingdon, Oxon: Routledge.

Brown, S. (2012), 'Censorship Under Siege: The BBFC in the Silent Era', in E. Lamberti (ed), *Behind the Scenes at the BBFC: Film Classification from the Silver Screen to the Digital Age*, 3–14, London: BFI/Palgrave-Macmillan.

'Cert "X" is O.K. by us, they say' (1950), *Daily Mirror*, 14 July.

Chibnall, S. (2012), 'From *The Snake Pit* to the *Garden of Eden*: A Time of Temptation for the Board', in E. Lamberti (ed), *Behind the Scenes at the BBFC: Film Classification from the Silver Screen to the Digital Age*, 29–52, London: BFI/Palgrave-Macmillan.

Davies, C. (1975), *Permissive Britain: Social Change in the Sixties and Seventies*, London: Pitman Publishing.

Davis, G. (2021), '"A Panorama of Gay Life": *Nighthawks* and British Queer Cinema in the 1970s', in R. Gregg and A. Villarejo (eds), *The Oxford Handbook of Queer Cinema*, 435–57, Oxford: Oxford University Press.

Durgnat, R. (1971), *A Mirror for England: British Movies from Austerity to Affluence*, New York: Praeger Publishers.

Dyer, R. (1976), 'Gays in Film', *Gay Left: A Socialist Journal Produced by Gay People* (2): 8–11.

Dyer, R., ed. (1977), *Gays and Film*, London: British Film Institute.

Farmer, R., L. Mayne, D. Petrie, and M. Williams, eds. (2019), *Transformation and Tradition in 1960s British Cinema*, Edinburgh: Edinburgh University Press.

Frith, P. (2020), '"Wholesome Rough Stuff": Hammer Films and the "A" and "U" Certificate, 1959–65', in D. Petrie, M. Williams, and L. Mayne (eds), *Sixties British Cinema Reconsidered*, 151–64, Edinburgh: Edinburgh University Press.

Gore, A. (1967), 'Sexual Offenses (No. 2) Bill', House of Lords debates, 21 July, *Hansard*, volume 285: column 522.

Green, J. (1988), *Days in the Life: Voices from the English Underground, 1961–1971*, London: Heinemann.

Griffiths, R. (2006), 'Sad and Angry: Queers in 1960s British Cinema', in R. Griffiths (ed), *British Queer Cinema*, 71–90, London: Routledge.

Halligan, B. (2022), *Hotbeds of Licentiousness: The British Glamour Film and the Permissive Society*, Oxford: Berghahn Books.

Hargreaves, T. (2012), 'The Trevelyan Years: British Censorship and 1960s Cinema', in E. Lamberti (ed), with J. Green, D. Hyman, C. Lapper, and K. Myers, *Behind the Scenes at the BBFC: Film Classification from the Silver Screen to the Digital Age*, 53–68, London: Palgrave Macmillan, British Film Institute.

Harper, S. and J. Smith, eds. (2012), *British Film Culture in the 1970s: The Boundaries of Pleasure*, Edinburgh: Edinburgh University Press.

Hearn, M. (2011), *The Hammer Vault: Treasures from the Archive of Hammer Films*, London: Titan Books.

Hill, J. (1986), *Sex, Class and Realism: British Cinema 1956–1963*, London: BFI Publishing.

Hill, S. (2016), *San Francisco and the Long 60s*, London: Bloomsbury.

Howes, K. (2006), 'Are There Stars Out Tonight?', in R. Griffiths (ed), *British Queer Cinema*, 61–9, London: Routledge.

Hunnings, N. M. (1967), *Film Censors and the Law*, London: George Allen & Unwin.

Hunt, L. (1998), *British Low Culture: From Safari Suits to Exploitation*, London: Routledge.

Hunter, I. Q. (2013), *British Trash Cinema*, London: BFI Publishing.

Hutchings, P. (1993), *Hammer and Beyond: The British Horror Film*, Manchester: Manchester University Press.

Hutchings, P. (2002), 'Beyond the New Wave: Realism in British Cinema, 1959–63', in R. Murphy (ed), *The British Cinema Book*, second edn, 146–52, London: BFI Publishing.

Jarman, D. with M. Christie, ed. (1993), *At Your Own Risk: A Saint's Testament*, London: Vintage.

'John Trevelyan Is New BBFC Secretary' (1958), *Kinematograph Weekly*, 29 May: 1.

Kelly, T., with G. Norton, and G. Perry (1966), *A Competitive Cinema*, London: Institute of Economic Affairs.

Lamberti, E., ed. (2012), *Behind the Scenes at the BBFC: Film Classification from the Silver Screen to the Digital Age*, London: Palgrave Macmillan.

Le Cheminant, P. (1967), Note to Harold Wilson, 25 July, PRO PREM 13/2152, Kew: National Archives.

MacCabe, C. (1996), *Performance*, London: British Film Institute.

Marwick, A. (1998), *The Sixties: Cultural Revolution in Britain, France, Italy and the United States, c. 1958–c. 1974*, New York: Oxford University Press.

Marwick, A. (2005), 'The Cultural Revolution of the Long Sixties: Voices of Reaction, Protest and Permeation', *The International History Review*, 27 (4): 780–806.

Mathews, T. D. (1994), *Censored*, London: Chatto & Windus.

McFarlane, B. (1997), *An Autobiography of British Cinema*, London: Methuen.

McKenna, R. (1912), 'Cinematograph Films (Unofficial Censorship)', House of Commons debates, 8 November, *Hansard*, volume 43: column 1612.

Medhurst, A. (1991), 'The Special Thrill: *Brief Encounter*, Homosexuality and Authorship', *Screen*, 32 (2): 197–208.

Murphy, R. (1992), *Sixties British Cinema*, London: BFI Publishing.

Nash, D. (2017), 'Blasphemy on Trial', *History Today*, 15 November. Available at: https://www.historytoday.com/miscellanies/blasphemy-trial (accessed 5 September 2022).

Newland, P. (2013), *British Films of the 1970s*, Manchester: Manchester University Press.

'Obituary: Mr John Trevelyan, Film Censor with the Diplomatic Touch' (1986), *Times*, 18 August.

Petrie, D., M. Williams, and L. Mayne, eds. (2022), *Sixties British Cinema Reconsidered*, Cambridge: Cambridge University Press.

Phelps, G. (1975), *Film Censorship*, London: Victor Gollancz.

Playdon, P. (2000), *The Black Presence in Performance: A Reading from the Margins*, Coventry: Coventry School of Arts and Design, Coventry University.

Robertson, J. C. (1993), *The Hidden Cinema: British Film Censorship in Action, 1913–1975*, London: Routledge.

Scovell, A. (2017), *Folk Horror: Hours Dreadful and Things Strange*, Leighton Buzzard: Auteur Publishing.

Shail, R., ed. (2008), *Seventies British Cinema*, London: BFI Publishing.

Simkin, S. (2012), 'Wake of the Flood: Key Issues in UK Censorship, 1970–75', in E. Lamberti (ed), with J. Green, D. Hyman, C. Lapper, and K. Myers, *Behind the Scenes at the BBFC: Film Classification from the Silver Screen to the Digital Age*, 72–86, London: Palgrave Macmillan, British Film Institute.

Stokes, M., M. Jones, and E. Pett (2022), *Cinema Memories: A People's History of Cinema-going in 1960s Britain*, London: BFI Publishing.

Sweet, M. (2005), *Shepperton Babylon: The Lost Worlds of British Cinema*, London: Faber and Faber.

Taylor, B. F. (2006), *The British New Wave*, Manchester: Manchester University Press.

Trevelyan, J. (1958), 'Censored! – How, and Why, We Do It', *Films and Filming*, July: 8, 33.

Trevelyan, J. (1967), 'Film Censorship in Great Britain', Appendix 5, *Report of the Joint Committee on Censorship of the Theatre*, London: Her Majesty's Stationery Office.

Trevelyan, J. (1970), 'Film Censorship in Great Britain', *Screen*, 11 (3): 19–30.

Trevelyan, J. (1977), *What the Censor Saw*, London: Michael Joseph.

Upton, J. (2017), 'Innocence Unprotected? Permissiveness and the AA Certificate 1970–82', *Journal of British Cinema and Television*, 14 (1): 64–76.

Walker, A. (1974), *Hollywood England: The British Film Industry in the Sixties*, London: Michael Joseph.

Walker, A. (1985), *National Heroes: British Cinema in the Seventies and Eighties*, London: Harrap.

Ward, J. (2015), *Not Gay: Sex Between Straight White Men*, New York: New York University Press.

Weedman, C. (2019), 'A Dark Exilic Vision of Sixties Britain: Gothic Horror and Film Noir Pervading Losey and Pinter's *The Servant*', *Journal of Cinema and Media Studies*, 58 (3): 93–117.

Weeks, J. ([1981] 1992), *Sex, Politics & Society: The Regulation of Sexuality Since 1800*, second edn, London: Longman.

1

Green Penguin Films

Kim Newman

The etymology is debated, but the print-the-legend version has it that French critic Nino Frank coined the term *film noir* to evoke the Paris publisher Gallimard's *Série Noire*, a thriller imprint known for its distinctive black covers. Similarly, the Italian crime-suspense-horror *giallo* genre got its name from the house of Mondadori, who published British and American mysteries with yellow jackets. The *giallo* design was inspired by popular UK paperback editions of the novels of Edgar Wallace, to the extent of insetting illustrations in a red circle – a device introduced for Wallace's *The Crimson Circle* (1922). *Noir* and *giallo* are mutant film forms, fusing earlier forms into something new – hardboiled American crime writing and German Expressionist cinema for *film noir*, Hitchcockian suspense and Hitchcockian horror for *giallo*. The genres have an infinitely rearrangeable set of themes, backdrops, characters, plots and images: gun-toting private eyes in trenchcoats (sweltering in California?) and fatal women in sheath dresses, as in *Out of the Past* (Jacques Tourneur 1947) or *Double Indemnity* (Billy Wilder 1944) … black-gloved stalker-psycho-killers and designer-outfitted distressed heroines, as in *6 donne per l'assassino* (*Blood and Black Lace*, Mario Bava 1964) or *Lo strano vizio della signora Wardh* (*Blade of the Ripper*, Sergio Martino 1971). There are isolated instances of *noir* and *giallo* from outside America and Italy: *The Small Back Room* (Michael Powell and Emeric Pressburger 1949) is a British noir and *Fragment of Fear* (Richard C. Sarafian 1970), set in Pompeii and London, is a British *giallo*. But, for the most part, these colour-coded genres arise from specific cultural circumstances and concerns.

In parallel with the Italian *giallo* boom of the 1960s and 1970s, Britain produced a cycle of stylized mystery/crime/horror movies – not the cosy crime epitomized by Margaret Rutherford's comic take on Agatha Christie's chilling Miss Marple (for whom murder might be most foul but earned a U certificate), but more adult fare aiming for the X certificate and a sense of the transgressive and disturbing. Straddling exploitation, social comment, horror and psychedelia, these gothicized, swinging thrillers and old dark house horror-farces might be considered fresh territory for genre mapmakers. If we follow the habit of colour-coding mystery movies with reference to a leading paperback publisher, these might be called Green Penguin Films. Penguin's crime line – inaugurated in 1935 with Dorothy L. Sayers's *The Unpleasantness at the Bellona Club* and Agatha Christie's *The Mysterious Affair at Styles* – used a green variant on the classic Penguin cover format to distinguish such light reading from the more serious novels issued in orange. Christie – an often-unheralded major influence on *giallo* – and her murder-in-the-manor competitors were a mainstay of the Green Penguin list, but so were Americans like Raymond Chandler and Ed McBain. Generations of British readers associated crime with green covers, as signalled by *Green for Danger* (Sidney Gilliat 1946), based on a 1942 novel by Christianna Brand, which, of course, was an often-reprinted staple of the Green Penguin line. The Green Penguin strain includes movies seen on their original release as plain genre fare and films conceived as arthouse indulgences – and some, like *Repulsion* (Roman Polanski 1965), which might have been both.

In the sense of a transgressive, stylized, calculatedly adult mutation of the British thriller, Green Penguin cinema perhaps began with *Peeping Tom* (Michael Powell 1960) – with its mix of tabloid sensationalism, sado-erotic kink, plodding police procedural, self-referential jokes ('you don't get pictures like that in *Sight & Sound*'), lightly parodied entertainment industry milieu (taking in Soho smut and horridly respectable middle-class comedies), EastmanColor delirium and horrific family drama. The lair of killer Mark Lewis (Carl Boehm) is a London mansion subdivided into pokey flats, where pockets of resentment linger in the protagonist's traumatic memories (stored in film cans) and the heroine's blind mother's alcohol-fuelled bitter insights. Like the Bates Motel, the murderer's home tells a story of downward mobility that parallels his mental malformation – a business sidelined by a new road, a formerly grand family residence splintered into multiple dwellings for rootless, less-monied city dwellers. We only see the house's garden in the home movie flashback footage in which Mark's psychologist father (Powell himself) is glimpsed as a fussy, inept, smiling Dad rather than the clinical sadist who turned his son into a monster while using him as a test subject for his studies in terror.

Thanks to a critical reassessment that has viewed the film as a late masterpiece rather than evidence of a precipitous drop from the quality level of the films Powell made with Pressburger, *Peeping Tom* is an outlier. It is paid respectful attention forever denied the misshapen, sleazy likes of *The Flesh Is Weak* (Don Chaffey 1957), *Cover Girl Killer* (Terry Bishop

1959), *Strip Tease Murder* (Ernest Morris 1961), *Night After Night After Night* (Lindsay Shonteff 1969), *The Fiend* (Robert Hartford-Davis 1972) and *The Playbirds* (Willy Roe 1978). Yet these X-certificate throwaways afford a mosaic picture of the Britain imagined by the *News of the World* and curtain-twitching moral reformers who would have despised the films themselves. There's always a disturbing bathos when performers associated with light entertainment appear among parades of starlets posing as pin-up models, prostitutes and strippers. It's startling to witness Harry H. Corbett (later of *Steptoe and Son*, 1962–74) as the seethingly repressed misogynist of *Cover Girl Killer* ('surely sex and horror are the new Gods in this polluted world of so-called entertainment') and Jack May ('Nelson Gabriel' on *The Archers*, 1950–) in *Night After Night After Night* as a high court judge who swaps his judicial wig for a drag queen leather look and prowls the red-light district in search of girls to murder. Typical of the way these films pull back the curtain of 'family entertainment' to reveal monstrous or perverse decay is *The Impersonator* (Alfred Shaughnessy 1961). Here, a sex pest (John Salew) – he asks a café owner for 'tea and a suggestive biscuit' – who becomes a serial rapist/murderer turns out to be the local pantomime dame. Unwigged on stage, he tries to make an escape by tearing through the scenery wall but smacks a brick wall – mistaking reality for the illusion of it. When the drag/transvestite tradition of British Christmas panto is explained, the American hero (John Crawford) asks, 'are you sure this show is suitable for kids?' The question resonates throughout an entertainment hinterland, from Tussaud's Chamber of Horrors through Edgar Lustgarten's true crime radio broadcasts to the simultaneous cosiness and sleaze of much British horror, comedy and smut.

The critical mauling *Peeping Tom* received on its original release makes it seem a one-off, but many of its elements recurred in the next decade and a half – notably the collision of seedy and swinging London which baffles even Alfred Hitchcock in *Frenzy* (1972). After Mark Lewis, a run of outwardly nice, cheerful, well-spoken, sensitive young men turn out to be homicidal threats to unwary women. Witness: Albert Finney (*Night Must Fall*, Karel Reisz 1964), Hywel Bennett (*Twisted Nerve*, Roy Boulting 1968), Martin Potter (*Goodbye Gemini*, Alan Gibson 1970), an entire class of public schoolboys (*Unman, Wittering and Zigo*, John Mackenzie 1971), Mark Lester (*Night Hair Child*, James Kelly 1972), Shane Briant (*Straight on Till Morning*, Peter Collinson 1972), Nicholas Clay (*The Night Digger*, Alastair Reid 1971) and Ralph Bates (*Persecution*, Don Chaffey 1974). A few of these are working-class fantasists – homicidal kin to Tom Courtenay in *Billy Liar* (John Schlesinger 1963) – and social climbing is the spur for murder in *Nothing but the Best* (Clive Donner 1964), with Alan Bates taking lessons from dissolute aristo Denholm Elliott, and *Endless Night* (Sidney Gilliat 1972), with Hywel Bennett reworking his chameleon psycho from *Twisted Nerve* (one of the nastiest British films ever made) in an adaptation of an atypical Agatha Christie novel. But most of these menaces are like Mark, of privileged background but come down in the world – all too often the last of their lines. An ur-type for this character is Lord Lebanon (Marius Goring) in *The Case of the Frightened Lady* (George King 1940), from an Edgar Wallace novel – a fey, aristocratic, thin-blooded strangler, joshing cheerfully with the police. Lebanon is sheltered by a dotty, doting mother (Helen Haye), who laments his death (while trying to kill the heroine) with 'a thousand years of being great – gone out, like a candle in the wind'. She doesn't just mean her family – she means Britain.

All the way back to James Whale's Hollywood-made *The Old Dark House* (1932), based on a novel of post-war malaise by J. B. Priestley, Britain is imagined as a crumbling mansion full of antique tat, inhabited by senile grotesques who snipe at each other when they aren't savaging callow guests who come into their home reeking of neurotic modernity. When Hammer Films, whose lushly colourful horror films instituted their own brand of splendidly disreputable cinema, branched out into shock-thrillers, the company's first impulse was to evoke *Les Diaboliques* (Henri-Georges Clouzot 1955) as much as *Psycho* (Alfred Hitchcock 1960). *Taste of Fear* (Seth Holt 1961), *Maniac* (Michael Carreras 1963) and *Crescendo* (Alan Gibson 1970) are set in rural France, a country associated in Britain with sexual licence and threat as demonstrated as late as *And Soon the Darkness* (Robert Fuest 1970), in which British girls on a cycling holiday in Brittany are stalked by a local killer. The Clouzot influence was not confined to Hammer – similarly cruel plots are deployed, mostly against neurotic women, in *Catacombs* (Gordon Hessler 1965), *Night Watch* (Brian G. Hutton 1973) and *Dominique* (Michael Anderson 1979). Very early in the cycle, *Midnight Lace* (David Miller 1960), an American film set in foggy London, fuses *Les Diaboliques* with *Gaslight*. Doris Day is harassed by a prank caller who is also a black-gloved killer and – as in many *gialli* to come – turns out to be her plausible, suave, impossibly cruel husband (Rex Harrison).

Beyond the influence of *Les Diaboliques*, Hammer – a company often based in dilapidated home counties' mansions – were also drawn to Priestley's grotesque caricature of the English country house weekend. They partnered with American showman William Castle in a comic remake of *The Old Dark House* (1963), which has credits drawn by Charles Addams and a dotty family of murderers and victims played by Robert Morley, Peter Bull, Joyce Grenfell (stabbed by her own knitting needles) and Fenella Fielding. Not entirely successful and often written off as an affront to the original, it's one of a run of British gothic comedies – *What a Carve Up!* (Pat Jackson 1961), *The Horror of It All* (Terence Fisher 1964), *Adventures of a Private Eye* (Stanley A. Long 1977), *Providence* (Alain Resnais 1977), *Sir Henry at Rawlinson End* (Steve Roberts 1980) and *The House of Long Shadows* (Pete Walker 1983) – on Priestley's theme, with families of aristocratic eccentrics slaughtered as their estates crumble and the modern world moves on happily without them. *What a Carve Up!* is a remake of *The Ghoul* (T. Hayes Hunter 1933), itself a British imitation of *The Old Dark House*. Jackson's film inspired Jonathan Coe's 1994 novel, which makes expressly political connections but also dives deep into a British popular cinema that offers Sid James and Kenneth Connor as bulwarks against the deadening, all-pervasive presence of the parasitic, landed Winshaw Clan.

In the 1950s, Hammer bought the rights to Josephine Tey's *Brat Farrar* (1949) – another Green Penguin title – with the intention of making an inroad into the carriage trade mystery field dominated by better-heeled production houses. Tey, source author for *Young and Innocent* (Alfred Hitchcock 1937), was a cut above the radio dramatists Hammer drew on for their pre-horror crime quota quickies. A Tey novel had become the eminently respectable (and interesting) *The Franchise Affair* (Lawrence Huntington 1951), from ABPC – the sort of outfit who could afford to look down on Hammer. However, *Brat Farrar* was one of several long-nurtured projects set aside after *The Curse of Frankenstein* (Terence Fisher 1957) prompted the company to fast-track more gothic horror. With Peter Cushing, Christopher Lee, splashes of blood and much heaving cleavage available, Hammer no longer felt a need to compete with the cut-glass drawing room tones of Michael Denison and Dulcie Gray. In a useful test case for what exactly constitutes Green Penguin cinema, Hammer eventually took the *Brat Farrar* rights off the shelf and had horror mainstay screenwriter-producer Jimmy Sangster retool the material as the *Psycho* soundalike *Paranoiac* (Freddie Francis 1963). In pursuing an X certificate, abjuring any pretence of respectability (even the novel's name is unmentioned in the credits) and shaping the mystery into something more explicitly shocking, Hammer might almost have set out to obliterate the tweedy, restrained world of films like *The Franchise Affair* to unloose a wild set of contradictory emotions that must eventually tear apart polite notions of character and story in a frenzy perfectly enacted by a sweaty, pop-eyed Oliver Reed.

Paranoiac drops the horse-breeding theme that takes up much of Tey's novel and stresses gothic effects: a corpse mummified behind a pipe organ, a hook-wielding slasher in choirboy's surplice and a grotesque papier-maché mask, eerie tape-recorded music played in support of a delusion (this unusual trope recurs at Hammer in Cyril Frankel's *The Witches*, 1967, and Sangster's *Fear in the Night*, 1972), a French nurse (a Clouzot reminder) drowned by night in the lake of 'High Tor', excuses for characters to wander perilously near clifftops (Francis frames deep focus widescreen images using optical effects to heighten the sense of threat from the landscape), a great deal of prowling around an old dark house and a last reel inferno in which the monster perishes and his rotting lair burns down around him. The Lord Lebanon figure is Simon Ashby (Reed), who knows the fortune hunter posing as his long-lost brother (Alex Davion) is an imposter because he killed the real Tony Ashby – a murder he admits he planned when he was about thirteen. While most successors to Lord Lebanon have to work hard to become threatening when they reach for the knife, Reed is as explosive here as he is in *The Curse of the Werewolf* (Terence Fisher 1961). In a horribly convincing scene, he loses his rag in a pub when his credit runs out and threatens a hale-fellow type who has dared to suggest he slow down by brandishing a fistful of darts as a weapon. Carried over from Castle's *The Old Dark House* is Janette Scott – demoted from demure murderess to the traditional Sangster role of heroine being systematically driven mad by a close relative out to claim a family fortune he wants to squander.

Sangster and Francis immediately followed *Paranoiac* with *Nightmare* (1964) and *Hysteria* (1964), further riffs on *Les Diaboliques* – with an ingénue (Jennie Linden) and an amnesiac (Robert Webber) manipulated by others as part of murder schemes. In *Nightmare*, another film fully committed to the gothic, the heroine's guardians make her believe she is being stalked in a nightmare by a woman she eventually stabs on sight in waking life ... and then the recurring dream transfers to the culprits, who are themselves driven mad by a counter-plot in the second half of the film. As ever, it's all about the inheritance. In *Psycho*, the stolen money is a feint and psychosis is the root of the horror. At the House of Hammer, where the Carreras family had their own dynastic/inheritance issues, even raving madmen like Simon Ashby are calculating, intent always on that secondary clause in the will that means a come-down-in-the-world, entitled (sometimes even titled) wastrel can live in the style to which he was born. This is a trait among many Green Penguin cinema shares with *giallo*, where apparently psychopathic violence is often just a cover for plain greed and gruesome murders are committed in order to gain an inheritance – wealthy spouses are especially liable to figure as ultimate victims – or even secure a business deal. In *5 bambole per la luna d'agosto/5 Dolls for an August Moon* (Mario Bava 1970), the killers are out to get a monopoly on a new type of industrial resin, an absurdly uninteresting McGuffin that's an excuse for some of Bava's strangest tableaux of beautiful death.

Hammer's psycho-thrillers shifted from black and white to colour with *Fanatic* (Silvio Narizzano 1965), confusingly based on a novel called *Nightmare* (Anne Blaisdell 1961). Sangster was replaced as screenwriter by the American Richard Matheson, who takes pains to differentiate the mod, modern, Americanized London media world associated with the American heroine from the old dark house in the Berkshire countryside where family horrors linger. Matheson also finds aristocracy inherently grotesque and *Fanatic*'s matriarch is genuinely insane rather than trying to drive her victim mad. Stephen Trefoile, the impotent last of his line, is dead before the film begins. His smothering mother (Tallulah Bankhead) invites the dead boy's ex-fiancée (Stefanie Powers) to stay, intent on marrying her to a corpse. As with Lady Lebanon, the useless aristocrat's mother is keeper of a dying flame (Sheila Burrell's incest-minded aunt has an equivalent role in *Paranoiac*).

Particular attention is paid to the culpability of the servants (a splendid triumvirate of character actors – Peter Vaughan, Yootha Joyce and Donald Sutherland) in the madness of their mistress. They know Mrs Trefoile is so demented that her scheme will rebound on them, but tradition, their own petty crimes and cosy positions in an unquestioned hierarchy lead them to stay onside, even as the corpses pile up.

Amicus, Hammer's closest rival, presents a mother (albeit a German immigrant) as the main menace in *The Psychopath* (Freddie Francis 1966), scripted by Robert Bloch – source author of *Psycho* – as a conscious rearrangement of the ingredients of his greatest hit. Here, the nice but creepy young man (John Standing) everyone assumes is the murderer is an innocent patsy. His not-really-wheelchair-bound mother (Margaret Johnson) is carrying out a string of revenge killings, always leaving dolls in the shape of her victims by their mangled corpses – a childish, macabre flourish. Hammer's further ventures into grande dame horror owe as much to the imagined role Mrs Bates plays in *Psycho* as to the career-reviving gothic of *What Ever Happened to Baby Jane?* (Robert Aldrich 1962). In the black and white, unsettlingly matter-of-fact *The Nanny* (Seth Holt 1965), from a novel by Evelyn Piper, Bette Davis is a sinister servant who calmly murders those who fracture her delusions and engages in a quiet battle with her determined young charge (William Dix). *The Anniversary* (Roy Ward Baker 1968), a colourful follow-up from a play by Bill McIlwraith, surrenders to then-modish camp. In a diamante eyepatch, Mrs Taggart (Davis) queens over a rare middle-class extended family of cowed, useless, doomed grown children who can't escape her, spitting venom and cackling. It's a short step from *The Anniversary* to two attempts to make films out of the sinister farces of Joe Orton (*Entertaining Mr Sloane*, Douglas Hickox 1970; *Loot*, Silvio Narizzano 1970), which have a similar uncomfortable tone, not quite funny, not quite horrific, and weirdly, inappropriately mod when the look of *Paranoiac* or *The Psychopath* would better fit Orton's savagery.

The theme of the old dark house as national or psychological metaphor metamorphoses and metastasizes in the likes of *The Servant* (Joseph Losey 1963), with its decadent master and aspirant butler changing places, and *One Way Pendulum* (Peter Yates 1965), from the play by N. F. Simpson, in which the eccentric Groomkirby family pursue demented hobbies (Jonathan Miller teaches speak-your-weight machines to sing 'You Can't Chop Your Mama Up in Massachusetts'). Harold Pinter, who scripted *The Servant* from Robin Maugham's novel, essayed dramas of obscure menace in drab settings, which came to the cinema in undervalued, talkative-disturbing form in *The Caretaker* (Clive Donner 1963), *The Birthday Party* (William Friedkin 1968) – one of the odder products of the Amicus House of Horror – and *The Homecoming* (Peter Hall 1973). Pinter's violence is almost exclusively verbal, but any of these would make an apt double-bill partner with the cruel pranking of *The Penthouse* (Peter Collinson 1967), the pulpy *The Haunted House of Horror* (Michael Armstrong 1969) or the extraordinary psycho-drama of *Mumsy, Nanny, Sonny & Girly* (Freddie Francis 1970). As in *The Anniversary* or *Fanatic*, all the charades, sneers and bickering eventually segue into knife-to-the-groin stabbings. These films all feel like acting-out group therapies that go too far. A recurring theme – it's even in the splendidly sinister Frankie Howerd vehicle *The House in Nightmare Park* (Peter Sykes 1973) – is of the outsider drawn into a long-standing family drama, bewildered by the relentless parade of inside jokes and routines they can't keep up with, liable to trip over ominous carnival or legacy-of-empire bric-a-brac, stumped by the hot-and-cold attitudes of possible lovers, somehow fascinated even by the meagre remains of inherited splendour, and always, always surprised when they become the target of a pent-up rage that ticks over in everyday family congress but turns to homicidal fury when relatives who hate each other unite against an upstart. It's usually a literal family, but it's also a social class – like the public school class in *Unman, Wittering and Zigo* who calmly inform a new master (David Hemmings) that they murdered his predecessor and would have no qualms about killing him too.

Shifting identities and found families come to dominate this sub-strand of British inheritance horror. Losey returned to an old dark house in *Secret Ceremony* (1968), with Mia Farrow as a child-woman who may (like Bennett in *Twisted Nerve*) be shamming mental incapacity and Elizabeth Taylor as a tart drafted off the streets for mother-daughter roleplay. The British genre kaleidoscope *Performance* (Donald Cammell and Nicolas Roeg 1970) also plays games in a decaying mansion which has nurtured a magical counterculture cell that undermines ancient certainties of class and decorum. The intruder, a gangster (James Fox), is enmeshed in the world – and eventually the look and personality – of a shut-in pop star (Mick Jagger) who, like Zaphod Beeblebrox (of Douglas Adams's *Hitch Hiker's Guide to the Galaxy* series of novels), seems to be on a cosmic voyage in his bedroom. In *Our Mother's House* (Jack Clayton 1967), from Julian Gloag's novel – and, later, *The Cement Garden* (Andrew Birkin 1993), from Ian McEwan's novel – a parent dies, leaving a brood of kids to make their own way in an old, large home which falls apart around them. Just as gangster Fox is dragged onto Jagger's trip, *Our Mother's House* has spiv Dirk Bogarde – the formerly absentee father – pulled into the enclosed, surprisingly dangerous world of a brood of children who have taken his name but refuse to be taken for fools. Stained glass windows allow Mario Bava lighting effects to filter into dusty, dark rooms and if you watch a bunch of these films one after the other you eventually come to think they're all set in the same huge house.

The gothic mansions and family cruelties of Hammer and lasting British classics like Thorold Dickinson's *Gaslight* (1940) and Robert Hamer's *Kind Hearts and Coronets* (1949) survive into the 1970s, but a rising generation runs wild in gaggles which straddle hippie commune and Satanic coven.

Tam Lin (Roddy McDowall 1970) transposes a folk tale to the hippie festival era, with Ian McShane ensnared by witch-mother Ava Gardner as her coterie of wild children (with comic mainstay Richard Wattis in a rare serious role as her poisonous, camp secretary). *Blue Blood* (Andrew Sinclair 1974) reprises elements of *The Servant* with brutal Oliver Reed and foppy Derek Jacobi in Longleat House; the script is based on *The Carry-Cot*, a novel by the stately home's eccentric owner Alexander Thynne, whose wife Anna Gael appears as one of the genre's many moon-children. Thynne could easily have been one of the inspirations for Jack, mad Earl of Gurney in Peter Barnes's play *The Ruling Class'*, filmed by Peter Medak in 1972. The Earl (Peter O'Toole) bursts into song, soliloquy and ultra-violence as he is cured of a delusion that he's Jesus Christ only to become convinced that he's Jack the Ripper. The twins (Judy Geeson and Martin Potter) of *Goodbye Gemini* and the would-be Peter Pan (Shane Briant) of *Straight on Till Morning* are prized by degenerates for their angelic looks, but are on a similar trajectory from childlike innocence to straight-razor slasher. All these films revel in freak-out party scenes, with prog or folk rock soundtracks and Austin Powers fashions, but catch the bleak, hungover desperation of groovers and ravers about to be swept aside by a brutal, intolerant world and new, even more vicious pop culture.

While the Bond films chased clean-lines and high-tech, represented by hovercraft and photocopiers, a rival strain engaged with clutter. The absurdist, junk shoppe element of the swinging sixties is most obvious in the 1967 Beatles LP *Sgt Pepper's Lonely Hearts Club Band* but an array of British pop culture detritus bobs up again and again in the songs of the Bonzo Dog Doo-Dah Band ('Hunting Tigers Out in India') or the novels of Michael Moorcock (*Dancers at the End of Time*). *Negatives* (Peter Medak 1968) is even set in a junk shop, where Peter McEnery, Glenda Jackson and Diane Cilento play sex charades based on the home of life of Dr Crippen and the aerial exploits of Baron von Richthofen. A particular curio is passed along between films – the skull of the Marquis de Sade is acquired by one collector of macabre antiques (Peter Cushing) in *The Skull* (Freddie Francis 1964) then turns up a year later among the treasures of another (Noël Coward) in *Bunny Lake Is Missing* (Otto Preminger 1965). The fact that props, sets, costumes and furniture tend to turn up in film after film adds to the sense of all these movies taking place in a shared universe, with recurring faces as well as situations. If there's a meta-frame to the world of Green Penguin cinema, it's the Amicus horror anthology *From Beyond the Grave* (Kevin Connor 1974), where Peter Cushing is the proprietor of Temptations, Ltd, a junk shop where every purchase comes with 'a big novelty surprise' like the spirit of Jack the Ripper – another frequently cited personage in this era – inside an antique mirror or a Restoration alchemist (Jack Watson) beyond an ornate door Ian Ogilvy unwisely decides to use for his stationery cupboard.

Such items often decorated the minimalist sets of *The Avengers* (1961–9), a series which evolved from realism to fantasy in parallel with the cultural shift from austerity to affluence. The most profound Green Penguin portrait of Britain may be 'The House That Jack Built' (1966), the episode in which Emma Peel (Diana Rigg) inherits a manufacturing company and takes a stand against cruel modernization by firing an automation expert who wants to replace workers with machines. This leads to the heroine, with it in her outfits and humane outlook, being pitted against a mechanized death trap disguised as yet another country house. Decorated with the usual waxed aspidistras and elephant's foot umbrella stands, this mansion also contains a buzzing, computerized artificial brain and an art nouveau murder maze. *The Haunted House of Horror*, which harbours a paisley-shirted man-child knife-killer rather than any spooks, is another Victorian death trap set to ensnare the dayglo-clad likes of Jill Haworth, Frankie Avalon and Richard O'Sullivan. *Curse of the Crimson Altar* (Vernon Sewell 1968) finds horror staples Boris Karloff, Christopher Lee and Barbara Steele hiding in quiet rooms while body-painted flower children freak out downstairs.

If the aristocrats of Green Penguin cinema are monsters, then the role of the middle classes is to be threatened – with an almost systematic sadism that underlines the precarious nature of social mobility. Suburban affluence, home-ownership, young families, ease of transport, and a post-ration book ease of consumption are fragile, frail and suspect because there are predators on the prowl. In *Never Let Go* (John Guillermin 1960), sales rep Richard Todd is reduced to insanity by the ripple effects of a car theft. When teddy boy Adam Faith steals his uninsured Ford Anglia, Todd becomes obsessed with reclaiming the vehicle from a criminal gang led by Peter Sellers – in a rare straight performance highlighted by grotesque cruelties (he stamps on an old man's beloved terrapin). His suit and tie dishevelled, the average man is repeatedly beaten, loses his job and wife and eventually becomes a brutal, monstrous match for Sellers in a final punch-up. Todd has a similar white-collar role in *The Very Edge* (Cyril Frankel 1963), scripted by Elizabeth Jane Howard and Leslie Bricusse, though the emphasis there is on a more usual sexual threat as a stalker/rapist (Jeremy Brett), who sometimes sports the fetishist leather outfit of an RAC motorcyclist, repeatedly targets Todd's ex-fashion model wife (Anne Heywood). Todd, of course, was a 1950s star, a staple of war films always found escaping from POW camps or leading daring missions. The characters he plays in *Never Let Go* and *The Very Edge*, the 'taxpayers' scorned by Colin Macinnes in his novel *Absolute Beginners*, are what might have happened to Todd's Second World War characters fifteen or twenty years on. Having suffered through the war, they've bought into the Affluent Society just in time for the credit squeeze to bite and for youth to rebel against his values.

Threat is especially directed against the daughters of these men, with an extended cycle of films about rapists and killers targeting young girls – children in *Never Take Sweets from a Stranger* (Cyril Frankel 1960) and *Don't Talk to Strange Men* (Pat Jackson 1962), and schoolgirls in *Assault* (Sidney Hayers 1971), *Revenge* (Sidney Hayers 1971), *Fright* (Peter Collinson 1971) and *Killer's Moon* (Alan Birkinshaw 1978). To underline the message, a child is abducted in *Bunny Lake Is Missing*, a student (Samantha Eggar) is imprisoned in *The Collector* (William Wyler 1965) and a blind girl (Mia Farrow) is stalked by a proto-slasher rapist in *Blind Terror* (Richard Fleischer 1971). These films tend to combine the tone of the 'awful warning' safety films of the era, which preached against 'stranger danger', with a seaminess that overlaps with the 'permissive' yet depressing era of the British sex film. *Take an Easy Ride* (Kenneth F. Rowles 1976) is literally this – put into a production as a short safety film about the perils of hitch-hiking, it was rethought mid-production as a rare British entry in the 'roughie' mode of adult movie, presenting a series of anecdotes about raped and murdered thumb-trippers. *I Start Counting* (David Greene 1970), from the novel by Audrey Erskine Lindop, is a far more considered, ambiguous work – though it also features a rapist-killer who is at once a nice young man (Simon Ward) and a supposedly reassuring feature of the British landscape (a bus conductor). The focus is on 14-year-old Wynne (Jenny Agutter), a potential victim, who suspects her 32-year-old adopted brother George (Bryan Marshall) is the killer, but doesn't let that damp the crush she has on him. Wynne, who is never filmed in the leering way Suzy Kendall and Susan George are in *Assault* and *Fright*, is a key character in British cinema, not only drawn to the mature man she believes to be a sex murderer but frequently taking the bus back to the derelict house from which her family has been moved to a high-rise flat. This abandoned place, waiting for demolition, is rich in personal history, and at fourteen, Wynne is already nostalgic, unwilling to let the past go ... even when it's dangerous. Cusp-of-the-1970s Britain (represented by Bracknell New Town), undergoing changes as traumatic as those of an adolescent girl, is captured with chilly bleakness.

The generation gap is insistently a theme, but only the minor *What Became of Jack and Jill?* (Bill Bain 1972), from Laurence Moody's novel *The Ruthless Ones* (1969), uses the resentment of the young against the old as a plot wellspring. Paul Nicholas (the rapist of *Blind Terror*) and Vanessa Howard (Girly in *Mumsy, Nanny, Sonny & Girly*) pull an elaborate *Diaboliques* plot to terrorize Gran (Mona Washbourne) into a heart attack by convincing her that a wave of 'out with the oldies' violence is sweeping the country. Again, it's all about the inheritance – though on a more modest scale. Gran's working-class thrift, toil and responsibility are rejected by a leather jacket lad who'd blow her savings on a hire purchase motorbike and fun in the sun holidays. Howard's mini-skirted Lady Macbeth is an instance of the 'killer dolly bird', an evolution of the amoral teenage temptress troublemakers played by Gillian Hills (*Beat Girl* 1960), Linda Hayden (*Baby Love*, Alastair Reid

1969) or Susan George (*Twinky*, Richard Donner 1970). Pamela Franklin and Judy Geeson are forerunners as schoolgirl murderesses in *The Third Secret* (Charles Crichton 1964) and *Berserk!* (Jim O'Connolly 1967), but the most vicious incarnation is Kim Butcher in *Frightmare* (Pete Walker 1974). Here, in an unusual collusion of the worst of young and old, a teenager and her cannibal grandmother (Sheila Keith) bond over electric drill murders. A dominant creative in the mid- to late 1970s, when Hammer Films floundered and many other Green Penguin filmmakers fled to television or fizzled out altogether, Pete Walker – with only the slightest trace of irony – called his production company Heritage Films. His films are deliberately, defiantly grotty rather than as self-consciously groovy as, say, *Goodbye Gemini*, but times had changed and Walker's only competition came from true crime one-offs like *The Black Panther* (Ian Merrick 1977), a chilling, calm, meticulous account of the career of hold-up man/kidnapper/murderer Donald Nielsen (Donald Sumpter). This is the end of the line for Green Penguin cinema – the essential element of whimsy is unsustainable set beside the blunt, blank malice of Nielsen's crimes.

The wellspring of Green Penguin Cinema, which flourished between the mid-1960s and the mid-1970s, was social upheaval. If *The Knack ... and How to Get It* (Richard Lester 1965) and *Morgan: A Suitable Case for Treatment* (Karel Reisz 1966) are mainstream expressions of the mood of times, these films are on the flipside, relishing freedom to be rude and dangerous but deeply worried. Fear of the young, rebellious and socially mobile recurs, as does a recognition that the wallpaper is peeling and the gas is cut off in what were formerly mansions. Sympathy is seldom with enfeebled, hypocritical traditionalists. In the grim 1970s, a backlash set in. Cruel and unusual punishments are doled out by aged establishment figures in Pete Walker's judicial *House of Whipcord* (1974) and clerical *House of Mortal Sin* (1976), which enact *Daily Mail* fantasies of corporal and capital punishment of young, long-haired representatives of the permissive society. Kids here are ciphers, who strip to feature in provocative front of house stills but never seem remotely sexy in the actual films. Walker's interest is in the fussy old establishment figures who are unable to keep up with the times, and pockets of the 1950s remain. Note how often Green Penguin films take a break from dazzling strangeness to check in on plodding police investigations conducted as if George Dixon or Gideon of the Yard were still on the beat.

Perhaps the most terrifying patriarchal monster is Walter Eastwood (Michael Gough) in *The Corpse* (Viktors Ritelis 1971), another take on *Les Diaboliques*. A managerial commuter belt tyrant, Walter brutally cows his wife (Yvonne Mitchell) and daughter (Sharon Gurney) around the breakfast table while raising his son (Simon Gough) to be his mini-me. Even dead, Walter is a terrifying, impossible-to-be-rid-of presence – but this is a film that gets the most out of its mundane cruelties, perverse touches (Walter feels up his daughter's warm bicycle seat) and acid politeness. I first saw *The Corpse* in an all-night programme at the Classic, Charing Cross Road, one of London's several Grindhouse venues, home to one strand of X certificate, barely a few seconds of BBFC cuts away from the Tatler Cinema Club that escaped the purview of the censors as did the Scala or the NFT. Yet, in its iciness, its Pinterish dialogue, even its roots in classic French-language cinema, it might equally have fit into the bill at the Hampstead Everyman, where the same X certificate signified another branch of cinema – more commonly associated with Alain Resnais, Joseph Losey and Roman Polanski than Hammer Films, Michael Gough and Pete Walker. Green Penguin Cinema is stamped with both kinds of X.

2

The Commercial Idealism of Controversial Cinema:

Raymond Stross and the Censorship of *The Flesh Is Weak*

Christopher Weedman

Raymond Stross (1916–88) built his reputation in British cinema as an independent producer of controversial social dramas. From the late 1950s through the early 1970s, a period of national history that saw the growing fissures within post-war conservatism give rise to the permissive attitudes associated with both Swinging London and the liberal social agenda of Prime Minister Harold Wilson's Labour government, Stross provoked the ire of the British film establishment by pushing topical boundaries. His films shone a spotlight on such then contentious sexual and social topics as prostitution (*The Flesh Is Weak*, Don Chaffey 1957), artificial insemination (*A Question of Adultery*, Chaffey 1958), paedophilia (*The Mark*, Guy Green 1961), rape (*The Very Edge*, Cyril Frankel 1963), homosexual desire (*The Leather Boys*, Sidney J. Furie 1964), adultery (*Třicet jedna ve stínu*/*90 Degrees in the Shade*, Jiří Weiss 1965) and transgenderism (*I Want What I Want*, John Dexter 1972). The British Board of Film Censors (BBFC) passed each of these films with an X certificate – except *The Very Edge* and *90 Degrees in the Shade*. Whereas *The Very Edge* received an A certificate, *90 Degrees in the Shade* was never classified by the BBFC for theatrical release.[1]

Stross and his frequent star and wife, Anne Heywood, achieved their greatest critical and commercial success in the United States with their 1967 film adaptation of D. H. Lawrence's 1922 novella *The Fox*. Directed by Mark Rydell and released by Warner Bros.-Seven Arts' arthouse subsidiary, Claridge Pictures, without a Motion Picture Association of America (MPAA) seal of approval during the final months of the Production Code (Penn 1968), *The Fox* earned an impressive $16 million at the US box office and broke narrative ground in mainstream studio cinema with its transgressive scenes of nudity, female masturbation, and lesbian and bisexual desire (Warga 1969). *The Fox*'s tremendous popularity and selection as 'Best English-Language Foreign Film' at the 1968 Golden Globe Awards brought Stross and Heywood (who earned a nomination for 'Best Actress') the industry acclaim in Hollywood that they seldom received in their native country.[2] 'In England I've always found that enthusiasm was lacking for various films I've made', Stross confessed (Gow 1971: 18). His discontent was not unjustified. While American critics and international festival juries tended to shower Stross's films with accolades, British critics and distributors remained less enthusiastic and, at times, dubious of the fact that the producer was capitalizing on controversial material. This scepticism arguably stemmed from lingering resentment over the thematic changes Stross brought to British cinema in the late 1950s.

The 1957 release of Stross's *The Flesh Is Weak* precipitated a new subversive era of British adult-themed films with its dark tale of Soho prostitution and vice racketeering. As Steve Chibnall explains, the combined success of *The Flesh Is Weak* and *The Curse of Frankenstein* (Terence Fisher 1957) commercially legitimized the BBFC's X certificate, which, from its advent in 1951 until 1957, had been shunned by most British production companies due to its sensationalist connotations and perceived lack of commerciality: 'Before *The Flesh Is Weak*, the number of British "X" films could be counted on the fingers of two hands. After its success, and that of Hammer's shockers, the certificate became an accepted part of British film culture and no longer a box-office handicap' (2012: 49). The commercial validation of the X certificate changed the prevailing industrial perception that British producers needed to make family friendly films like the Rank Organisation's hit comedies *Genevieve* (Henry Cornelius 1953) and *Doctor in the House* (Ralph Thomas 1954) to be domestically profitable.[3]

The press surrounding *The Flesh Is Weak* and Stross's follow-up production, *A Question of Adultery*, foregrounded late 1950s British conservative anxiety about sexually frank films developing a mainstream audience.[4] Throughout most of the decade, X certificate films, primarily American and Continental European imports, played to limited audiences at arthouse and independently owned venues. This narrow market emanated from the reluctance of the two major cinema circuits, ABC and Rank, to exhibit 'adults only' features after they lost money distributing the violent

American noirs *The Enforcer* (*Murder Inc.*, Bretaigne Windust 1951) and *Detective Story* (William Wyler 1951). Whereas ABC subsequently booked only a handful of esteemed X certificate films, Rank steadfastly refused to release any in their cinemas (Harper and Porter 2003: 221–2; Perry 1974: 158). During this early period of the X certificate before the arrival of such landmark British films as *Room at the Top* (Jack Clayton 1959), *Peeping Tom* (Michael Powell 1960) and *Saturday Night and Sunday Morning* (Karel Reisz 1960), Stross's films seemed to make some members of the British press feel uncomfortable. This distress, arguably, stemmed from the fact that his films were both domestically made and for a mass audience – hence eroding the 'high' and 'popular' art divide that generally curbed the number of British patrons viewing sensual 'adults only' French imports like *La Ronde* (Max Ophüls 1950) and *Et Dieu ... créa la femme* (*And Woman ... Was Created*, Roger Vadim 1956).

By using controversial sexual subjects and 'name' American stars (John Derek in *The Flesh Is Weak* and Julie London in *A Question of Adultery*) as selling points to lure British audiences away from their television sets, Stross found himself attacked by the press, which labelled him a 'shrewd showman' profiteering from 'the kind of muck which has no place on the cinema screen' (Evans 1957: 31; Player 1958: 12). Always outspoken and unafraid to stand his ground against these denigrations, Stross retorted, 'I am not peddling animated dirty postcards. Of course I make pictures to make money. I'm not a fool. But I do not exploit sensationalism for purely mercenary reasons. I believe it is important to make pictures with an adult theme, pictures that give audiences something to discuss' (Helliwell 1958). Stross's words highlighted his firm belief that art and commerce need not be mutually exclusive. He felt that films could be both socially conscious and possess an acceptable level of sensationalism to make them marketable to a wider audience. The fusion of these goals was indicative of what Stross dubbed his 'commercial idealist' temperament (Eichelbaum 1978). After establishing himself as a producer of controversial films with *The Flesh Is Weak*, Stross lived up to this self-description by consistently making thematically provocative films with a dual artistic and populist sensibility.

Despite playing a key role in popularizing mainstream adult-themed films across Britain and the United States with *The Flesh Is Weak* and *The Fox*, Stross remains underrecognized within film scholarship. His oeuvre as a producer has garnered only minimal attention: notably brief discussions by Raymond Durgnat and Brian McFarlane, as well as an in-depth 1971 interview by Gordon Gow.[5] I aim to rectify this neglect, which stems, in part, from an inability of some critics to look past the sexual themes and sensational publicity for greater social significance. By examining the evolution of Stross's career with particular attention to the censorship history and reception of *The Flesh Is Weak*, I posit that he is a thematically groundbreaking producer, who utilized controversial social topics and the new narrative freedoms afforded by the X certificate to both rebel against post-war British cultural conservatism and explore the lives of alienated people living on the margins of society.

The Evolution of a 'Commercial Idealist'

Born in Leeds in 1916, the highly ambitious Stross worked his way up through the ranks of the British entertainment industry. Stross received his start backstage at the Q Theatre in West London ('Son' 1949), but, by 1933, he secured an entry level position at Sound City Film Producing and Recording Studios in Shepperton (Luft 1967). Sound City provided him with valuable experience as a grip, cutter, story reader and assistant cameraman on several early talkies (Gow 1971: 19). At twenty years old, Stross formed his own company, Sturt-Stross Film Productions, and produced as well as directed the low-budget short *The Show's the Thing* (1936), which he followed up with his second (and last) directorial effort, *The Reverse Be My Lot* (1938). A melodrama about a physician engaging in illegal human experimentation to cure an influenza epidemic, *The Reverse Be My Lot* was cited by its distributor, Columbia Pictures, as having 'a provocative and daring theme … [and] unusual, yet wholly entertaining, situations' – a description that suggests Stross's early predilection for commercial stories about controversial topics ('Columbia's Nine' 1938: 53). After a stint in Columbia's London front office, Stross ventured into film exhibition and amassed a prosperous chain of Raymond Stross Theatres across the UK (Luft 1967).

By the 1950s, Stross returned to filmmaking with the comedic melodrama *Hell Is Sold Out* (Michael Anderson 1951) and established himself as a maverick in a generally circumspect British film industry. His reemergence as an independent producer coincidentally coincided with the advent of the BBFC's X certificate in 1951. Yet due to the initial stigma surrounding the adult rating, Stross's early films tended to possess thematically conventional narratives without the controversial content indicative of his later work. While Stross was proud of his crime melodrama *The Man Who Watched Trains Go By* (Harold French 1952) (A. Heywood 2022, personal communication, 17 January), he dismissed most of his early films as creative compromises made to appease British executives (Gow 1971: 20).[6] Nevertheless, as Durgnat asserts, these inchoate productions provided glimpses of a rebellious storyteller fighting to emerge: 'during the early fifties, certain of [Stross's] films, even if in the end they succumbed to the conformist straightjacket, were visibly squirming and struggling and heaving convulsively around inside it. It is for precisely that originality that serious criticism considered them *infra dig*' (1971: 245). Durgnat aptly cites *Tall Headlines* (Terence Young 1952) as a harbinger of Stross's subsequent work. An adaptation of Audrey Erskine Lindop's 1950 novel about a seemingly respectable British family coming to terms with the fact that their eldest son, Ronnie, went to the gallows for murdering a woman, the film reveals, as Durgnat notes, the 'paralysing middle-class shame which serious Ealing movies unquestioningly affirmed' (1971: 245). Building upon Durgnat's observation, the family's callous and misinformed 'slut shaming' of their other son's working-class bride, Doris Richardson (Mai Zetterling), demonstrates how they are guilty of prejudging people with the same cruelty that others have inflicted upon them due to Ronnie's crimes.

Not only does *Tall Headlines'* depiction of women navigating culturally repressive attitudes about gender and sexuality anticipate the more developed explorations of this theme in *The Flesh Is Weak*, *A Question of Adultery*, *The Very Edge*, *The Fox*, *I Want What I Want*, and Stross's final American film *Good Luck, Miss Wyckoff* (Marvin J. Chomsky 1979), but representations of middle-class hostility against socially and sexually 'Othered' characters figure prominently in the plights of the recovering paedophile Jim Fuller (Stuart Whitman) in *The Mark*; the lesbian Jill Banford (Sandy Dennis) and the bisexual Ellen March (Heywood) in *The Fox*; the gender transitioning Wendy Ross in *I Want What I Want*; and the genophobic rape victim Evelyn Wyckoff in *Good Luck, Miss Wyckoff* (both played by Heywood). Despite the discernible roots of these recurring themes and character tropes in *Tall Headlines*, it took *The Flesh Is Weak* for Stross to fully establish the type of controversial adult-themed cinema that became his métier.

Setting the Stage for *The Flesh Is Weak*

A seminal X certificate film, Stross's *The Flesh Is Weak* was a major box-office success in Britain in 1957–8, but until the more recent scholarship of Viv Chadder (1999), Melanie Bell (2006, 2010), Chibnall (2012) and Jingan Young (2022) was usually excluded or minimized in conventional historiographies of post-war British cinema and the adult rating.[7] This study builds upon these prior analyses by providing an in-depth examination of *The Flesh Is Weak*'s censorship history and reception (aspects only briefly discussed by Bell, Chibnall and Young) to show how the film marked a crucial turning point in Stross's career by redefining his image as a purveyor of what McFarlane cites as 'anodyne comedies' to a producer of 'sensationalist dramas, often dealing with cutting-edge sexual attitudes' (2003: 644). Moreover, as will be demonstrated, the outcry surrounding *The Flesh Is Weak*'s banning in the seaside town of Worthing, West Sussex stoked debate about whether the local censorship committee should have the power to overrule the BBFC's decisions on which X certificate films were suitable for adult audiences.

Adapted by screenwriters Leigh Vance and Roger Falconer from Deborah Bedford's 1956 play *Daughter of Desire*, *The Flesh Is Weak* concerned Marissa Cooper (Milly Vitale), a naïve 21-year-old woman, who relocates to London seeking greater prosperity. She takes a job as an escort in a seedy Soho nightclub, but quits after meeting and falling in love with a handsome businessman, Tony Gordon (John Derek). Within weeks of their engagement, Tony emotionally blackmails Marissa into prostitution to supposedly pay off his gambling debts. After enduring the humiliation of walking the streets of Soho, Marissa is shocked to discover Tony's actual identity from a journalist, Lloyd Buxton (William Franklyn), writing an exposé on the Giani crime family. Buxton informs Marissa that her fiancé is instead Tony Giani, a well-known gangster who grooms young women to populate the prostitution ring that he operates with his brothers, Angelo (Martin Benson) and Benny (Roger Snowdon). As a result of this revelation, Marissa is forced to choose between remaining with the Gianis or risk her life helping Buxton put them behind bars.

The Flesh Is Weak drew upon the recent criminal exploits of the Messina Brothers, who ruled the London underworld from the late 1930s through the 1950s. Before escalating public scrutiny (sparked by journalist Duncan Webb's exposé in the 3 September 1950 issue of *The People*) put an end to their criminal enterprise, the Sicilian-born Messinas ran roughly five hundred prostitutes in the West End (Arnold 2011: 307–8; Webb 1950). As depicted in both the stage and film versions, they groomed young women into prostitution by showering them with gifts, dinners and promises of marriage (Morton 2012: 180). Before filming this true crime material, Stross produced Bedford's play, which premiered at the Kings Theatre in Southsea on 7 May 1956 ('Drama' 1956: 13). After a successful week-long engagement at the Kings, Stross took *Daughter of Desire* on a twenty-six-week run across the provinces (M. R. 1956), but, according to its star Janet Munro, the producer fell short of his goal of bringing it to the West End (W. W. 1959).

Likely cognizant of the growing audience for adult-themed narratives, Stross announced his intention to make a film version of Bedford's play a month into its provincial run ('It's Not' 1956). When the play's British lead, Munro, proved unavailable, Stross pressed ahead with the Italian Vitale, who was cast alongside American star John Derek in an apparent attempt to increase the film's international marketability. As a result of Vitale's casting, the female protagonist was altered from an experienced British Women's Auxiliary Air Force veteran to a naïve Italian paternal orphan ('Drama' 1956: 13).[8] This alteration in *The Flesh Is Weak* eliminated the post-war social commentary of the play by removing the implication that the character's turn to prostitution stemmed, in part, from her inability to economically reacclimate to civilian life. Moreover, the change in characterization, as Bell argues, 'position[s] the woman as an outsider' and 'intensif[ies] her marginal status' by 'displac[ing] active female sexuality onto a "foreign other"' (2010: 132). The trope of the sexualized continental woman reoccurs in numerous 1950s British films, including the coquettish French nightclub singer Hélène Colbert (Brigitte Bardot) in *Doctor at Sea* (Thomas 1955), the duplicitous Mediterranean gypsy bride Belle (Melina Mercouri) in *The Gypsy and the Gentleman* (Joseph Losey 1958) and the despondent French adulteress Alice Aisgill (Simone Signoret) in *Room at the Top*. As Sue Harper notes, the 'narrative function' of this strain of female characterizations 'was to operate as sexual proxies for respectable British girls' (2000: 99).[9] Vitale's casting in *The Flesh Is Weak* conformed to these foreign female stereotypes but, at the same time, her presence enabled the film to further foreground its connections to the Messina case due to the fact that the real-life gangsters primarily targeted continental women (Arnold 2011: 307).

Negotiating the BBFC Censors

Whether the BBFC played any part in Stross's decision to cast a continental actress as Marissa is unclear, since the censorship file on the film is incomplete. No correspondence remains from Stross's conversations with the BBFC prior to his letter to Board secretary John Nicholls on 3 May 1957; by then an early, incomplete work print (missing the final reel due to purported retakes involving the 'bandaged head' of Vitale) had been submitted for review (Stross 1957). Nonetheless, it is clear that Stross and the BBFC communicated before filming commenced in mid-March 1957. Not only did *The Birmingham Post & Gazette* report that the Board 'vetted the script before work began' (Walker 1958a) but Stross stated in *Kinematograph Weekly*'s on-set production article that the censors were 'extremely cooperative and very reasonable' and, in at least one instance, 'encouraged us to go further than we imagined we could. He [Nicholls or his recently departed predecessor Arthur Watkins] suggested that we actually show our girl's first pick-up, emphasising her embarrassment and shame' (Evans 1957: 31).[10] Although Stross's remarks reveal the BBFC's unexpected willingness to permit him to depict the act of sexual solicitation, a close examination of the scene suggests that the producer and his collaborators were compelled to work within narrow narrative parameters that did not overtly challenge traditional British sexual mores.

In the pick-up scene, the film's director Don Chaffey and cinematographer Stephen Dade frame Marissa in a slightly elevated, knee-level shot of her high heels as they walk across the rain-soaked pavement. The camera initially tracks with Marissa and then abruptly stops as she continues towards the phone box to wait for her first male client. The decision against showing Marissa's face both conveys the 'embarrassment and shame' of her character (as the BBFC purportedly suggested) and keeps the audience at a firm distance to prevent them from fully identifying with the character. The scene is later revealed to be a partial narrative cheat, since her British middle-class client (Jack May) finds himself unable to engage in the sexual act. Showing a similar uneasiness when he enters her flat, the client expresses no discernible interest in illicit sex and reveals that he picked her up at the suggestion of his male co-workers, who told him that a tryst with a prostitute would enable him to forget his former girlfriend.

Stross's late 1950s and early 1960s films sometimes employed narrative cheats or, when adapting literary or dramatic properties, altered the source material to navigate through volatile themes due to the BBFC's restrictive censorship practices. *The Mark* diverged from the 1958 novel by Charles E. Israel to indicate that Fuller never gave into his paedophilic impulses, while *The Leather Boys* changed the homosexual relationship of the male motorcyclists, Reggie (Colin Campbell) and Pete (Dudley Sutton), from the 1961 novel by Gillian Freeman (who wrote the script) to make it clear that only one of them was gay and same-sex acts never transpired. Likewise, *The Very Edge* implied but never confirmed the rape of model-turned-housewife Tracey Lawrence (Heywood), whose seemingly happy marriage becomes strained due to her newfound fear of sexual intimacy after she is attacked in her home by a stalker (Jeremy Brett). These instances display Stross's tendency to treat transgressive subjects with a simultaneously daring yet reserved approach, which helped facilitate both getting through the censors and appealing to a wider audience.

The narrative cheat in *The Flesh Is Weak*'s pick-up scene enabled Stross and his collaborators to dramatize the act of solicitation but, at the same time, avoid the risk of affronting the BBFC by overtly associating British middle-class men with illegal, non-marital sex. As Nicholls did not mention the pick-up scene in the list of required cuts (referenced in Stross's 3 May 1957 letter), one may assume that the Board approved of this discreet treatment (Stross 1957). However, as Bell notes, the client's admission to Marissa ('You're not what I expected. You're nice and sort of ... well, you could almost be like me') retains subversive implications. Bell interprets these lines as problematizing the distinction between 'prostitutes' and 'ordinary women', two categories that the Wolfenden Report subsequently strove to delineate in its 1957 recommendations on how to curb prostitution (2010: 129–30, 134). Building upon Bell's observation, the words 'you could almost be like me' aligns the male client with effeminacy and, by extension, non-heteronormative sexuality given his soft voice, disinterest in sex with Marissa, and need to prove his masculinity to his co-workers. As a result, the coded subtext of the characterization makes the scene an early antecedent of Stross's subsequent and increasingly more conspicuous explorations of non-heteronormative sexuality in *The Leather Boys*, *The Fox* and *I Want What I Want*.

Despite the purportedly easygoing nature of their early script negotiations, the working relationship between Stross and the BBFC exhibited strain after the producer submitted the work print. According to Stross's only letter to Nicholls, the two men had a 'heated conversation' on 1 May 1957, which indicates that they were in strong disagreement about the required cuts (Stross 1957). Stross expressed his reluctance to make any changes that either damaged the film's artistic integrity or required reshoots, an economically difficult proposition for an independent producer working on a limited budget. He stressed, 'I am sure that you will appreciate my acute anxiety at all times not to damage this picture by editing that is not practical, and we have spent two days now looking at the cuts required by you' (Stross 1957). The required cuts centred around depictions of violence and sex in two scenes. The first scene involved a chase sequence featuring members of the rival Salvi crime family pursuing a Giani minder, Saradine (Denis Shaw), down a dark Soho alleyway. Unbeknownst to Saradine, the Salvis seek vengeance against the Gianis for Tony's prior razor slashing of Billy Sachetti, a member of their organization, during a turf dispute. Shot in a noir style with low-key black-and-white lighting, Saradine runs for his life as the Salvis pursue him in their Humber Super Snipe sedan. After cornering the minder at the entrance of a stairwell, the Salvis grab Saradine and toss him through a storefront window.

The BBFC appears to have ordered trims to this scene to tone down the violence. However, Stross and his collaborators instead made the decision to completely remove it rather than damage the continuity: 'We fully appreciate the censor's point of view concerning this and, unfortunately, the cutting required leaves us no alternative other than to take the entire sequence out', the producer told Nicholls (Stross 1957). This deleted scene is present in the 2009 UK DVD release from Odeon Entertainment.[11] By contemporary standards, the violence in the chase scene barely raises an eyebrow and, even for its own time, would not look out of place in any 1950s Hollywood noir or gangster film. The most sensational elements (the slashing of Sachetti, and Saradine falling through the window) transpire offscreen. While the former is discussed during a phone conversation between Angelo and Benny, the latter cuts back to the stairwell with only the sound of shattering glass heard in the distance. Nevertheless, the BBFC's request to trim the chase scene is unsurprising. The Board frowned upon depictions of realistic violence in the mid to late 1950s, particularly following the controversy that greeted *Cosh Boy* (Lewis Gilbert 1953), an X certificate juvenile delinquent drama released shortly after the high-profile hanging of 19-year-old Derek Bentley for the shooting death of a Croydon police constable (Chibnall 2012: 42–4).

The second scene involved an implied sexual encounter between the two lovers, which showed Marissa unbuttoning Tony's shirt and sensually rubbing and kissing his chest as they lay in bed together. Initially, Stross told Nicholls that they would trim this scene by 'entirely remov[ing] the undoing and lifting of the shirt and merely le[aving] the modicum of stroking of Tony's chest necessary for continuity' (Stross 1957). Not satisfied with Stross's proposed compromise, Nicholls replied on 7 May 1957 informing him that the Board refused to permit any 'chest or body stroking' (Nicholls 1957a). An examination of the scene (again seemingly intact on the 2009 DVD) suggests the Board was likely uncomfortable with both the indication of Marissa's own sexual desire and the implied act of oral sex. At the beginning of the scene, Marissa displays sexual agency by both lying on top of Tony and initiating foreplay, but the gangster then re-exerts his dominance by grabbing her hair and pulling her head closer to him as she kisses his stomach – imagery subtly suggesting oral sex, as Bell has noted (2010: 137). While this crucial scene indicates Marissa's willingness to submit to Tony's sexual desires (anticipating her eventual coercion into prostitution), the imagery proved too sexually transgressive for the Board and, by all appearances, was heavily trimmed before the British theatrical release.

Once the BBFC approved the additional cuts on 9 May 1957, Nicholls informed Stross that an X certificate would not be granted until the Board viewed the final edit with a full soundtrack, as well as the publicity and front of house stills that the distributor, Eros Films, planned to use for the film's domestic advertising campaign (Nicholls 1957b). Despite subsequently passing the film with an X certificate on 19 June 1957, Nicholls stressed to Stross that he did not want to see 'any of the more glaring forms of advertising' (Nicholls 1957c). Little heed appears to have been paid to the BBFC's unenforceable recommendations, since *The Flesh Is Weak*'s UK poster boasted a large key art image of a cigarette-smoking Marissa/ Vitale standing provocatively against a brick wall, while draped in a formfitting black dress with matching long gloves and handbag. A small insert image of her male journalist saviour, Buxton/Franklyn (the film's fictional reconfiguration of Webb from the Messina case), was included in the lower right-hand corner. The poster's bold tagline ('They Threatened Us. Don't Make this Film!') complimented the sexually charged design by both underscoring the culturally dangerous nature of the narrative, and serving as a direct reference to Stross's claims to the press that he took out a £20,000 insurance policy on his life after receiving death threats from the London crime underworld while making the film ('Another Gimmick?' 1958).

Commercial Success and Worthing Censorship Controversy

No matter whether Stross's claims about the death threats were true or, as *The Cheshire Observer* questioned, just 'Another Gimmick?', the advertising campaign by the producer and Eros proved highly effective at attracting

British mass audiences ('Another Gimmick' 1958). Shortly after its 2 August 1957 premiere at London's Cameo-Royal on the Charing Cross Road, *The Flesh Is Weak* exceeded all box-office expectations as it broke the cinema house's attendance record by drawing capacity, or near capacity, crowds during its first twenty-one screenings over the Summer Bank Holiday weekend. According to *Kinematograph Weekly*, Cameo-Royal's daily screening of the film 'starts at 10:00 a.m. and if the management had its way the hall would remain open all night, so large and persistent is the demand for seats. And to those who are sceptical of the film's chances in average houses, let me remind them that it's been pulling in as many women as men' (Billings 1957: 13). This account is supported by advertising images showing long lines of men and women standing outside the Cameo-Royal with its marquee declaring, 'At Last! The Shame of London Exposed. But You Must Be Over 16 to See It. Come In – Then Go Home and Warn Your Daughters! It's Happening Now as You Watch the Film' ('Eros' 1957: 22). As opposed to supporting clichéd cultural notions of X certificate films being primarily targeted to male audiences and 'not the ideal choice of an evening's entertainment for maiden aunts' (Newlands 1958) – a patronizing comment made in the *West London Press*'s film review – both the images and *Kinematograph Weekly*'s account show that interest in late 1950s adult-themed films was, in this case, significantly more diverse.

Critical responses to *The Flesh Is Weak* proved highly divisive. *The Daily Herald* praised the production as being 'exciting in parts' and 'a painstaking reconstruction of the Messina Brothers case' (Carthew 1957), and *The Star* declared it 'a brave picture that should shock London, and scare the provincials' ('The Flesh' 1957). Nevertheless, the bulk of the reviews remained mixed to negative with several critics taking aim at the decidedly downbeat and sensational nature of the subject matter. While *Picturegoer* conceded that 'it took some courage to tackle the subject of vice and prostitution in London's back streets', the narrative was 'all so unutterably dreary it ought to deter any girl from joining the oldest profession' (Hinxman 1957: 17). Likewise, *The Monthly Film Bulletin* drew parallels between *The Flesh Is Weak* and the controversial British gangster film *Brighton Rock* (John Boulting 1948) by finding Derek's performance as a 'Graham Greene-style boy gangster ... [to be] played with appropriate menace', but, overall, judged the film to be 'crudely melodramatic ... dealing with, but not one feels very gravely concerned about, the real life problem of organized prostitution' ('Flesh Is' 1957: 114). The latter review indicates a reservation that *The Flesh Is Weak* did not possess a more overtly moralizing tone, which suggests that some critics may have been uneasy with the subject of prostitution being dramatized first as entertainment and only second as social commentary.

The subsequent release of the Wolfenden Report in September 1957 and its stringent legal recommendations to combat prostitution further fuelled the film's success, in part due to the fact that Stross and Eros did not shy away from capitalizing on the report in their promotion of the film. An alternate UK poster design for *The Flesh Is Weak* drew explicit connections between the film and the press coverage of the Wolfenden Report by showing a collage of tabloid newspapers boasting stills from the film with headlines declaring, 'Vice Report: This Is the Full Story', 'Sex Law Clash Ahead' and 'Prostitution – These Facts Have Not Yet Been Faced'. Due to this fortuitous stroke of timing, *The Flesh Is Weak* continued to be a lucrative moneymaker and, after its twelve-week run at the Cameo-Royal, went into a wider release on the ABC circuit in January 1958 (The Stroller 1957: 5).

Despite the film's commercial success in London, *The Flesh Is Weak* did not always have an easy time getting booked in provincial cinema houses, since local licensing boards possessed different sensibilities and, in some cases, employed stricter censorship practices than the BBFC. This chasm is exemplified by the film's failed booking at the Plaza Cinema in Worthing, West Sussex. After seven members of the Worthing Watch Committee (a subcommittee of the town council that oversaw a wide-range of local licensing from petrol storage to Sunday shop openings) attended a pre-screening on 13 September 1957, they voted to ban the film 'on the ground that it contains matter which, if exhibited, would offend against good taste or decency or would be likely to be offensive to public feeling' (Worthing Watch Committee 1957). This decision compelled the cinema manager, Eric Blaker, to cancel the film's scheduled engagement (starting 22 September 1957) and replace it with the safe American musicals *High Society* (Charles Walters 1956) and *The King and I* (Walter Lang 1956) (Hunt 1957; 'The "Flesh" Is Too Strong' 1957). The ban raised numerous eyebrows in Worthing. Not only had the Watch Committee previously received criticism for sending a failed resolution to the town council 'deprecat[ing] the exhibition of [X certificate] films in the borough' ('A Censure' 1956) but the neighbouring communities of Brighton and Hove had already passed *The Flesh Is Weak* without protest ('The "Flesh" Is Too Strong' 1957).

When Worthing residents complained about the disparity in the censorship standards, the committee chairman, Councillor Harold W. Roberts, told the press, 'What happens there has not necessarily any bearing on what happens in Worthing. The matter was debated for some time; we had a long discussion. This film was banned because the committee considered that certain things in it might be offensive' ('The "Flesh" Is Too Strong' 1957). Residents remained unswayed and judged the Watch Committee's views on X certificate films to be both out of touch and inexpert in comparison to the BBFC. The Watch Committee purportedly did not pre-screen all X certificate films and instead relied on distributor synopses – as well as negative reports from other communities – to decide which ones to closely examine ('Troublesome X' 1958). Furthermore, the

Watch Committee possessed a track record of holding British X certificate films to a stricter standard than international imports with comparable depictions. In addition to previously passing the Italian prostitution-themed melodrama *Donne proibite* (*Forbidden Women*, Giuseppe Amato 1954) in early 1957 (Hunt 1957), they also approved the more overly sexual Bardot vehicle *Et Dieu ... créa la femme* a month after *The Flesh Is Weak*'s banning (Dean 1957).

These criticisms spurred increasing protest against the Watch Committee and its ability to locally ban films already vetted by the BBFC. As suggested in a letter to the editors of the *Worthing Gazette* on 25 September 1957, the committee's decision was imbued with an ill-conceived paternalism that insinuated Worthing residents were incapable of making their own film viewing decisions. The author of the letter questioned:

> Why should men who gave years of their lives, and some of their limbs to crush the dictator Hitler, be dictated to in their own homes, as to what films they are allowed to see? Once a film has been passed by the [BBFC], that should be good enough. It is about time Worthing realised this is the 20th century, and not the age of Victorian narrow-mindedness, and that we are grown-up people who have minds of our own.
>
> (Disgusted 1957)

A similar letter seconded this viewpoint and maintained that the Worthing ban was only sending revenue to other surrounding communities:

> How better can our Watch Committee send trade away from the town? The film is showing at Brighton and Hove and I expect British Railways and the Southdown bus company have done roaring trade running to and from Brighton. I should have thought the citizens of Worthing were quite capable of selecting the type of picture they wish to see, and not let the judgment rest on narrow-minded old cronies.
>
> (Off to Brighton 1957)

After the Worthing Labour Party's general management committee passed a resolution condemning the banning ('Banned' 1957), the Watch Committee increasingly lost credibility and, on 6 January 1958, agreed to stop reviewing X certificate films ('Watch Committee Resigns' 1958). They instead decided to abide by the BBFC's censorship decisions, so adult-themed films would not be compelled to satisfy, in the words of the *Worthing Gazette*, 'more than one set of censors' ('Troublesome X' 1958). However, the move did not clear a path for *The Flesh Is Weak* to be screened in Worthing, since the Watch Committee refused to reconsider any of its past decisions on banned X certificate films (Worthing Watch Committee 1958).

Roadblocks and Greener Pastures

Following the popular success of *The Flesh Is Weak* and the subsequent British New Wave hits *Room at the Top* and *Saturday Night and Sunday Morning*, adult-themed films with sexual storylines proved so lucrative that, by the early 1960s, Rank realized it could no longer afford to concentrate solely on family audiences. Not only did Rank start distributing X certificate films from outside production companies on its cinema circuit but this vertically integrated film corporation also greenlit its first in-house 'adults only' production, *No Love for Johnnie* (Thomas 1961). Nevertheless, these changing attitudes did not make it any easier for Stross to secure wide distribution for his films. In December 1960, Stross carefully negotiated with Nicholls's successor, John Trevelyan, to get *The Mark*'s sensitive treatment of paedophilia and psychotherapy passed by the BBFC with an X certificate (Trevelyan 1961). Yet despite *The Mark*'s selection as Britain's entry for the prestigious Palme d'Or at the 1961 Cannes Film Festival, ABC and Rank promptly banned the film from their cinema circuits due to its controversial subject matter ('The Mark' 1961: 22). Rank's managing director, John Davis, attempted to justify the decision by citing *The Mark* as being 'too sordid for popular consumption' (Nathan 1961), a notion further undermined when the film earned American actor Stuart Whitman a 'Best Actor' nomination at the 1962 Academy Awards.

Stross lambasted *The Mark*'s banning by pointing out the hypocrisy of Rank's willingness to exhibit other highly transgressive X certificate films, particularly those boasting A-list Hollywood stars. 'They showed *Suddenly, Last Summer* which dealt with cannibalism and sodomy', Stross noted. 'If I had Elizabeth Taylor instead of Maria Schell – with every respect to her – would they still have turned it down?' (Nathan 1961). As the decade continued, Stross faced additional roadblocks and routinely watched as his productions were shelved without a prompt circuit release. Many British independent producers accused ABC and Rank of using this tactic to squeeze them out of the domestic film market (Bishop 1963). *90 Degrees in the Shade* never received distribution in Britain (Bentley 1968), while *The Leather Boys* and the atypical sci-fi/horror venture *Ein Toter sucht seinen Mörder* (*Vengeance*, Freddie Francis 1962) waited several months to obtain a release on the ABC circuit (Bishop 1963; Walker 1974: 249–50).

The BBFC's censorship practices may have become more tolerant during Trevelyan's tenure, but, as evident from Stross's experiences in the early to mid-1960s, the production of controversial adult-themed films remained a perpetually challenging and precarious endeavour. By 1967, Stross and Heywood relocated to Hollywood to produce their smash hit *The Fox*, which – outside of a momentary return to London to make the seminal 1972 transgender film *I Want What I Want* – signalled the end of their long careers in British cinema. Despite his various adversities, Stross remained optimistic and ardently committed to his filmmaking convictions. He insisted to Gow:

> In Hollywood they said to me, 'Kid, you've got good taste'. But everybody's got taste – bad taste, indifferent taste, appalling taste, tastelessness. What we have to have in this industry is a lack of fear, integrity – but above all, superlatively good taste at all times. And then there is nothing – *nothing* – that we can't do'.
>
> (1971: 22)

Sadly, a series of health problems in the 1970s curtailed Stross's career at its peak (Pollock 1978: 6). He and Heywood made only one more film together, an adaptation of William Inge's rape-themed 1970 novel *Good Luck, Miss Wyckoff*, in the United States in 1979. Nevertheless, the husband-and-wife team continued collaborating on multiple unfilmed projects up until his death in 1988 at the age of seventy-two (A. Heywood 2022, personal communication, 11 October). While seldom given the credit his groundbreaking filmography warrants, Stross deserves proper recognition for expanding the thematic possibilities of the X certificate and opening the door for subsequent British cinema mavericks such as Ken Russell, Nicolas Roeg, Jane Arden and Derek Jarman by fearlessly tackling sexual topics once deemed unfilmable.

Author Note

Special thanks to Anne Heywood and the Stross family, Julian Grainger, Diane Ladlow (West Sussex Record Office), and Jacob Smith (BBFC) for both their support and assistance accessing rare archival materials for this chapter.

Notes

1   *90 Degrees in the Shade* later received the BBFC's 12 classification (suitable for audiences twelve and older) for home video release in 2010.

2   Despite partial finance from US film companies (Warner Bros.-Seven Arts and Motion Pictures International), *The Fox* qualified as a Canadian production due to being filmed in Kleinburg, Ontario.

3   Chibnall (2012: 29–52) and Harper and Porter (2003: 220–2) provide valuable background on the X certificate in the early to mid-1950s.

4   This uneasiness is evident in Alexander Walker's remarks about the 'vulgar' and 'common' nature of *A Question of Adultery* (1958b). Likewise, Arthur

Helliwell, despite finding some 'integrity' and 'restraint' in the film when he viewed it in rushes, insisted that 'it still adds up to Sex with a capital "S" – which means another Stross box-office winner. So who does he think he's kidding? Not me!' (1958).

5   For further analysis of Stross's career, see Durgnat (1971: 244–5), Gow (1971: 18–22) and McFarlane (2003: 643–4).

6   Representative compromised Stross films include *Rough Shoot* (Robert Parrish 1953), *Star of India* (Arthur Lubin 1954), *As Long as They're Happy* (J. Lee Thompson 1955), *An Alligator Named Daisy* (Thompson 1955), *Jumping for Joy* (John Paddy Carstairs 1956) and *A Touch of the Sun* (Gordon Parry 1956).

7   For previous readings of *The Flesh Is Weak*, see Bell (2010: 123–47), Chadder (1999: 75–7), Chibnall (2012: 48–9) and Young (2022: 123–4, 126–33). Bell (publishing as Bell-Williams) penned a previous version of her chapter in 2006.

8   Marissa was named Morna Blakeney in Bedford's play ('Drama' 1956).

9   For analysis of Vitale's casting and its association with the trope of the sexualized 'other', see Bell (2010: 132–3), Bell-Williams (2006: 271) and Young (2022: 126–7).

10   In his brief discussion of the film's censorship problems, Chibnall mentions that Vance's script was likely submitted during Watkins's tenure, which ended in January 1957 (2012: 49).

11   It is unclear if Odeon's DVD of *The Flesh Is Weak* (licensed from the London-based Euro London Films) was sourced from a US or international release print.

References

'Another Gimmick?' (1958), *The Cheshire Observer*, 1 March.

Arnold, C. (2011), *The Sexual History of London: From Roman Londinium to the Swinging City – Lust, Vice, and Desire Across the Ages*, New York: St Martin's Press.

'Banned, But It Was Advertised Here' (1957), *Worthing Gazette*, 25 September.

Bell, M. (2010), *Femininity in the Frame: Women and 1950s British Popular Cinema*, London: I.B. Tauris.

Bell-Williams, M. (2006), '"Shop-soiled" Women: Female Sexuality and the Figure of the Prostitute in 1950s British Cinema', *Journal of British Cinema and Television*, 3 (2): 266–83.

Bentley, J. (1968), 'Queen Anne Strips to Conquer', *Sunday Mirror*, 1 September.

Billings, J. (1957), 'Your Films', *Kinematograph Weekly*, 22 August: 13.

Bishop, P. (1963), 'Why They're All on the Shelf', *The People*, 8 December.

Carthew, A. (1957), 'Rest of the New Films', *The Daily Herald*, 2 August.

'A Censure on "X" Films Bounces' (1956), *Worthing Gazette*, 3 October.

Chadder, V. (1999), 'The Higher Heel: Women and the Post-war British Crime Film', in S. Chibnall and R. Murphy (eds), *British Crime Cinema*, 66–80, London: Routledge.

Chibnall, S. (2012), 'From *The Snake Pit* to the *Garden of Eden*: A Time of Temptation for the Board', in E. Lamberti (ed), *Behind the Scenes at the BBFC: Film Classification from the Silver Screen to the Digital Age*, 29–52, London: BFI/Palgrave-Macmillan.

'Columbia's Nine for Trade Show' (1938), *Kinematograph Weekly*, 20 January: 53.

Dean, P. (1957), 'Is She Annoyed?', *Worthing Gazette*, 30 October.

Disgusted [pseud.] (1957), 'Angelic Worthing?', *Worthing Gazette*, 25 September.

'Drama of a Girl's Downfall' (1956), *The Stage*, 10 May: 13.

Durgnat, R. (1971), *A Mirror for England: British Movies from Austerity to Affluence*, New York: Praeger Publishers.

Eichelbaum, S. (1978), 'To Stockton, for a Film About a Virgin', *The San Francisco Examiner*, 16 April.

'Eros Films Wins a Wager!' (1957), *Kinematograph Weekly*, 15 August: 22.

Evans, P. (1957), 'Stross Defends His Social Document', *Kinematograph Weekly*, 21 March: 31.

'Flesh Is Weak, The' (1957), *Monthly Film Bulletin*, September: 114.

'The "Flesh" Is Too Strong for Worthing' (1957), *Worthing Gazette*, 18 September.

'The Flesh Is Weak' (1957), *The Star*, 2 August.

Gow, G. (1971), 'Love Yourself Sufficiently', *Films and Filming*, March: 18–22.

Harper, S. (2000), *Women in British Cinema: Mad, Bad and Dangerous to Know*, London: Continuum.

Harper, S. and V. Porter (2003), *British Cinema of the 1950s: The Decline of Deference*, Oxford: Oxford University Press.

Helliwell, A. (1958), 'Follow Me Around!', *The People*, 12 January.

Hinxman, M. (1957), 'The Flesh Is Weak', *Picturegoer*, 21 September: 17.

Hunt, P. D. (1957), 'This "X" Film Has a Moral', *Worthing Gazette*, 25 September.

'It's Not Just One of Those Things' (1956), *The Newcastle Journal*, 8 June.

Luft, H. G. (1967), 'As We See It: Presenting Movie Maker Stross', *B'Nai B'rith Messenger*, 22 December.

'"The Mark", Cannes Entry, Has Booking Trouble' (1961), *Variety*, 5 April: 22.

McFarlane, B. (2003), *The Encyclopedia of British Film*, London: BFI/Methuen Publishing.

Morton, J. (2012), *The Mammoth Book of Gangs*, Philadelphia: Running Press.

M. R. [pseud.] (1956), Untitled photo caption, *The Sunday Dispatch*, 20 May.

Nathan, D. (1961), 'Zero Night for Stross and His Banned Film', *The Daily Herald*, 9 May.

Newlands, W. (1958), 'The Seamy Side', *The West London Press*, 17 January.

Nicholls, J. (1957a), 'Letter to Raymond Stross', *The Flesh Is Weak* files, 7 May, London: BBFC archive.

Nicholls, J. (1957b), 'Letter to Raymond Stross', *The Flesh Is Weak* files, 9 May, London: BBFC archive.

Nicholls, J. (1957c), 'Letter to Raymond Stross', *The Flesh Is Weak* files, 20 June, London: BBFC archive.

Off to Brighton [pseud.] (1957), 'Send Trade Away', *Worthing Gazette*, 25 September.

Penn, S. (1968), 'Bid to Cash in on Market Held by Imports', *The Wall Street Journal*, 22 March.

Perry, G. (1974), *The Great British Picture Show: From the 90s to the 70s*, New York: Hill and Wang.

Player, E. (1958), 'Home Screen Film Parade: Lifelike', *Picturegoer*, 26 April: 12.

Pollock, D. (1978), 'Raymond Stross'[s] Comeback; To Shoot (Black Rapist) Inge Novel', *Variety*, 28 June: 6.

'Son of a Former Dewsbury Director' (1949), *The Yorkshire Post and Leeds Mercury*, 9 November.

The Stroller [pseud.] (1957), 'Long Shots', *Kinematograph Weekly*, 8 August: 4–5.

Stross, R. (1957), 'Letter to John Nicholls', *The Flesh Is Weak* files, 3 May, London: BBFC archive.

Trevelyan, J. (1961), 'BBFC Memo: Second Screening Report', *The Mark* files, 30 December, London: BBFC archive.

'Troublesome X' (1958), *Worthing Gazette*, 15 January.

Walker, A. (1958a), 'Street Scene', *The Birmingham Post & Gazette*, 20 January.

Walker, A. (1958b), 'Sagan Again', *The Birmingham Post & Gazette*, 15 September.

Walker, A. (1974), *Hollywood UK: The British Film Industry in the Sixties*, New York: Stein and Day.

Warga, W. (1969), 'Anne Heywood Playing Oscar Game by the Rules', *The Los Angeles Times*, 3 February.

'Watch Committee Resigns as Censor' (1958), *Worthing Gazette*, 15 January.

Webb, D. (1950), 'Arrest These Four Men', *The People*, 3 September.

Worthing Watch Committee (1957), 'Licensing of Cinemas – Film "The Flesh Is Weak"', Watch Committee meeting minutes, 13 September, catalogue no. BO/WO/3/29/1, Chichester: West Sussex Record Office.

Worthing Watch Committee (1958), 'Licensing of Cinemas – "X" Films', Watch Committee meeting minutes, 10 February, catalogue no. BO/WO/3/29/1, Chichester: West Sussex Record Office.

W. W. [pseud.]. (1959), 'Santa Disney Fills Janet's Stocking', *Kensington Post*, 9 January.

Young, J. (2022), *Soho on Screen: Cinematic Spaces of Bohemia and Cosmopolitanism, 1948–1963*, New York: Berghahn Books.

3

Colour, Realism and the X Certificate:

Horrors of the Black Museum and *Peeping Tom*

Sarah Street

In 1959 two films, *Horrors of the Black Museum* (Arthur Crabtree 1959) and *Peeping Tom* (Michael Powell 1960), elicited comments not only about their controversial content but also their strategic use of colour. *Monthly Film Bulletin* remarked that '[f]or all its contemporary setting, the plot of this lurid melodrama [*Horrors of the Black Museum*] relies almost entirely on hackneyed Gothic paraphernalia', concluding that the film 'gains any persuasion it may have from the Eastman Colour-and-Cinema-Scope trappings rather than from Michael Gough's conventional portrayal of menace' ('*Horrors*' 1959: 59). The *Kinematograph Weekly*'s review of *Peeping Tom* quoted Michael Powell's observation that to achieve a contemporary setting 'Otto Heller is using colour in a very different way ... with sets almost devoid of colour' ('*Peeping Tom*' 1959: 22). These comments on two X certificate films reference colour as a distinctive element of their contemporary mise en scènes. Both films were shot in Eastmancolor, a relatively cheap stock introduced in the early- to mid-1950s that could be used in any camera, during a period when the majority of British films were still produced in black and white. During the years 1957–62 Hammer's horror films 'provided the BBFC with a testing ground through which they were able to reflect upon some of the key issues arising from the shift to colour' (Frith 2019: 246). Concerns were raised even at the script stage of their evaluations, such as with *Dracula* (Terence Fisher 1958) for which it was advised that 'strong cautions will be necessary on shots of blood' (Reader's report 1957). The third Hammer film (but first in colour) to be granted an X certificate was *The Curse of Frankenstein* (Fisher 1957), and concerns about the script, black-and-white print, and final colour version similarly revolved around the presentation of blood, in particular 'Frankenstein wiping the blood off on his overall after severing the head' (Watkins 1957). But it was two non-Hammer films that proved to be the most controversial cases involving questions of colour. When John Trevelyan reflected on his time as Board secretary of the BBFC in 1958–71, he commented that colour emphasized and increased 'the potentially dangerous ... sadistic and nasty' elements of *Horrors of the Black Museum* and *Peeping Tom* (1973: 159).

This chapter considers the contribution of colour to both films' reputations as risqué, boundary-pushing fictions that were caught between a desire to showcase, even celebrate colour, and the risks of showing an all-too-graphic representation of violence. Although released at the beginning of the 1960s, the films anticipated representational and aesthetic shifts that became identified with a decade of uncompromising 'Adult' entertainment: by the end of the decade this was in full, 'living' colour. Members of the production teams of both films had previously worked on significant Technicolor films. Desmond Dickinson, cinematographer on *Horrors of the Black Museum*, shot *The Importance of Being Earnest* (Anthony Asquith 1952), a notable film for its strategic crafting of costume and colour (Street 2012: 167–8). Arthur Lawson, art director on *Peeping Tom*, worked on Powell and Emeric Pressburger's seminal Technicolor films *The Red Shoes* (1948), *The Elusive Pimpernel* (1949), *Gone to Earth* (1950) and *The Tales of Hoffmann* (1951). Both Dickinson and Heller went on to experiment with lighting and Eastmancolor in different genres including Dickinson's work on the science fiction film *Konga* (John Lemont 1961) and contemporary drama *Baby Love* (Alastair Reid 1969), and Heller's innovative application of artificial lighting featured in *The Ipcress File* (Sidney J. Furie 1965).

The relatively novel status of colour in British cinema challenged filmmakers to explore its aesthetic and generic possibilities, and *Horrors of the Black Museum* and *Peeping Tom* are exemplary films in this regard. Colour was referenced in the posters advertising both films, with *Peeping Tom* in particular naming Eastmancolor as the process that delivered this attraction. In addition, the hyping of the theatrical gimmick 'Hypnovista' in posters for *Horrors of the Black Museum* stood out prominently for its red lettering and with an eye depicted inside the enlarged letter 'O'. The eye was perhaps a symbolic means of accentuating the cinema experience at a time when television set ownership was increasing but colour television was not introduced in Britain until the late 1960s. The eye acquires an additional resonance in respect of the film's shocking opening scene which featured eyes and caused the censors great concern. While Arthur Crabtree was using colour for the first time in a feature film, Michael Powell drew on his past experience of filming in Technicolor, a factor that Trevelyan took into consideration when making considerable efforts to ensure that *Peeping Tom* was not banned (Aldgate 1995: 54–5). Both films used colour as an essential element of their designs, analysis of which can be related to prevalent debates about realism, the visualization of horror and the impact of colour on censors, critics and audiences. Their controversial reputations also related to their contemporary settings which captured 'the tatty world of cheap sensationalism' involved in their plots and locales, which separated them from Hammer's arguably more removed, historical settings (Pirie 2008: 114). My analyses will show how, quite apart from enhancing the films' most horrific scenes, colour was integral to their stylistic designs. By considering the impact of colour over a film text as a whole rather than fixating, as the censors did, on particular moments and scenes, I argue that colour functions as a more remarkable, impressive and resonant orchestration than they acknowledged. In the case of *Peeping Tom* especially, the full impact depended on complex schemes of interrelated, chromatic patterning that are part of the film's world while at the same time using techniques that permit us to maintain critical distance at key points.

Colour and the Film Text

Theories on the relative power of colour are useful to understand how colour operated throughout a film, rather than during arresting moments. Sergei Eisenstein wrote about colour as an organic system in which films could exhibit a particular design structure with potential to play with, or even divorce colours from their more usual cultural/symbolic meanings. As Eirik Frisvold Hanssen explains, for Eisenstein colour was an integral part of a film's 'organic unity' involving expressive elements such as montage and music: 'Colour should be used at given moments when it can be employed to accentuate specific themes and ideas within the totality of the film' (2004: 219). For Edward Branigan, colour is profoundly relational and can be likened to a 'tracking' camera which shifts as sequences of colours occur within a shot or through framing and reframing. This permits a colour to exert influence on nearby colours, as well as enabling colour matches or mismatches employing off-screen space. Both critics stress the fact that because images move, theorizations of colour must take into account shifting patterns and parallels among textual layers and relational structures. In addition, Branigan's interest in colour perception is suggestive of how the patterns and structures of a film interact with a spectator's 'working' memory of colours, their varied and various associations (2018: 114).

These ideas elucidate how colour operates in *Horrors of the Black Museum* and *Peeping Tom* and in relation to the shots and scenes the BBFC was most concerned about when making their X certificates. Three themes have been selected for particular concentration: the films' opening 'shocker' sequences, pivotal scenes in which artificial coloured lighting subsumes the screen, and colour's function in authenticating the physical environments and locales within which the films are set. Although the films are very different in tone, they share some similarities, particularly relating to their contemporary settings and respective worlds of pulp fiction and pornography, as noted by David Pirie: 'Their visual inspiration is 1950s pornography while their central preoccupation is with the British public's insatiable appetite for crimes of violence' (2008: 114). The latter was a particular concern for the BBFC, with one reader of the script for *Horrors of the Black Museum* commenting: 'We should not, I think, lose sight of the fact that a sharp increase in crimes of violence has accompanied a relaxation in our standards [...] we cannot be *sure* that more violence and horror in films has not in some degree contributed to the decline of self-control among young grown-ups' (Script report 1958).

A similar uncertainty about the impact of horror films pervaded the BBFC, as Trevelyan revealed in his memoirs when he admitted he had misjudged *Peeping Tom*'s script in not preparing him for the full shock of its disturbing realization on film: 'I had been sent the script and had thought that the film would contribute to a public understanding of mental illness, but the film seemed to be totally different. Having accepted the project at script stage we did not feel able to reject the film, so we made extensive cuts and hoped for the best' (1973: 159). Mark Kermode points out, however, that '[c]omparisons between the submitted script and its celluloid realization demonstrate very little deviation from what was originally approved by the Board', demonstrating how 'something happens from a script to a projected film but it is intangible' (2002: 12). Trevelyan had not anticipated the full impact of *Peeping Tom* or its infamous negative critical reception, such as Derek Hill's review in *Tribune* – 'Obviously, there's a legitimate place in the cinema for genuine psychological studies. But this crude, sensational exploitation merely aims at giving the bluntest of cheap thrills' – that more or less put Powell out of work for many years (1960: 55).

Opening Sequences and Their Resonance

Both films have highly distinctive opening sequences that involve terror and a victim's vision. From the BBFC's reports it is clear that these elements were considered to be the most potentially harmful, and cuts were suggested to reduce their impact. *Horrors of the Black Museum* opens with an establishing shot that locates the London setting with iconic red buses and cars on a busy road. The camera follows a red postal van which stops outside a house to deliver a parcel. Inside, two women open it to discover a pair of binoculars with no note indicating who has sent them. Gail, the woman to whom the parcel was addressed (Dorinda Stevens), goes towards the window to look through them, and as she does, the camera cuts away from her, focusing for a moment on her friend Peggy (Malou Pantera). We hear a scream and the camera cuts back to Gail, hands over her face with blood running through her fingers. She falls to the floor, the binoculars beside her on the carpet but now showing spikes coming out of their viewing lenses, fatal spikes which have pierced her eyes (see Plate 2). Peggy runs out of the flat, and a close-up shows the binoculars again with bright-red blood on the spikes and carpet that confirm the sickness of the crime. The version referred to here is the 2013 Network DVD release by Studio Canal (no. 79538860), which includes two pre-censored shots of the binoculars on the carpet.

The BBFC's report on this sequence confirms that cuts were made to the film, John Trevelyan being particularly concerned about the blood seeping through the woman's hands, and the close-up of the binoculars and blood on the carpet. He wrote to Herman Cohen of Anglo-Amalgamated Films, the company that distributed *Horrors of the Black Museum*: 'If you must have blood perhaps it could be confined to the shot of the binoculars on the floor, although even this is very unpleasant' (Trevelyan 1958b). Cohen nonetheless managed to persuade Trevelyan that the shots were necessary for the meaning of the plot to be understood, an argument Trevelyan reluctantly accepted with the proviso that 'the close shot of the binoculars on the carpet with the spikes covered with blood' was removed (Trevelyan 1959). An X certificate was granted and the approved version 'cuts the scene to the binoculars on the floor to the bare minimum of just the dissolve' (Cohen 1959).

The fixation of the BBFC on showing blood is typical of their concern over specific details, rather than the impact of an entire sequence. The binoculars and blood on the carpet when seen for the first time, for example, have arguably more impact than the close-up that simply shows the same but larger. In terms of chromatic sequencing and resonance, there is a distinct build-up in the sequence, whereby the muted mise en scène and costuming makes the red blood appear startling in comparison. The hallway of the house that has been divided into flats is drab, decorated with brown wallpaper and blueish-painted dirty walls seen when the postman delivers the parcel. Once inside, the living room has mauve walls, a 'cool' colour, and the women are dressed somberly. Gail is blonde, wearing a black top and shiny black skirt, and Peggy is a redhead in a brown dress. This overall composition allows the blood to have maximum shock value when it is seen, first running through Gail's pale fingers, and then revealing the horrific mechanism of the killer binoculars. Writing in the *Kinematograph Weekly*, the film trade paper aimed at exhibitors, Josh Billings noted that 'the highlights, served with lashings of tomato ketchup, stretch credulity to near breaking point' (Billings 1959: 15). This statement, commenting on the release as sanctioned by the BBFC, shows that the shots had impact, even in their restricted state. Stretching credulity implies that the blood was exaggerated, unreal 'ketchup', yet critics were clearly nervous about what realistic, or as in this case hyper-realistic colour, might add to scenarios that were already disturbing. British horror films of the period typically used 'Kensington Gore' (theatrical blood made up of a basic recipe of syrup, corn flour and food colouring) to create such effects (Hills 2015: 419). The film's trailer created anticipation of the scene's shocking visual impact by stating that it could not be shown 'as it appears in the picture' because it was as a U (Universal) certificated trailer advertising an X certificate film.

Horrors of the Black Museum was released with the theatrical gimmick of 'Hypno-Vista', a novelty that consisted of a thirteen-minute short film prologue to the feature film added by US distributors American International after the film's initial UK run. Intended to hype the film's appeal to American audiences, the prologue was presented by Emile Franchel, a psychologist specializing in hypnotism. He demonstrated the impact of visual colour effects, particularly as they related to hypnotism, emotional responses and the power of suggestion. The short film matched colours to sounds, for example 'cool' blue was accompanied by freezing sounds, while red, described as a 'hot' colour, was associated with scorching heat. This indicates how the novelty of colour was being presented as an additional pleasure in the film, encouraging audiences to respond to its various effects. It is also reflective of contemporary interest in using these techniques to market other products to the public. When advertising companies began to deploy 'subliminal' methods through psychological suggestion in the late 1950s, critics became concerned about the sinister and ethical impacts of 'the hidden persuaders' on people's consciousness (Packard 1957). This resulted in a ban in 1958 imposed by the Institute of Practitioners in Advertising, the UK's leading trade and professional association, on its members using experimental and subliminal advertising techniques (Schwarzkopf 2007: 139). Even so, concerns persisted in the context of contemporary brain science research into the hallucinatory and emotional impact of stroboscopic lights (Walter 1953).

The idea that colour could engage audiences in an almost subliminal way is demonstrated in the film's opening sequence, with the gradual build-up to the shock of the red blood that so disturbed John Trevelyan. When we first see red in the film, following the opening credits which have a blue background, it is for London buses and a postal van that travel through the streets in a perfectly innocuous, normal way. Once inside the flat red is absent, with the exception of the hair colour of Gail's friend which is copper-toned natural red, rather than dyed or bright, until the blood spills through Gail's fingers as she holds them in horror to her face, calling out 'my eyes ... my eyes'.

The suddenness of the intrusion of a red that is shocking and fearsome recalls Eisenstein's observations on colour and context:

> What is unique in an image and what can blend essentially with it are absolute only in the conditions of a *given* context, of a *given* iconography, of a *given* construct ... Red! The colour of the revolutionary flag. And the colour of the ears of a liar caught red-handed. The colour of boiled crayfish – and the colour of a 'crimson' sunset. The colour of cranberry juice – and the colour of warm human blood.
>
> (2006: 107, Eisenstein's italicization)

In this opening sequence the meaning of red has been transformed, delivering what Murray Pomerance has referred to as 'deep' colour that can be likened to the effect Barthes described in *Camera Lucinda* as of a *punctum* that arrests the spectator: 'Deep colour triggers memory [...] a prickling point of emerging affective contact' that is highly saturated and brilliant (Pomerance 2017: 5). When Cohen urged Trevelyan not to cut the shots of the blood, he was insisting on their importance to the film's 'entire meaning', a statement affirming colour's centrality to the film's core sensibilities and ideas. A woman's sight, and her life, has been destroyed in a single moment, triggering our primal fears of losing vision and control. Context changes meaning when a parcel purporting to be a curious, welcome gift from an unknown stranger turns out to be a deadly weapon. We later discover the murder is typical of the modus operandi of Edmund Bancroft (Michael Gough), the crime writer who used items such as the binoculars purchased from an antique shop to commit a series of macabre killings which he subsequently documented in his private 'museum' of horrors. Although not applicable to this fictional situation, as some members of the film's audience would have understood, unsolicited letters or packages in the post invariably meant trouble since they could be associated with sexual blackmail or as a means of gaining subscribers to pornographic publications (McLaren 2002).

Peeping Tom has a similarly intriguing and remarkable opening which also invites questions of vision, looking and horror. Like *Horrors of the Black Museum* the opening credits are shown with a blue background, and similar design principles are subsequently deployed, whereby primary colours such as red show up vividly, in comparison with otherwise more muted sets Powell referred to as 'almost devoid of colour'. A startling close-up of an eye, first shut but then opening to show a blue iris opening very widely, as if in fear, follows in a blatant announcement of the film's voyeuristic theme, recalling the iconic first shots of *Un Chien Andalou* (Luis Buñuel 1928) and *Vertigo* (Alfred Hitchcock 1958) that also place a close-up of an eye within an unconventional representation, respectively, a slit across the eye, and a swirling pattern emanating from the pupil. In *Peeping Tom*, the opening then progresses to a long shot of a dirty-looking dark street where Dora (Brenda Bruce), a blonde-haired woman wearing a red skirt, gold hooped earrings, a fur shawl and blue jumper with a shiny belt, is looking into a shop window. A man in a light brown duffle coat walks into shot – we see him from behind and hear him whistling. Next is a close-up of camera lenses, almost hidden in his coat as he walks forward and a whirring noise is heard, giving the impression that he is secretly filming the scene. Then we see the camera's viewpoint with its cross-hairs visible, closing in on Dora as she looks into the shop window that sells stockings, hats, maybe underwear. As the camera gets closer it tilts down to her red skirt and up her body as she turns and says, 'It'll be two quid' in a tired voice, as if she has spoken the words many times before. She walks on and we follow her through the viewfinder as she walks through Newman Passage, a dark and deserted London location referred to by Powell as 'a narrow arched passageway that gives you goosepimples just to look at it. They say it was associated with Jack the Ripper' (2000: 217). The area was generally linked to clandestine activities such as a former refuge for communists and location of brothels.

The camera tilts down to a bin into which the man throws a yellow Cine-Kodak Plus X (16) film magazine box, information that implies he is an amateur filmmaker. Dora walks upstairs, the camera showing her skirt and the backs of her legs, the low angle accentuating her black-lined stockings and high-heeled shoes. An older woman dressed in beige/browns descends the stairs, giving a look of disapproval as she passes Dora. Once inside her shabby room, Dora lights the electric fire, sits on the bed, takes off a gold anklet and unzips her skirt in a routinized way, saying nothing. To emphasize the fact that we are seeing what the camera shoots, we hear a noise as it tilts down momentarily before we hear a click. When the camera tilts up again Dora looks puzzled by the noise, and she is now illuminated by a flickering light that settles on her face. She looks terrified as her eyes widen, she leans backwards on the bed and screams as the camera gets closer; we do not see what has frightened her. The sequence then cuts to a whirring film projector, with a red accent on the shot. A man is watching a film of Dora, and we see the same shot of her looking into the window that opened *Peeping Tom*, but this time in black and white. It is clearly the film we have seen being made of a possible crime being watched later by the perpetrator. *Peeping Tom*'s credits then appear in blue lettering, shadowed with white.

The BBFC's report on *Peeping Tom* is limited to details given on their website (the original files are believed lost), as a 'case study' film:

When the film arrived at the BBFC in 1960, seven cuts were made in order to allow the film to be classified at X. These included curtailing scenes of the murder of a prostitute and of Mark's suicide; the removal of shots of a nude woman; removal of sight of a woman's disfigured face; reducing the scene in which Vivian is murdered, in particular the focus on the spike that kills her; removing shots and dialogue references to a woman's bruises and some dialogue cuts in a conversation between police officers; reducing emphasis on the killer spike in a conversation between Mark and Mrs Stephens and removing shots of Millie on a bed.

(Peeping Tom file)

The horror of *Peeping Tom* is in the unseen, horrific idea of the way the women are murdered by the amateur photographer Mark (Carl Boehm) with his spiked tripod, filming them as they see their own distorted, mirrored reflection as they die. This opening sequence of Dora sets up the question: what have the women seen that is so terrifying and why does Mark film them? We do not learn the full horror of the killing method until Mark tells Helen (Anna Massey) towards the end of the film. Like the report on *Horrors of the Black Museum* the BBFC's emphasis is on particular shots, their duration and the 'killer spike', even if only mentioned in conversation. As Trevelyan's testimony later revealed, they 'hoped for the best', but this was no preparation for how the film would turn out with its effective central performances, psychological exploration of Mark's disturbed childhood and the film's deliberate avoidance of crude, 'tomato ketchup' effects.

There are similarities between *Peeping Tom* and *Horrors of the Black Museum* in their early presentations of colour. While the censors did not mention colour explicitly in the case of *Peeping Tom*, Trevelyan recalled colour as being problematic (1973: 160). It is used to present the world of the film, and Mark's world view, graphically. The strategy of accentuating red, for example, occurs in both films, especially for stereotypical representations of sexuality. Red is emphasized by its strategic appearance, which sets up associative connections and resonances throughout the rest of *Peeping Tom*. While Mark's ordinariness is emphasized by his brown duffle coat, the women he murders or takes salacious photographs of wear vibrant colours, including Dora's red skirt in the opening sequence, and the red net cape with black lace, pink corset and black suspender belt worn by Milly (Pamela Green), one of the models in the studio where he works. Bancroft's victims in *Horrors of the Black Museum* are also seen wearing red, which becomes part of both films' depictions of their seedy environments. Yet it is important to understand the relational function of colours, particularly how red is contrasted with other colours, and the patterning that is evident throughout the film. Drawing on Branigan's 'tracking' methodology, this becomes a core element of the film's aesthetic design while also a means of conveying the film's 'adult' sensibility, power to shock and disturb. The following discussion of how artificial coloured lighting is associated in both films with the unknown and danger demonstrates how colour is a crucial means of representing the main protagonists' murderous activities.

Artificial Colours, Affect and Horror

Horrors of the Black Museum and *Peeping Tom* use artificial colours to help depict their contemporary settings, the 'adult' milieus within which the horrors are created. Branigan notes that: 'A color may literally or figuratively change by acquiring new sets of relations and meanings when it appears on a new level while "moving" through a text' (2018: 269). The ways in which colours 'move' in both films involve their presentation at key points as artificial, or 'surface' colours that appear to conspire with, and underscore, the horrific actions depicted. Artificial colours are often associated with ephemeral cultures of modernity, such as neon-lit cities. David Batchelor has described these 'non-natural' forms of colour as elusive and transitory: 'The places, actual and imagined, where colour enters and leaves, where it begins and ends, and begins again, and ends again, in an endless play of light and shadow' (2014: 17). In *Horrors of the Black Museum* Bancroft's secret horror museum, located in the basement of his home, thrives on electricity to power the flashing coloured lights of his mysterious new machinery. Bancroft even uses electrical current to murder the visiting doctor who suspects that he is the killer.

The most striking sequence involving artificial colours occurs when Bancroft's assistant Rick (Graham Curnow) and his girlfriend Angela (Shirley Anne Field) visit the Battersea funfair. To secure Rick's total loyalty, Bancroft has injected him with an experimental fluid that inculcates the 'gift of obedience', which takes its full effect when he rides in the 'Tunnel of Love' with Angela. We observe the couple sitting in the ride's car as it enters the tunnel, and once in the dark a series of artificial, coloured lights fill the screen, switching between red, green and blue. The colour changes, experienced by the characters as part of a thrilling ride at the funfair, involve the shock of witnessing Rick's physical transformation (his face becomes disfigured) into a stabbing monster who kills Angela. It is as if the colours have contributed to this dramatic effect, exemplifying a mutability that shifts in an instant from eliciting pleasure to horror. Red is particularly central to how the funfair sequence develops. Wearing a red jacket, Rick's extraordinary powers, fuelled as the drug starts to take hold, are demonstrated when he surprises onlookers by hitting the bell in a 'strongman' contest. Angela suggests they go on the 'Tunnel of Love' ride, the entrance of which is indicated by a red neon sign. Once inside, the changing colours bring on Rick's transformation, and red is particularly evident in triggering the process. It is as if red has been growing in intensity throughout, until its total suffusion of the screen signals its most potent power (see Plate 3).

The funfair's reputation as a locale for thrilling, dangerous rides illuminated by brightly coloured signage that glows in the dark is exploited here to both deliver plot information and maximize the sequence's affective impact. Colour's centrality to Rick's transformation captures something of the film's preoccupation with 'Hypno-Vista', as visual suggestion and hypnotism are expressed by Bancroft's control over Rick as his murderous accomplice who he has instructed to take Angela to the funfair. Other films which bathe the screen entirely with one colour similarly use the technique to show characters losing control and to signal trauma, such as a red screen when Sister Ruth loses consciousness in *Black Narcissus* (Powell and Pressburger 1947), and as the trigger for Marnie's extreme emotional reactions in *Marnie* (Hitchcock 1964). *Taxi Driver* (Martin Scorsese 1976) also uses red to suffuse the screen, most notably in an extreme close-up of Travis Bickle's (Robert De Niro) eyes as he observes the seedy nocturnal streets of New York from inside his cab. While the red has a realistic function in reflecting the city's neon lighting, Scorsese, influenced by Michael Powell, uses it as an expressive prefiguring of Travis's violent actions at the film's climax (Stern 2005: 47). In such scenes the characters quite literally 'fall into colour', in the sense that Batchelor identifies when describing the effect as: 'a drug, a loss of consciousness, a kind of blindness – at least for a moment. Colour requires, or results in, or perhaps just is, a loss of focus, of identity, of self' (2000: 51).

In *Peeping Tom*, coloured lighting features in Mark's photographic studio, and also in one of the key murder scenes that takes place in a film studio where Mark works part-time as a focus puller. When Helen visits his rooms in the house he owns and in which she is a lodger, she asks to see his films. Laura Mulvey has described this as 'one of the most beautiful scenes in the whole film. The red darkroom light fuses with her red hair and red dress, and the scene is shot with a crane so the camera can follow Helen fluidly, without the distraction of cuts; now nothing can distract her in this strange new world that she finds so exciting' (2005: 146). Mark shows Helen home movies shot by his father (Michael Powell) which document his preoccupation with reactions in the nervous system to fear, using his son for experiments in photographing fear that involve similar intermittent, flashlight effects to those later used by Mark in his own versions. Disturbed by the shots of the young Mark being frightened, Helen's anger is visibly underscored by the red light in the dark room illuminating her face, causing the same effect described above of red enveloping her, suffusing the entire screen (see Plate 4). The scene is central to the film's attempt to offer an explanation for Mark's sickness in his abuse as a child. The vivid, artificial red contrasts with his father's home movies which, like Mark's, were also shot in black and white. But Helen is unable to view them from the perspective of a distant observer, or as an interesting documentary experiment. The fact that colour is used to depict the 'real' world of the murders, as opposed to Mark's black-and-white recordings of them, and in Helen's 'seeing red' reaction to his father's experiments, marks a key difference between their viewing practices. While Mark is seduced by the clinical spirit of experimentation that for him indicates the success of his own 'home' movies, Helen's angry reaction to his father's films challenges any notion of exoneration implied by those conventions. The red darkroom's function of developing private films can also be linked in this context to the colour's cultural associations with sexuality and violence.

In the film studio scene Moira Shearer plays Viv, an extra who when filming for the day is over, tells her co-workers she is going on a date. We later learn this is Mark who has promised to illicitly film her for a screen test she can subsequently use to get work. Their rendezvous is located in the deserted studio, and she hears whistling as she enters. Successive bright lights – pink, green and white – obscure her vision as she looks for the source and sees that it is Mark up on a mechanical rostrum which he then lowers so he can begin the test. Once again, we are shown the viewpoint of Mark's own camera filming Viv as she dances to warm up. The same horrified expression is visible/witnessed as with Dora's murder, and red light intrudes into Viv's last moments as she is overcome by the horror of what she is seeing.

In these two sequences artificial red light has again been dominant as a means of accentuating loss of control, as if its vividness is connoting the seeping, saturated impact of Mark's horrific pastime, which also involves blinding his victims with light. It signals Helen's realization that 'all this filming isn't healthy', urging that he needs help, and then in the film studio sequence, we see Mark using a succession of coloured lights to build up suspense when Viv at first cannot see him, and then in her final, fatal moments. The extremity of the effect would appear to contrast with Mark's persona as rather mild-mannered, typically dressed in beige, browns and with brown/blonde hair. In addition to red, blue is also significant in this scene, as noted by Mulvey in her analysis of *Peeping Tom*. As a primary colour that is complementary to red, blue gains importance when we see Viv preparing for her screen test in her dressing room. Her make-up case is 'a pale yet saturated blue' and 'so prominent that this insignificant object catches the spectator's eye' (2005: 148). Yet we later appreciate this object's obtrusive appearance as prefiguring the blue trunk in which Mark places Viv's body, causing consternation when it is subsequently discovered during filming at the studio. Blue is used for an intimate, personal accessory – the make-up case – while the trunk, used to conceal her body, is a very different kind of intimate container. In tracking the symmetry of such moments of affective and poignant chromatic resonance, *Peeping Tom* fully exploited the potential of Eastmancolor. Sequences such as these undoubtedly contribute towards the film's pervading atmosphere of tension. They also expose the BBFC's fixation on blood, or the length and number of particular shots, as a profoundly limited understanding of how a film, and its colours, can skilfully build up tension and horror. The full impact of colour would not have been evident to Trevelyan when reading the script, yet its cumulative, visual force was fully present in the print.

Colour and the Authentication of Locale and Culture

The reviews cited at the beginning of this chapter highlight the importance of colour in delineating the two films' respective locales. William Johnson noted how in *Peeping Tom* 'Colour and sound conspire to create a visceral atmosphere inside Mark's house to suggest that these rooms and halls, and especially the secret world of his darkroom, are an extension of his body. Glistening browns and purples stand out from the shadows of the hall and stairway; vari-coloured lamps punctuate the gloom of the darkroom' (1980: 9). As noted by Pirie, both films captured 'the tatty world of cheap sensationalism', and the contribution of colour to establishing this all-pervasive atmosphere will now be discussed (2008: 114). It is against these backgrounds that the films' horror gains hold as it emerges from an accumulating sensibility of suspense and dread, involving much more than a few seconds of censored screen time.

The interior spaces of *Horrors of the Black Museum* are varied, reflecting the different occupations and social status of the characters. The murders take place in intimate, interior spaces, caused by devices designed to perform their deadly function when the murderer is absent, and the victim is caught unaware. Gail's murder takes place in her home, and a subsequent victim, Joan Berkley (June Cunningham), is gruesomely despatched by a guillotine contraption that has been rigged on her bed. The motive is revenge for Bancroft's humiliation and rejection by a woman to whom he clearly feels socially superior. In the previous scene Bancroft and Joan, who are involved with each other, quarrel. When he refuses to give her money, she grabs his walking cane and calls him 'half a man'. Joan then goes to a bar, wearing a red dress, dances to the jukebox and tells the barman that she is now free of any man wanting to own her. As she walks home two policemen accompany her; it would appear she is completely safe. Inside her flat she relaxes, puts on music and takes off her dress and black underwear. The lighting is dark, and she puts on a pale blue nightgown, a soft, unassuming item of clothing compared with her more seductive earlier appearance. As she lies on the bed she looks up and sees the contraption, but it is too late to avoid the blade's sudden drop, skilfully triggered by the weight. The scene gains poignancy since for all her bold strike of independence from Bancroft, she becomes his victim when she is most vulnerable in the intimate space of her own bedroom. The dark mise en scène and colour changes ensure that the second murder we see is just as memorable as the first. Trevelyan at the BBFC was anxious about this scene, commenting: 'We should like to avoid any shots of the severed head and to keep blood to a minimum' (Trevelyan 1958a). As with the opening murder, the censors' emphasis is on the death, and mode of killing, rather than on how a sequence is developed to build up the tension that makes its climax all the more impactful.

Another murder takes place in the antique shop where Bancroft ostensibly purchases items for his crime research. The shop is dark and cluttered; it is a mise en scène dominated by browns and greys. Bancroft kills the owner with a pair of ice tongs when she realizes the binoculars she had recently sold him were used to murder Gail. Her interest in the murders and in his occupation as a crime writer gives their interactions an air of familiarity since Bancroft is a regular customer, but she has to be eliminated when she confronts him with her suspicions and attempts bribery. Once again, the selected location is where its occupant feels safe and is off her guard; this dramatic device can be thought of as a pattern, a repetition of circumstance that builds up throughout the film.

In *Peeping Tom* colour is used to vivify Mark's occupation as a part-time photographer of soft-pornographic images which are illicitly sold at a newsagent's shop in Soho. Upstairs Mark takes pictures of women dressed in gaudy costumes: one in a red net cape with black lace and underneath a pink corset and black suspender belt, while another has a black tango hat with a red carnation. The lighting for this scene is harsh and bright, creating a contrast with the darkness of Newman Passage seen earlier. The studio is small, with amateurish-looking props and poster backdrops for the set featuring exotic locales (see Plate 5). It is later the location for Mark's final murder. By contrast his house is spacious, permitting him to have his own photographic studio as well as lodgers such as Helen and her mother, who are totally different from the women he photographs and kills. This distinction, between Mark's private 'experiments' and his otherwise unassuming public demeanor, is reflected in the spaces he inhabits, although his home studio – his own private interior space where he finally kills himself – blurs the boundary and contributes towards the film's all-pervasive, visceral atmosphere. In this way, colour is central to establishing and reworking the realism of both films' distinctive 'adult' mise en scènes. This point makes further sense of their status as part of the voyeurism-preoccupied 'Sadian' trilogy of films (the third film is *Circus of Horrors,* Sidney Hayers 1960) distributed by Anglo-Amalgamated that critics described as representative of a 'new type of cinematic realism' (Quigly 1960: 224).

Conclusion

Released in the same year, the films fared very differently at the box office. *Horrors of the Black Museum* was very successful, whereas following its adverse critical reception *Peeping Tom* received a limited release and interest was only revived following Martin Scorsese's championing of the film in the 1970s and its subsequent video (1989) and DVD (2007) release. Yet both films were subject to similar evaluative processes which reveal the BBFC's typical method of basing its judgements initially on script versions, and of focusing comments on selected shots, particularly if they involved showing blood. As a natural substance associated with life and death, blood was to be expected in horror films, while other forms of vibrant colour received less attention. As this chapter has demonstrated, tracing the complex presentation of colour in both films extends far beyond the shots and scenes identified by the BBFC as sufficiently graphic to be excised. Colour is integral to their aesthetic designs which can only be fully appreciated when considered as complex patterns that interact, resonate and shock in variable intensities and at different moments. While the films have often been linked for their common themes of voyeurism, vision and blindness, the role of colour has not been acknowledged for its centrality to their vivid representation.

As we have seen, both films speak to the early 1960s contexts, in which they were produced and released. Their realistic settings and themes resonate with concerns about the power of the image and its impact particularly on young audiences. The example of how artificial coloured lighting is used in both films, particularly in vivid, intermittent flashes, connects them with contemporary fears about how such techniques might undermine self-control and influence consciousness. While 'Hypno-Vista' was a gimmick, its bold promotion played on fears of losing control through colour, and the use of red in both films took this idea to extremes in provocative ways. Although the films' respective probing of the impact on the brain of subliminal colour effects and the psychology of fear could be seen as attempts to connect them with legitimate discourses on mental processes, their popular cinematic forms made them untrustworthy as authoritative commentaries. As colour films became more numerous in subsequent years, the BBFC rarely singled it out as objectionable, although its disquieting presence clearly exposed an inability to articulate its full impact. In retrospect, *Horrors of the Black Museum* and *Peeping Tom* are Eastmancolor classics demonstrating how 'colour conscious' directors could use it skilfully to enhance the true realism, suspense, shock and horror associated with 'adult' films.

References

Aldgate, A. (1995), *Censorship and the Permissive Society: British Cinema and Theatre, 1955–65*, Oxford: Clarendon Press.

Batchelor, D. (2000), *Chromophobia*, London: Reaktion Books.

Batchelor, D. (2014), *The Luminous and the Grey*, London: Reaktion Books.

Billings, J. (1959), 'Horrors of the Black Museum', Review of *Horrors of the Black Museum*, *Kinematograph Weekly*, 16 April: 15.

Branigan, E. (2018), *Tracking Color in Cinema and Art: Philosophy and Aesthetics*, New York: Routledge.

Cohen, H. (1959), Letter to J. Trevelyan, *Horrors of the Black Museum* files, 9 March, London: BBFC archive.

Eisenstein, S. (2006), 'On Colour', in A. Dalle Vacche and B. Price (eds), *Color: The Film Reader*, 105–17, Abingdon: Routledge.

Frith, P. (2019), '"The Curse of the Thing Is Technicolor Blood: Why Need Vampires Be Messier Feeders than Anyone Else?": The BBFC and Hammer's Colour Films, 1957–62', *Historical Journal of Film, Radio and Television*, 39 (2): 233–50.

Hanssen, E. F. (2004), 'Eisenstein in Colour', *Konsthistorisk tidskrift/Journal of Art History*, 73 (4): 212–27.

Hill, D. (1960), 'Peeping Tom', Review of *Peeping Tom, Tribune*, 29 April: 55.

Hills, M. (2015), 'The Horror!', in M. Conboy and J. Steel (eds), *Routledge Companion to British Media History*, 414–24, Abingdon: Routledge.

'Horrors of the Black Museum' (1959), Review of *Horrors of the Black Museum*, *Monthly Film Bulletin*, 26 May: 59.

Johnson, W. (1980), 'Peeping Tom – A Second Look', *Film Quarterly*, 33 (3): 2–10.

Kermode, M. (2002), 'The British Censors and Horror Cinema', in S. Chibnall and J. Petley (eds), *British Horror Cinema*, 10–22, London: Routledge.

McLaren, A. (2002), *Sexual Blackmail: A Modern History*, Cambridge, MA: Harvard University Press.

Mulvey, L. (2005), 'The Light that Fails: A Commentary on *Peeping Tom*', in I. Christie and A. Moor (eds), *Michael Powell: Perspectives on an International Film-Maker*, 143–55, London: British Film Institute.

Packard, V. (1957), *The Hidden Persuaders*, New York: Doubleday.

'Peeping Tom' (1959), Review of *Peeping Tom*, *Kinematograph Weekly*, 19 November: 22.

Peeping Tom file (1960), BBFC case study, n.d. Available online: https://www.bbfc.co.uk/case-studies/peeping-tom (accessed 2 September 2021).

Pirie, D. (2008), *A New Heritage of Horror: The English Gothic Cinema*, London: I.B. Tauris.

Pomerance, M. (2017), 'The Colour of Our Eyes', *New Review of Film and Television Studies*, 15 (1): 2–8.

Powell, M. (2000), *A Life in Movies: An Autobiography*, London: Faber and Faber.

Quigly, I. (1960), 'Peeping Tom', Review of *Peeping Tom, The Spectator*, 15 April: 224.

Reader's report (1957), second draft screenplay, *Dracula* files, 14 October, London: BBFC archive.

Schwarzkopf, S. (2007), 'They Do It with Mirrors: Advertising and British Cold War Consumer Politics', *Contemporary British History*, 19 (2): 133–50.

Script report (1958), *Horrors of the Black Museum* files, 14 August, London: BBFC archive.

Stern, L. (2005), 'From the Other Side of Time', in I. Christie and A. Moor (eds), *Michael Powell: Perspectives on an International Film-Maker*, 36–55, London: British Film Institute.

Street, S. (2012), *Colour Films in Britain: The Negotiation of Innovation 1900–55*, London: British Film Institute/Palgrave Macmillan.

Trevelyan, J. (1958a), Letter to S. Levy, *Horrors of the Black Museum* files, 22 August, London: BBFC archive.

Trevelyan, J. (1958b), Letter to H. Cohen, *Horrors of the Black Museum* files, 2 December, London: BBFC archive.

Trevelyan, J. (1959), Letter to H. Cohen, *Horrors of the Black Museum* files, 5 March, London: BBFC archive.

Trevelyan, J. (1973), *What the Censor Saw*, London: Michael Joseph.

Walter, W. G. (1953), *The Living Brain*, New York: W.W. Norton.

Watkins, A. (1957), Memo to A. Hinds, *The Curse of Frankenstein* files, 6 February, London: BBFC archive.

4

Mediating Desire:

Karel Reisz's Adaptation of *Saturday Night and Sunday Morning*

Simon Lee

When the Warwickshire County Council Cinematograph Licensing Committee voted to ban screenings of Karel Reisz's film adaptation of Alan Sillitoe's *Saturday Night and Sunday Morning* (1960), their rationale was telling. The committee chair, G. N. Sperryn of nearby Sutton Coldfield, declared, 'Those of us who saw the film were unanimously of the opinion that it should be banned as harmful to public morals' ('County Ban' 1961). Despite the film's international acclaim, its apparent crime was that 'It concerns the adultery of a factory worker with a colleague's wife, and presents a most unsavory picture of factory morals' ('County Ban' 1961).[1] Sillitoe, who developed the screenplay with Reisz, anticipated trouble, recalling in his autobiography how he tabled his inclination to 'tell the censorship goons to fuck off' and accepted changes to the script to ensure release despite 'end[ing] with a much watered down version of the book' (1995: 259). In an earlier, unpublished draft of this same text, though, he registered regret by asking whether 'a proper rendering of the film will ever be made' (Sillitoe n.d.c: 350).[2]

Reisz's adaptation is generally heralded as an exemplar of the British New Wave, with its X certificate stemming from the film's embrace of adult themes, coarse language and use of violence. *Saturday Night and Sunday Morning*'s surprising success and its subsequent cult following validates how both critics and audiences found the film to be refreshingly honest. *The Nottingham Evening Post* claimed that 'Sillitoe knows from the heart how young men like Arthur Seaton act and feel' ('Queen of Films' 1960), and the *Illustrated London News* noted that there is 'a kind of honesty about this film's blunt realism' (Dent 1960: 858). Filmgoers were similarly impressed by the realistic portrayal of working-class life, with Arthur Marwick insisting that 'the filtering out of the eccentricities and ambiguities of Sillitoe's novel' helped guarantee a 'much greater impact with mass audiences' (1984: 146). *Saturday Night and Sunday Morning* proved to be a box-office smash, becoming one of the most popular British films released that year. And yet, in this chapter, I will suggest that the film was just as dedicated to its own commercial viability by dint of its ties to the popular 'angry young man' phenomenon.[3] As Georg Gaston remarks, the nature of Sillitoe and Reisz's collaboration makes it difficult to parse their particular roles in the development of the screenplay (1980: 32). However, Colin Gardner suggests that distinctions persist, not just through changes made to the script as part of the adaptation process but in the way that Reisz's formal and stylistic decisions curtail the more belligerent aspects of Sillitoe's protagonist-cum-avatar (2006: 119). While both Gaston and Gardner register tension in Sillitoe and Reisz's process, neither investigates the specifics of this tension nor its larger significance. This chapter considers discrepancies between the novel and the film, especially the way Reisz's adaptation appears to temper Sillitoe's adversarial impulse. It begins by showing how censorial outcries like that of the Warwickshire County Council were more invested in regulating social behaviour than shielding viewers from images deemed obscene. Next, it argues that cultural production associated with the British New Wave weaponized such concerns as part of its aesthetic and commercial agenda. The texts associated with this specific style are marked by their frank embrace of adult themes and taboo topics, vacillating between the provocative and the political in a manner supported by the collaborative input of the British Board of Film Censors (BBFC). As such, the chapter explores how Reisz – while honouring his own vision for the film – mediated a range of competing desires: the author's desire to antagonize 'the establishment', the censor's desire to regulate content, the production company's desire to turn a profit and the audience's desire for exciting yet conscientious entertainment. That is to say, *Saturday Night and Sunday Morning* played a pivotal role in Reisz's career, allowing him to transcend the relatively niche world of Free Cinema and move into the realm of commercial, mainstream filmmaking.

The Nature of Censorial Outrage

While censorship in the arts has generally centred on images considered obscene, the Warwickshire County Council's ban reveals a more complicated set of concerns. As Su Holmes suggests, early X certificates were aligned with films that deviated from traditional norms or challenged an ideological consensus of morality. Holmes refers to the circulation of foreign-language films such as Max Ophüls's *La Ronde* (1950), a film that the censor felt raised concern due to depictions of infidelity and promiscuity (2005: 232). Similarly, the Warwickshire committee's contention with Reisz's film was driven more by the implications of the protagonist's behaviour than anything considered prurient.[4] Due to outcry and protest over the initial vote to ban the film, a second screening was organized and a decision was made to permit the release contingent on the removal of two minutes of footage ('County Still Insist' 1962). With cuts in place, the committee would agree to an X certificate with exhibition in the county. The scenes in question – two instances of implied rather than depicted sex – confirm that the original ban centred on policing conduct rather than minimizing access to anything explicit or pornographic. Still, this traditional form of censorship differed from how the censor saw its role in post-Second World War society. Tony Aldgate cites then-BBFC secretary Arthur Watkins to show how the new X certificate intended to promote 'films which, while not being suitable for children, are good entertainment and films which appeal to an intelligent public' (2003: 133).[5] In this sense, an ideological rift emerged between a relatively progressive, liberalized censor such as the BBFC and independent conservative groups such as Sperryn's committee, who felt that the BBFC lacked objectivity and traditional values. Although filmmakers generally avoided X certificates to mitigate licensing and distribution problems, the films of the British New Wave were well suited for the new censorship system introduced by the BBFC in 1951. The 'kitchen sink' sequence's embrace of adult themes and its frank approach to social issues were largely validated by the X certificate's goals to 'appeal to an intelligent public'.[6]

The novels and plays that served as the foundation for many of the British New Wave films also used adult themes as a central tenet of the kitchen sink agenda. In fact, taboo content is arguably more pronounced in these texts – a point that illuminates the censor's role in the development of the sequence. As Dominic Shellard argues, the office was more responsive to cultural change than might be assumed. Discussing Shelagh Delaney's 1958 play, *A Taste of Honey*, Shellard writes, 'The Lord Chamberlain, ever mindful of public opinion, was sensitive to the increasing debate about reform of the law, and quietly decided that the portrayal of Geoffrey as an openly gay character, but one who was unthreatening and not proselyting, could stand' (2003: 222). Delaney's play champions progressive ideals, using controversy as a way to promote discourse rather than to sensationalize. The BBFC, it seems, recognized this function and the films based on the original kitchen sink texts help position the censor as a proponent of social advancement.

Sensationalism, though, was still mobilized for commercial appeal – even at moments when the source material called for sensitivity. While it might be assumed that depictions of sex and violence drove censorial concerns, the language remained a priority. For instance, the censor's issues with Jack Clayton's 1959 adaptation of John Braine's 1957 novel *Room at the Top* were rooted in the author's use of regional dialect and coarse language, with words like 'lust' and 'bitch' swiftly excised from the final cut.[7] But once cuts were made and the final version passed scrutiny, the offending dialogue was reinstated as part of the promotional material, which advertised the film as 'A Savage Story of Lust and Ambition' (Aldgate 2005: 108). In the case of the Warwickshire debacle, nearby Birmingham cinemas capitalized on the uproar over Reisz's film, with one cinema manager noting how the ban 'turned a success into a fabulous success' ('Cinema Winning' 1961). Long Eaton's Palace Theatre marketed *Saturday Night and Sunday Morning* as 'The most talked about film of the year … Banned from the Cinema screens in Warwickshire by the Warwickshire County Council … Were they right to do this? … Come and judge for yourself!' ('Long Eaton' 1961). According to John Trevelyan, Watkins's successor at the BBFC, transportation was arranged to bus viewers out of Warwickshire and into Birmingham to see the film as part of the marketing (1973: 107). In this regard, films like *Saturday Night and Sunday Morning* are commensurate with the BBFC's transformation from a seemingly tyrannical entity into a more productive force, especially in the way serious subject matter and frank themes could be used to balance gravitas with excitement. Such films mark a moment in which filmmakers worked alongside the censor rather than from a place of opposition.

Sillitoe's Antagonism and Strategic Provocation

Sillitoe, nevertheless, failed to recognize this transformation and still viewed the censor as an oppressor. While discussing changes made to the novel's infamous abortion scene, he adds that 'it seems to me that censorship in the British film industry is in its own way as hidebound as that of Soviet Russia' (1960: 59). And in a draft of an essay titled 'Chauvinistic', he equates critics with censors too, noting in particular what he viewed as a registered prejudice against writers from the industrial north, which was presumably shared by these two groups. In a voice meant to ventriloquise that of a finger-wagging critic, he remarks, 'The proletarian writers have crowbars instead of pens and wield them in the china-shop of the English language' (n.d.a: 4).

His general contention here was less about the denigration of working-class voices and more about access and circulation – the impact of the critic on a text's success: 'Bad reviews are good for writer, painter, composer ... Yet they are bad for the people who read them, bad I am sure for the reviewer himself, and possibly bad for the publisher who may (or may not) sell a few less copies of the book whose production he has organized' (n.d.a: 11).[8] Responses to the novel were mixed, with Sillitoe himself commenting that many early reviews appeared uncharitable or plain dismissive. In *The New York Times*, Gilbert Millstein signalled the distinction between the representation of working-class life in *Saturday Night and Sunday Morning* and the kind of proletarian fiction that had come prior: 'The class-conscious writers of the Thirties would find him [Arthur] reprehensible – a [*sic*] nihilistic, irresponsible, and uncomfortably full-blooded, and no man to fit a predetermined thesis' (Millstein 1959). But in his autobiography, Sillitoe congratulates himself on his ability to upset critical sensibilities in a manner that mirrors Holmes's characterization of the X certificate as anti-tradition: 'The antipathy from those who did not like the book showed that the character created out of my imagination had genuine differences of attitude to the normal run of people depicted in novels of that time' (1995: 252). The author's animus was tangible, and he clearly viewed the text as an affront to the artistic elite. After all, his previous efforts at publishing – several manuscripts of complete novels – were roundly rejected by major publishing houses. It was this full-throated antagonism and drive to offend both censors and critics that Reisz had to ease in order to ensure the film's existence.[9]

The film opened in London on 27 October 1960 and received a number of award nominations from the British Academy with Reisz winning Best British Film, Albert Finney for Most Promising Newcomer and Rachel Roberts for Best British Actress. Although the novel's reviews were mixed, by the time the film came out, Britain was much more attuned to the rise of gritty working-class voices following the success of Clayton's *Room at the Top* and Tony Richardson's adaptation of John Osborne's 1956 play *Look Back in Anger* (1959). Still, Sillitoe and Reisz had been uncertain how the film would be received, or whether it would be understood as intended. Inevitably, the author felt that such preliminary concerns were misplaced since 'Critics who didn't like it were not able to ignore it' (1995: 270). Barely able to contain his cynical rancour, he noted how controversy heightened public intrigue:

The Watch Committees of certain counties banned it, like Colonial District Commissioners who didn't want the natives to be suborned by the idea that they had any value in the world. How anyone could object to such a film puzzled rather than annoyed me, but the publicity created by intolerance helped to fuel interest and speculation.

(1995: 270)

Given that Clayton's film greased the wheels, critical responses were more uniformly enthusiastic than those of the novel. Bosley Crowther, writing for *The New York Times*, observed that 'there is a solid human fiber and a sense of hopefulness in this film' that underscores 'a confidence in the working class that is as matter-of-fact and severe as the long rows of workers' brick houses and the bank of beer spigots in the pub' (1961). Alton Cook noted in the *New York World-Telegram* how the film shared *Room at the Top*'s 'vicious cynicism', concluding that the film was 'a brilliant debut for a new director, Karel Reisz, who has been in minor echelons of English film since the war' (1961). Such reviews can certainly be read as indicative of rapid cultural change, but they also specify shifts attributable to Reisz's ability to curb Sillitoe's bitterness. In other words, the film's positive reviews point towards a slightly more palatable version of the narrative than appears in the novel.

Accompanying the positive reviews was a growing public awareness of the film's X certificate, as well as attempts to censor its distribution. Newspapers such as *The Birmingham Post* ran headlines not about the film itself but about both its local and national controversy.[10] Such headlines, in turn, prompted letters from the public opposing attempts of censorship. For instance, a perceptive letter written to the *Guardian* concerning attempts to ban the release in Sillitoe's hometown remarked, 'I am not surprised that Lieutenant-Colonel Cordeaux, the conservative member for central Nottingham, dislikes the film [that], he complains, gives the impression that young men in industrial towns – and in Nottingham in particular – are ill-behaved, immoral, drunken Teddy-boys. Certainly, the work is calculated to upset the traditionally minded' ('Itself Unveiled' 1961). The letter concludes with its writer documenting their own experience seeing the film in a working-class part of London: 'The impressive thing was the public's absorption in the picture of a life very like its own, shown without benefit of comic or other filters. A large part of the nation must be looking at itself unveiled for almost the first time' (2006: 102). Despite the liberal application of the X certificate to the films of the time, the associated controversy does indeed point towards censorship and strategic provocation as another key tenet of the kitchen sink era, sustaining both intrigue and socially relevant messaging as a genre motif.[11] The trick, it seems, was to strike the right balance between controversy and commercial appeal.

Collaboration and Mediation

Gardner notes how Richardson's success with the stage production of Osborne's *Look Back in Anger* offered him a rare opportunity 'to worm himself and his old Free Cinema buddies into the film industry' (2006: 102).

This perhaps explains Reisz's own desire to develop *Saturday Night and Sunday Morning* as a more commercially viable film than his prior work in Free Cinema. *Look Back in Anger*'s acclaim helped Richardson launch Woodfall Productions, which operated as an independent company with pre-established buzz due to the play's popularity. Reisz was drawn to the artistic control offered through Woodfall, principally the company's commitment to include the original authors in the process of adaptation (2006: 102).[12] Gardner adds that the screenplay took twelve months to develop with many revisions along the way (2006: 103). Nonetheless, Sillitoe would go on to register embarrassment over the film's final cut, specifically noting his anxiety about its release and regret about his willingness to cede so much control to Reisz's vision (1995: 266). This was perhaps due to the fact that Arthur was somewhat of an autobiographical avatar: Sillitoe expressed his satisfaction of seeing 'Albert Finney as Arthur Seaton working in the Turnery Department of the Raleigh factory, as if he too had been there since he was fourteen. The spot was the same I had stood on at that age, in another world, at another time, and certainly as someone else' (1995: 268–9). Yet, setting and general circumstances aside, *Saturday Night and Sunday Morning* is not a retelling of Sillitoe's life; it is perhaps better understood as a manifestation of the author's id – a hypothetical bridge between Sillitoe's dissidence and a general sentiment of alienation felt by young working-class people at the time. For many, Arthur provided catharsis through a fantasy of defiance, one emblematic of new voices and new methods of representation the kitchen sink sequence sought to elevate. In fact, Reisz would comment on the appeal of such anti-establishment outsider voices by noting how many of the British New Wave's films were 'made by writers who had never written, directors who had never directed, and actors who had never acted' (Welsh and Tibbetts 1999: 27). While such claims of amateur collaboration may appear hyperbolic, the sentiment is apt: films like *Saturday Night and Sunday Morning* were highly collaborative endeavours foregrounding historically marginalized voices – the upshot of an especially dynamic moment in British cultural production in which unencumbered drives and inspiration merged with commercial viability.

Sillitoe sought to preserve the integrity of his plot, but the novel and the film do depart in ways that speak to Reisz's goal of a commercially viable product that still pushes the envelope. The most notable distinction is the closing scene, which alters the tone of the entire narrative albeit with subtlety. John Hill, in his discussion of working-class narratives, observes how plots often turned on 'socially or sexually transgressive desire' in which 'the central character either "opts out" of society or else adapts and adjusts to its demands' (1986: 57).[13] In the novel, Arthur's subversive proclivities persist even in the light of his presumed resignation to the daily grind, recognized through a rousing monologue that builds on the protagonist's earlier and most celebrated entreaty: 'don't let the bastards grind you down'

(Sillitoe 1958: 37). In the film version, however, the final scene suggests that Arthur and Doreen have indeed capitulated to the status quo of home ownership and, by extension, a ground-down life of labour in the factory. Looking down over the new housing estate, Arthur throws a rock in its direction, prompting Doreen to ask, 'What did you do that for? Maybe one of those houses will be for us'. He reaches down to help her up from her supine position on the grass, adding, 'Come on, duck, let's go down'. Although the gesture of the thrown rock might be considered antagonistic, the larger implication is that compliance wins out over insubordination, inferring to the viewer that submission is complete. While the film maintains some of the novel's rebellious charge in that Arthur remarks how the thrown rock will likely not be his last, this final scene does imply that the bastards have indeed ground him down. In contrast, the novel closes with Arthur asserting agency, winding in and manipulating the reel of the fishing pole that operates as a fairly obvious metaphor for entrapment. Here, the character's independence is upheld, and his insubordinate attitude is sustained.

It is challenging to pinpoint Sillitoe and Reisz's individual contributions and concessions, but the altered ending does point towards Reisz's distinct role as a subtle mediator. Aldgate and Richards sum up some of the back and forth between the screenwriters and the BBFC in a manner that certifies the collaborative effort that went into the script (1983: 133–7). Gaston maintains that the film's ending is frequently misunderstood, noting how one critic found it 'sweet and happy' (1980: 43).[14] Drawing on a 1972 claim by Reisz that the now-resigned and subordinate Arthur operates as a symbol of an ineffectual post-war Britain, Gaston suggests that even Sillitoe himself misunderstood the film's closing scene (1980: 44). This seems unlikely. While Arthur did serve as an embodiment of frustration, his championing of independence and autonomy challenges any notions of nationalistic collectivity. Furthermore, Reisz backpedalled from this supposed metaphor in a 1977 interview, confessing that the film version does indeed depict Arthur as a character who 'begins to conform, to face personal defeat' (Gardner 2006: 116). Alexander Walker, stressing the director's regret, agrees with Reisz's confession, noting that

> the film ends with a dim perception of how a way of life has claimed [Arthur], as it's claimed generations before him, and will eventually tame him into social conformity in spite of his half-hearted gesture of chucking stones in the direction of the new housing estate whose middle-classness beckons so temptingly to his girl-friend.
>
> (1974: 84–5)

In this sense, the film can be read as a relatively tepid critique of capitalism, but this pales in comparison to the novel's much more dissident agenda.

While developing the screenplay, Sillitoe evidently tried to retain Arthur's insubordinate nature to counter Reisz's push for the character's submission to social responsibility. Gaston suggests that Sillitoe's primary contribution to the process was likely the 'vivid dialogue' (1980: 32) which Gardner posits was one of the first features to be tamed (2006: 104). Sillitoe also penned a wedding scene that was removed from the final cut in which Arthur marries Doreen but makes a mockery of the whole institution (1960: 58).[15] An additional closing factory sequence was also cut in which Finney recites parts of the novel's closing admonition of authority figures (1960: 58). While the novel implies maturation, Sillitoe retains his character's defiance through the strategic use of ambiguity; the closing polemic could easily be interpreted as acquiescence or as a continued rejection of society. The film inverts this message by grafting much of the novel's closing polemic into the opening sequences, an effect that surely helped ease the censor's concerns of social responsibility but deforms the narrative in the process. Whereas the novel ends with a tone of rebellion, the film opens with rebellion in a manner that sensationalizes it yet closes with a suggestion that the rebellion is over. In a 1972 interview, Sillitoe claimed that this socially acceptable ending was just a momentary lapse in Arthur's anarchic ways, calling the thrown stone 'just Round One' (Walker 1974: 85). The sense of regret registered in his autobiography, though, suggests that this claim was likely more of an attempt to assuage his own concessions about the adaptation process. While the film still drew the ire of regional censors, it does appear that Reisz softened the novel's more insubordinate message to create a film that, while still marketable as a spectacle of rebellion, ultimately sides with social responsibility and acquiescence. As such, the film demonstrates not just a tempering of subversion but a sensationalizing of insubordination that is inevitably, strategically subdued.

Continuing to discuss the film's development, Sillitoe stated, 'I wanted a hand in the kind of film it was going to be' (1960: 58), suggesting a pre-emptive suspicion of the adaptation process. Whereas Reisz sought to preserve the general narrative, Sillitoe was as invested in his protecting his protagonist's integrity to keep him from 'getting transmogrified into a young workman who turns out to be an honest-to-goodness British individualist – that is, one who triumphs in the end against and at the expense of a communist agitator or the trade unions' (1960: 58).[16] If censorial concerns did indeed centre on depictions of anti-social behaviour or insubordination, then subtle changes certainly paint Reisz's as a diplomatic mediator, shielding the project's commercial potential from Sillitoe's more anti-social impulses. Sillitoe himself claimed the process of collaboration a challenge, noting that after a year's work on the screenplay, 'I also felt, and still feel strongly, that I don't work at my best when collaborating with other people' (1960: 58). While discussing his feelings about Finney as Arthur, Sillitoe would note that 'the whole film should have been rougher, more brutal' to better match the image he held of Arthur in his own mind (Walker 1974: 83).

Beyond the final scene which alters the novel's closing ambiguity, additional changes reveal Reisz's circumspect mediation. Perhaps the most salient distinction between the novel and film's major set pieces is the illicit bathtub abortion. During the screenplay's development, the BBFC advised the writers that a solitary, passing mention of the scene would be permissible as long as the film gave no indication of the abortion's success and that no agency on the part of the character seeking the abortion was recognized (Sillitoe 1995: 259). The novel describes Brenda's procedure in detail and certifies its completion (Sillitoe 1958: 102). The film, though, masks the procedure and inevitably deems it a failure. Although Brenda agrees to visit a doctor for a second attempt, she later tells Arthur she changed her mind and wants to keep the child instead. Here, Reisz's negotiations are rendered clear through judicious sequencing. Because Brenda's mention of keeping the child happens much later in the film and is only brought up in passing, the audience is led to believe that the abortion did take place successfully after all.[17] Reisz addresses the censor's concerns, but frames the event with enough strategic ambiguity to uphold the novel's original charge. While both the novel and the film directly address the topic of abortion – a prominent concern in Britain at the time – the differing outcomes provide an example of censorial concession but also a degree of technical negotiation.

Furthermore, the film's adaptation of the novel's violence not only remains intact but is conspicuously overstated, especially the scene in which Arthur is accosted by 'two big swaddies'. This is noteworthy considering the initial BBFC reports flagged the violence as a potential concern (Aldgate and Richards 1983: 134). The fight itself occurs in a darkened alley, obscuring much of the attack from the viewer. Once the 'swaddies' have fled the scene, though, the camera zooms in on Arthur's bloody and swollen face, tracking him closely as he crawls his way back to the main street only to collapse midway. Given that Arthur's attack stems from his promiscuity and infidelity (the attack comes after his friend and colleague Jack learns that Arthur has been having an affair with his wife), Reisz's decision to extend the moment of Arthur's suffering can be read as a device by which to placate concerns about socially acceptable behaviour. Because the camera pauses on and frames Arthur's injuries for an uncomfortably long stretch of time, the effect reads as a warning against adultery and boorishness. As the initial BBFC reports on the screenplay felt that the fight might be too much of a spectacle, it is particularly interesting that the final cut not only obscures the fight from view but transforms the aftermath into a didactic spectacle. When combined with the altered ending which suggests that Arthur has learnt from his mistakes and is now willing to conform, the film's overall message appears less ambiguous. While the film is still quite violent, allowing distributors to sensationalize violence as part of the marketing, the directorial decision seems clear: the moment appears to be less of a fight scene and more of a lesson in social responsibility.[18]

From Free Cinema to the Mainstream

Trevelyan refers to *Saturday Night and Sunday Morning* as an example of 'film-makers becoming a little more daring' in the light of the BBFC's liberalization (1973: 107).[19] This may be true, but it fails to account for the degree of concessions and calculations required to keep the project afloat. Gardner hints at such deliberations, noting how 'Woodfall immediately developed a harmonious relationship with Trevelyan, who was willing to be pragmatic in order to promote British films of quality' (2006: 104). Trevelyan discusses this in terms of his preference for pre-production consultation, or what he refers to as 'a constructive form of censorship which many serious film-makers value' (1973: 108). Reputation as a permissive censor notwithstanding, his qualms about the early screenplay anticipated the concerns raised by the Warwickshire County Council. While Sperryn's attempted censorship suggests anxiety about worker insubordination, Trevelyan was worried that the film might act as an invitation for young people to behave irresponsibly (Gardner 2006: 105). In turn, Reisz responded with careful compromises to safeguard the film's release, cloaking the novel's more dissident sentiments in ambiguity to appease the censor and, in turn, sustain production. While the film is still quite radical for the time, it is clear that the novel's transgressive subtext saw the most censorship in the process of adaptation.

Sillitoe never meant his work to be insurrectionary, commenting in a single-page draft of an essay that 'I never put in a political message, yet hoped the stories and novels would, somewhere, carry a moral message' (1996). Yet, in an interview with a Japanese publisher, his tone was notably more insurgent. Discussing his thoughts on the purpose of literature in culture, he points towards the social function of narratives, stating: 'It seems to me that literature to be most effective has to corrupt – that is to say, it has to undermine conservative traditions that bind the country and the culture in chains of subservience forged too long ago. To corrupt is to destroy, and to destroy is to change. It is this process that literature has to accelerate' (Sillitoe n.d.d: n.p.). Sillitoe's philosophy runs counter to Sperryn's conservatism and also departs from the BBFC's contingent permissiveness. That the film was produced and distributed at all is testament to Reisz's ability to navigate a path between the censor's concerns and Sillitoe's desire to corrupt.

It is perhaps of interest that during the Warwickshire County Council fiasco, neither Reisz nor Sillitoe appeared to have much to say on the topic.

It was David Kingsley of British Lion, backed by Osborne and Richardson, that responded to Sperryn and his committee ('No Cuts' 1961). Had the issue registered on a more national level, one cannot help but wonder if Reisz might have agreed to remove the scenes the committee found 'harmful to public morals' ('County Ban' 1961) and potentially convince Sillitoe to sign off on the cuts as well. Reisz did not like Arthur and rejected any parallels made between himself and the character.[20] In this sense, perhaps he did not feel as protective over Arthur and did not share either Sillitoe or his protagonist's rejection of compliance. He referred to the character as 'a sad person, terribly limited in his sensibilities, narrow in his ambitions and a bloody fool into the bargain' (Walker 1974: 85). But this is quite different to the way the film's audience experienced the character, especially in terms of the novel. Given the ease by which Arthur can be read as a hypothetical projection of Sillitoe's and post–Second World War youth culture's collective id, the director's role as the ego to the censorial superego is apparent.

Conclusion

Reisz's role suggests great diplomacy and an awareness of what it means to walk the line. It also reinforces Richardson's claim that Woodfall provided an opportunity for Free Cinema directors to advance their style and, by extension, their own careers (Gardner 2006: 102). In a 1958 essay for *Universities and Left Review*, Reisz argued that film is an ideal vehicle by which to disseminate socialist ideals (1958: 66). In this regard, strategic mediation and circumspect concession carries a dissident valence of its own. Whereas Sillitoe embodied the impudence of the novel, Reisz brought compromise but with a craftier subversive charge that can be interpreted as a key aspect of his own development. What might be viewed by some as a craven softening can also be understood as a sly bid to sustain the 'kitchen sink' commitment to controversial content while placating censorial concerns. Despite Sillitoe's ultimate feeling that the narrative was compromised, Reisz deserves much credit for balancing oppositional desires of the author and the censor. He managed to pacify Sillitoe's adversarial predispositions while navigating the censor's concerns of 'public morals'. In doing so, the adaptation of *Saturday Night and Sunday Morning* remained relatively intact and would go on to help broaden representation of historically marginalized voices in the arts while laying the groundwork for future advances. Reisz, it seemed, had a clear grasp of this particular cultural moment, demonstrating a prudent understanding of the need to find common ground between controversy and social impact.

Notes

1   The narrative of the Warwickshire ban is as dramatic as Sillitoe's story, much of which is tracked throughout this chapter in snippets. In 1960, a small committee of Warwickshire County Council representatives began reviewing all X certificate films to gauge their suitability for Warwickshire citizens ('Coventry Will See' 1961). While technically a blip on the radar of the film's release, what this whole ordeal highlights is the transformation of the censor's role in British culture.

2   The manuscript draft reveals a number of hesitant edits to his coverage of *Saturday Night and Sunday Morning*'s production in the published autobiography, several of which point towards Reisz's impact on the screenplay. It seems clear from Sillitoe's original notes that Reisz acted as a mediator between the author and the censor: 'My acceptance of the world (or some of it) had brought my nihilistic proclivities to the fore, but the fact was that Karel, perhaps sensing this, played down the censorship problems with regard to me until the script was no longer an issue' (Sillitoe n.d.c: 350). The published text, though, lessens the burden on Reisz, making deliberations seem more like shared concessions: '… but such nursery rules had to be followed if the film was to go on release at all' (Sillitoe 1995: 259). Materials drawn from the Alan Sillitoe papers are courtesy of the Lilly Library, Indiana University, Bloomington, Indiana.

3   A brusque handwritten note in Sillitoe's archive remarks, 'AYM. It enabled them – us, if you like – to make more money than might usually have been the case' (n.d.b). I read this note as less of an admission of a cynical cash grab and more as a critique of the way the term was levied to market sensational material. However, criticism of the British New Wave as a commercial afterthought to kitchen sink novels and plays is not uncommon, with Peter Wollen remarking how 'film-makers fetishized the second-rate novels of regionalists, realists, and reactionaries' (2006: 32).

4   It is worth noting, though, that Sperryn and his committee had ulterior motives. Sperryn's bias and lack of expertise were laid bare when he mentioned that the film was the first he had seen in a decade since he 'gave up regular film-going ten years ago because of the amount of rubbish shown' ('County Ban' 1961). Sperryn confirms that objectional content was the reason. He would go on to allege that films like *Saturday Night and Sunday Morning* were tied to increases in crime ('Resignation Over Film Ban' 1961), adding that 'Brutality and illegitimacy are leaping up. We believe we have put our finger on one of the reasons and that something must be done quickly with regard to both film and television' ('Censored Films' 1961). His view on John Schlesinger's 1962 adaptation of Stan Barstow's 1960 novel, *A Kind of Loving*, is particularly telling: 'I have heard about *A Kind of Loving* and I am trying to find whether it has been submitted to us at all. Unfortunately, my committee would have to see it, but we should certainly ban this type of film if we can possibly do so' ('Councillor Attacks' 1962). As Mike Hally observes, such local committees operated alongside the BBFC but ultimately

made decisions based on what they deemed appropriate for the regions they
served. Furthermore, the committees themselves were managed by local police
departments who also attended screenings (2016: 3) with shifting political
winds tending to dictate the severity of decisions made (15). Sperryn and his
supporters obviously had an agenda. It seems likely that the intent was to use
Saturday Night and Sunday Morning as a scapegoat to initiate a new censorial
system, one distinct from the BBFC that could operate on a national rather
than regional level ('Committee Calls' 1961).

5   Pertinent to Holmes's discussion, Aldgate adds that while the X certificate
    sought to promote the circulation of films aimed at discerning adults, it only
    increased the flow of international cinema with British producers struggling
    to keep up (2003: 133). Furthermore, the BBFC was 'intent upon fostering
    its own concept of national cinema and had therefore looked with growing
    interest at new wave films for that very purpose' (Aldgate and Richards
    2009: 194). The implication, it seems, is that the apparent liberalization of
    censorship under Trevelyan looks more like the BBFC acting as a producer
    (1973: 105).

6   It was the overall 'frankness' and 'gravitas' of the film's style that John
    Trevelyan cited as the reason why otherwise-innocuous scenes that infer
    (but do not depict) sex were considered obscene (1973: 106). Describing the
    censorship categories available at the time, he writes, 'In a "U" film we could
    allow a man and a girl to be seen going together to a bedroom door; that in an
    "A" film they could be seen going into the bedroom and up to the bed' (1973:
    105). An X certificate film could show a couple 'in or on the bed engaged in
    what appeared to be sexual intercourse provided that there was reasonable
    discretion in what was shown' (1973: 105). Arguably, the two scenes that the
    Warwickshire County Council protested are much closer to an A than an X,
    so Trevelyan's suggestion that the genre's emphasis on frankness transformed
    the scenes in the minds of Sperryn's viewers makes much sense. For clarity,
    the first scene involves Albert Finney (Arthur) and Rachel Roberts (Brenda)
    heading upstairs, presumably to bed. They awaken together the next day
    and embrace. The camera, however, pauses on a dresser-top framed picture
    of Bryan Pringle, who plays Arthur's co-worker, Jack, as a way to signal the
    severity of the moral transgression that leads to Arthur's beating. The second
    scene features a fully clothed embrace between Finney and Shirley Anne Field
    (Doreen) with the couple rolling onto the floor of Doreen's parents' living
    room before the scene cuts to Arthur in the factory. Clearly, the offense is
    registered through the implications of Arthur's behaviour – adultery and
    premarital sex – rather than the specific details that Trevelyan outlines under
    the X certificate.

7   This also proved to be a major concern with *Saturday Night and Sunday
    Morning*, as Trevelyan noted in a letter to Harry Saltzman: 'I appreciate that
    words of this kind are normal in the speech of the type of people that the film
    is about but I have always found, strange though it may seem, that these are
    the very people who most object to this kind of thing on the screen' (Aldgate
    and Richards 1983: 135).

8   In this regard, it does seem that Sillitoe was concerned with commercial viability – at least in terms of distribution.

9   Aldgate and Richards note that by 1960, 'Sillitoe was already viewed by some BBFC examiners as a "socially irresponsible" writer' (2009: 195–6). To clarify, Aldgate and Richards revised their study of Sillitoe by replacing the essay on *Saturday Night and Sunday Morning* in the 1983 edition of this text with an essay on *The Loneliness of the Long Distance Runner* in the 2009 edition.

10   In the Warwickshire case, outrage and protest stemmed from the imposed priggishness about an internationally acclaimed film, but also because Sperryn's original decision undermined the democratic nature of the committee. For the first viewing, only four of the twenty committee members were present and the vote was forced through ('Film Ban Attacks' 1961). The fiasco was considered an embarrassment for both the council and the county leading to a move to deplore the ban as well as some very-public resignations from the council based on the claim that 'The committee's ban makes us all look fools' ('Resignation Over Film Ban' 1961).

11   It is perhaps worth noting how David Kingsley of British Lion Films responded to Warwickshire's request to remove two sex scenes not only by refusing the cuts but by referring to the members of the council as 'Mrs. Grundies' adding, 'We are glad to say that our decision has the full support of the producing company and its directors Mr. John Osborne and Mr. Tony Richardson' ('No Cuts' 1961). Sperryn responded in turn by framing Kingsley's comment as 'the outburst of an angry child' ('No Cuts' 1961) – a comment that curiously echoes the sensational 'Angry Young Man' appellation.

12   It is generally understood that the British New Wave included original authors as part of its aesthetic regime, but Walker suggests that Sillitoe's invitation came about because Harry Saltzman, one of the original founders and producers of Woodfall, 'had no money to pay a scriptwriter of any reputation' (1974: 80).

13   It should be noted that *Saturday Night and Sunday Morning*, like the majority of the texts associated with kitchen sink realism, moved class representation from the kind of caricatures and stereotypes associated with late nineteenth- and early twentieth-century class-conscious texts towards a more authentic, dedicated representation grounded in notions of community (Lee 2023). In the case of the British New Wave, this is likely the result of the documentary motifs associated with Free Cinema but can also be understood through the BBFC's championing of realism as a 'serious' modality. As Aldgate and Richards note, the film 'presented a realistic picture of an industrial working-class environment in a way that had rarely been evident in British cinema before' adding how 'To its credit, the film did not argue that the working class was thereby becoming more middle-class [*sic*] in its values or cultural behavior. It was not patronizing in that respect and, if anything, stood out modestly against any kind of simplistic "embourgeoisement" thesis' (1983: 143).

14   Aldgate and Richards summarize critical responses to the film demonstrating that it did indeed produce a variety of assumptions about Arthur's future.

They write, 'In view of this evident divergence of opinion, one might be
forgiven for thinking that, as is often the case, the critics quite simply saw the
film that they wanted to see and extrapolated those "messages" from it that
they might naturally have been predisposed to extrapolate' (1983: 140). As
with the abortion sequence, the authors claim this to be an unintended error.
But I would suggest that, in the light of the novel's strategic use of ambiguity
as a device, the effect should be read more as a feature than as a bug.

15   This scene was removed because all involved felt it was out of character
     for the now-reformed Arthur to humiliate his bride in such a way
     (Sillitoe 1960: 59).

16   Sillitoe is being cagey here, but the statement seems to corroborate the notion
     that while Arthur has matured by the end of the narrative, he retains his
     antagonistic side. In a follow-up sentence, Sillitoe states, 'I didn't want him to
     become a tough stereotype with, after all, a heart of moral gold which has in it
     a love of the monarchy and all that old-fashioned muck. Not that I imagined
     Woodfall Productions wanting to tamper in any way with what "ideological
     content" the story possessed' (1960: 58). Clearly, the novel's closing ambiguity
     of whether Arthur will concede or continue to fight is what the author
     considers to be its 'ideological content'.

17   Aldgate and Richards point to such instances as part of their claim that the
     adaptation lost its focus and unintentionally confused viewers (1983: 142–3).
     Given Trevelyan's intervening direction on how to handle the abortion
     sequence, it seems far more likely that the writers developed the screenplay in
     a manner that retains the sequence by masking the outcome.

18   Gardner suggests a parallel motif, noting how the film fleshed out a number
     of characters that Arthur 'victimizes' (such as Doreen) to further emphasize
     the felt impact of actions beyond that of the novel (2006: 113). In doing so,
     Reisz injects concerns of consequence, whereas the novel maintains a certain
     antagonistic belligerence tied to Arthur's insubordination.

19   Trevelyan cites Clayton's *Room at the Top* as a kind of watershed moment,
     suggesting once more that kitchen sink texts deploy strategic impertinence as
     shared motif (1973: 107). Aldgate and Richards note how Trevelyan's response
     to *Room at the Top* established the censorial criteria 'and helped to determine
     the critical consensus that existed across the industry when judging "quality"
     film thereafter' (2009: 195). In addition, Mike Hally discusses the way locally
     appointed censors measured their own conservatism against shifting trends in
     British culture, noting that attempts to shape and control public sentiments
     were largely futile (2016: 15).

20   Hally outlines the way local authorities exercised region-specific forms of
     censorship beyond the capacity of the more-prominent BBFC regulations. He
     notes how such groups consulted with the BBFC but positioned themselves
     as the ultimate arbiters of taste for the discrete areas they served (2016:
     3). The fact that such committees emerged and operated in tandem with
     the police force once more helps explain why *Saturday Night and Sunday
     Morning*'s emphasis on insubordination proved to be a major concern for the
     Warwickshire committee.

References

Aldgate, T. (2003), 'From Script to Screen: *Serious Charge* and Film Censorship', in I. MacKillop and N. Sinyard (eds), *British Cinema in the 1950's: An Art in Peacetime*, 133–42, Manchester: Manchester University Press.

Aldgate, T. (2005), 'Room at the Top', in B. McFarlane (ed), *The Cinema of Britain and Ireland*, 105–12, London: Wallflower.

Aldgate, A. and J. Richards (1983), 'The Seeds of Further Compromise: *Saturday Night and Sunday Morning*', in *Best of British: Cinema and Society from 1930 to the Present*, 131–45, Totowa, NJ: Barnes and Noble Books.

Aldgate, A. and J. Richards (2009), 'New Waves, Old Ways, and the Censors: *The Loneliness of the Long Distance Runner*', in *Best of British: Cinema and Society from 1930 to the Present*, new edn, 185–200, London: I.B. Tauris Publishers.

Brown, N. (2017), *British Children's Cinema: From the Thief of Bagdad to Wallace and Gromit*, London: I.B. Tauris.

'Censored Films: "Ridicule Well Worth While"' (1961), *The Birmingham Post*, 23 November.

'"Cinema Winning" Struggle With TV' (1961), *The Birmingham Post*, 24 February.

'Committee Calls for New Censorship Body' (1961), *The Birmingham Post*, 12 June.

Cook, A. (1961), 'An Angry Young Man on a Weekend Prowl', *New York World-Telegram*, 4 April.

'Councillor Attacks "A Kind of Loving"' (1961), *The Birmingham Post*, 14 January.

'County Ban on Film Described as Shocking' (1961), *The Birmingham Post*, 14 January.

'County Still Insist on Cuts in Film' (1962), *The Coventry Evening Telegraph*, 20 October.

'Coventry Will See Banned "Shocking" Film' (1961), *The Coventry Evening Telegraph*, 14 January.

Crowther, B. (1961), 'Screen: Different Briton', *The New York Times*, 4 April.

Delaney, S. (1958), *A Taste of Honey*, New York: Grove Press.

Dent, A. (1960), 'Rotten to the Core', *The Illustrated London News*, 12 November: 858.

'Film Ban Attacks Likely in Council' (1961), *The Birmingham Post*, 6 February.

Gardner, C. (2006), *Karel Reisz*, Manchester: Manchester University Press.

Gaston, G. (1980), *Karel Reisz*, Woodbridge, CT: Twayne Publishers.

Hally, M. (2016), 'Local Authorities and Film Censorship: A Historical Account of the "Naughty Pictures Committee" in Sale and Manchester', *Entertainment and Sports Law Journal*, 11: 1–21.

Hill, J. (1986), *Sex, Class, and Realism: British Cinema, 1956–1963*, London: BFI Publishing.

Holmes, S. (2005), *British TV & Film Culture of the 1950s: Coming to a TV Near You*, Bristol: Intellect.

'Itself Unveiled' (1961), *Guardian*, 6 February.

Lee, S. (2023), *The Intersection of Class and Space in British Post-war Writing: Kitchen Sink Aesthetics*, London: Bloomsbury.

'Long Eaton Palace' (1961), *Long Eaton Advertiser*, 3 February.

Marwick, A. (1984), 'Room at the Top, Saturday Night and Sunday Morning, and the "Cultural Revolution" in Britain', Journal of Contemporary History, 19 (1): 127–52.

Millstein, G. (1959), 'Books of The Times', The New York Times, 20 August.

'No Cuts, So County Will Not See Film' (1961), The Coventry Evening Telegraph, 24 January.

'"Queen of Films" Comes Back Home to Nottingham' (1960), The Nottingham Evening Post, 8 November.

Reisz, K. (1958), 'A Use for Documentary', Universities and Left Review, 3 (Winter): 23–4 and 65–6.

'Resignation Over Film Ban' (1961), The Birmingham Post, 23 February.

Shellard, D. (2003), Kenneth Tynan: A Life, New Haven, CT: Yale University Press.

Sillitoe, A. (1958), Saturday Night and Sunday Morning, New York: Alfred A Knopf.

Sillitoe, A. (1960), 'What Comes on Monday?', New Left Review, no. 4 (July): 58–9.

Sillitoe, A. (1995), Life Without Armour, London: HarperCollins.

Sillitoe, A. (1996), 'Responsibility', Article draft, Mss. II, Box 22, Bloomington, IN, Alan Sillitoe Papers, Lilly Library, Indiana University.

Sillitoe, A. (n.d.a), 'Chauvinistic', Article draft, Mss. II, Box 21, Bloomington, IN, Alan Sillitoe Papers, Lilly Library, Indiana University.

Sillitoe, A. (n.d.b), 'Note on AYM', Mss. II, Box 12, Folder 27, Bloomington, IN, Alan Sillitoe Papers Lilly Library, Indiana University.

Sillitoe, A. (n.d.c), 'Revised Typescript of Life Without Armour', Mss. II, Box 2, Folder 14, Bloomington, IN, Alan Sillitoe Papers, Lilly Library, Indiana University.

Sillitoe, A. (n.d.d), 'Typed Interview with Chuokoron-Sha, Inc. Publishers', Typed interview, Mss. II, Box 25, Interviews folder, Bloomington, IN, Alan Sillitoe Papers, Lilly Library, Indiana University.

Trevelyan, J. (1973), What the Censor Saw, London: Michael Joseph.

Walker, A. (1974), Hollywood UK: The British Film Industry in the Sixties, New York: Stein and Day.

Welsh, J. M. and J. C. Tibbetts, eds. (1999), '"Let's Talk About Tony": Interviews with Colleagues (Karel Reisz, Kevin Brownlow, David Watkins, and Angela Allen)', in J. M. Welsh and J. C. Tibbetts (eds), The Cinema of Tony Richardson: Essays and Interviews, 23–48, Albany, NY: State University of New York Press.

Wilson, C. (1956), The Outsider, London: Victor Gollancz.

Wollen, P. (2006), 'The Last New Wave: Modernism in the British Films of the Thatcher Era', in L. D. Friedman (ed), Fires Were Started: British Cinema and Thatcherism, second edn, 30–44, London: Wallflower Press.

5

Lolita, Censorship and Controversy:

The Archival Remains of the Dispute Between Canon L. J. Collins and Stanley Kubrick

James Fenwick

In 1958, the Harris-Kubrick Pictures Corporation, the independent production company of the filmmaking partners James B. Harris and Stanley Kubrick, acquired the filming rights to Vladimir Nabokov's 1955 novel *Lolita*. At the time, the book was banned in some countries due to its controversial subject matter: the story of a middle-aged professor's sexual obsession, domination and abuse of a thirteen-year-old girl (Ladenson 2007: 188). It took Harris and Kubrick four years from acquiring the rights to releasing a film based on *Lolita*. The main resistance to the film's production and distribution came not from regulatory censorship bodies in the United States (the Production Code Administration, [PCA]) and the UK (the British Board of Film Censors [BBFC]), but rather from private religious and political organizations. *Lolita*'s subject matter, along with the film's sexual commodification of its young title star, Sue Lyon – she had just turned fourteen when she was cast in the role – raised the ire of the United States' National Legion of Decency and the UK's Moral Law Defence Association and Christian Action.

MGM had declared that it would not distribute the film in the United States without the Legion's approval ('Trade' 1962: 11). At least thirty seconds of footage had to be cut to steer clear of the C category (C for condemned). The Legion eventually gave *Lolita* a separate certificate that advised caution about the film's content, after receiving MGM's confirmation that advertising would stipulate that no one under the age of eighteen would be admitted. Upon learning of Harris and Kubrick's plans to adapt *Lolita*, the Christian and conservative sections of British society protested the production with the aim of ensuring it was left unmade or unreleased. Moral reform campaigners believed Nabokov's novel – and by extension Harris and Kubrick's film – was an indicator of moral degradation contributing to the decay of moral standards among teenagers and, worse, promoting and normalizing sexual relations between adult men and underage children (Abrams 2016: 31–2; Ladenson 2007: 218–19). By early 1961, the chairman of Christian Action, Canon Lewis John Collins, was leading the organization's campaign against *Lolita*, which included lobbying the BBFC to ban the film. Collins was a radical political campaigner and used Christian Action as a pressure group on issues ranging from pacifism to apartheid in South Africa. Collins's campaign proved ultimately unsuccessful and *Lolita* was released with an X certificate in the UK.

Research into the censorship of *Lolita* is extensive, focused largely on the ways in which Harris and Kubrick interacted with the PCA and the BBFC during the script-writing and pre-production stages of the project (Biltereyst 2015; Fenwick 2020). Scholarship to date has tended to emphasize the adaptation process and the sexual aspects of the story that were left out of the script, or revised in order for it to receive both PCA and BBFC approval (Corliss 1994; Duckett 2014). Research shows that Harris and Kubrick shared a favourable relationship with the BBFC's John Trevelyan (Biltereyst 2015) and Martin Quigley, author of the Production Code (Fenwick 2020). These relationships were crucial throughout the script-writing and pre-production phases in order to guarantee the film's release. The pair was also closely supervised by the production company financing the project, Seven Arts, with its chief executive, Eliot Hyman, in constant dialogue with Harris and Kubrick to ensure they followed the PCA and BBFC's recommendations. *Lolita* was controversial and therefore a high-risk project. Even if approved for distribution by censorship bodies, it was always likely to receive an X certificate because of its subject matter and the reception of the book in the late 1950s (Ladenson 2007: 196–7), when it became an instrumental case study on literary censorship. As Ann Feeney argues, Nabokov's novel is 'one of the most frequently mentioned works in discussions of censorship' (1993: 67). Within Kubrick studies, arguments emphasize that it is Nabokov's book that is the source of the controversy surrounding Kubrick's film, not the film itself. The focus on adaptation and on interpreting and textually analysing the film against and within Kubrick's broader filmography leads to continual suggestions that *Lolita* the film is less sexually provocative than the book, that Kubrick was forced to compromise his artistic vision in order to have the script approved and that the film was not controversial enough (Abrams 2018; Corliss 1994; Kolker 2017; Metlić 2019).

This chapter intercedes in this debate by focusing on the Christian Action campaign led by Collins to pressure the BBFC into banning the film. The chapter utilizes archival sources, mainly correspondence from Collins to Kubrick and the BBFC located in the Lambeth Palace Archives and the Stanley Kubrick Archive, which have to date been overlooked. Rather than focusing on the film itself and the adaptation process, the chapter instead focuses on the arguments put forward by Collins and the means by which he suggested Harris and Kubrick were purposely cultivating a controversial reaction as part of the film's publicity campaign. What the archival remains of this dispute indicate is how Collins was not responding to the film's content (he had, after all, not seen it) but rather to the way in which Harris and Kubrick were framing the film in publicity material. Far from being less sexually explicit or provocative than Nabokov's novel, Harris and Kubrick's *Lolita* exploited and sexually commodified Lyon through press releases, photo shoots, and interviews (Fenwick 2020: 113–15). This in turn incensed religious and political organizations like Christian Action, leading to a discourse focused on wider issues of moral decay, teenage delinquency, and sexual depravity. This chapter lays out a selection of the archival remains of the dispute, contextualizing Collins's letters with reference to wider discussions and references in the UK media in the 1950s and 1960s. In doing so, the chapter considers whether Christian Action sought to ban just one film – *Lolita* – or whether it aimed to challenge the BBFC's X certificate itself. By exploring Collins's correspondence, the chapter examines how Christian Action wanted the BBFC to recognize that the X certificate was not adequate in protecting against potentially problematic representations of a paedophilic relationship and the exploitation of a child star, and to acknowledge that a film like *Lolita* risked normalizing abusive sexual relationships between adults and minors.

Context

Before setting out the archival evidence, it is necessary to consider three key contexts: 1) the brief history and controversy surrounding Nabokov's book, 2) the production history of Harris and Kubrick's *Lolita*; and 3) the history and motivations of Christian Action and Collins. Doing so will provide a greater understanding of the argument that took place between Collins and Kubrick in late 1961, prior to the film's UK release in September 1962.

Both Nabokov's novel and Harris and Kubrick's film adaptation are the story of a paedophile. The central character, Humbert Humbert, has a sexual obsession and desire for pre-pubescent girls under the age of fourteen. The age of consent in most parts of the US and UK at the time of the novel's setting – the mid-1950s – was sixteen (except in Georgia, where the age of consent remained fourteen until 1995) ('Raising' 1995: D4). To engage in sexual activity with a child under sixteen, as Humbert does, was therefore statutory rape. Humbert describes his predilection for 'nymphets' – girls between the age of nine and fourteen that 'bewitched' men 'many times older than they' (Nabokov 1955: 10), and confesses that he is 'consumed by a hell furnace of localized lust for every passing nymphet' (11). Nabokov originally struggled to find a publisher for the book. Four US publishers had rejected the manuscript in 1954, with Nabokov speculating that none of them had read the book to the end (Phillips 2016: 233). He eventually resorted to Olympia Press, a Paris-based publisher with a reputation for 'stark pornography with no literary pretensions – books with titles like *White Thighs*, *The Sexual Life of Robinson Crusoe*, and *The Chariots of Flesh*' (Millinship 1962: 8). (Though, it must be noted that Olympia also published the work of renowned authors, such as Samuel Beckett, William S. Burroughs, Henry Miller, and Pauline Réage.)

Lolita's association with Olympia further contributed to its pornographic (or, at the very least, erotic) reputation. Given that Olympia exclusively published in English, despite being based in Paris, it regularly received complaints from the British government (8). *Lolita* was published in 1955 and exported to countries around the world, including the United States, without censorship. But the UK government ordered the confiscation of copies of the novel being imported into the country. Following pressure from the British Home Office, the French government prohibited the book from being sold in English in 1956 (Cranston 1957: 5). Yet, at the same time, the book was to be translated into French and published in Paris. As the critic Maurice Cranston noted, this created an absurd paradox in which, '"Lolita" can be imported into the United States, but not exported from France; it cannot be sold in English in France, but it will soon be sold in French in France' (1957: 5). As the book's notoriety grew, so did publisher interest. Nabokov eventually found a US publisher, GP Putnam's Sons, and the first mainstream print became an instant bestseller, selling 100,000 copies in the first three weeks of its release (Biltereyst 2015: 142). Still, even once the book was published in the UK, there were many groups opposed to it. A number of Conservative Party MPs were determined to prohibit the sale of publications such as *Lolita* and 'others of a like nature', which they believed had a 'harmful effect on the morals and outlook of the younger generation, especially in view of the cheap prices at which they sell' ('MPs want Ban' 1961: 2).

A combination of the novel's scandalous reputation – John Gordon, editor of the *Sunday Express*, described it as 'the filthiest book I have ever read. Sheer unrestrained pornography' (1956: 6) – and high praise from fellow authors – Graham Greene called it one of the best books of 1955 in a review in the *Sunday Times* (Phillips 2016: 233) – showed there was considerable interest in optioning the book for a film adaptation. Harris acquired the filming rights to *Lolita* for $150,000 and subsequently secured financing from Seven Arts (after MGM, United Artists, and many other major US studios had turned down the project [Fenwick 2020: 108–9]). Seven Arts, to mitigate the financial risk of the project, brought in a script consultant, Martin Quigley, who recommended changes to the script and dialogue (112–13). Quigley co-authored the Hollywood Production Code introduced in 1930 as a set of guidelines as to what was, and more importantly what was not, acceptable for on-screen representation in the United States. Quigley suggested edits to any controversial dialogue or material in the script. Similarly, in the UK, Harris and Kubrick worked closely with John Trevelyan, secretary of the BBFC. According to Daniel Biltereyst, Trevelyan's initial objections to the script were more about the fact that it 'differed from the novel by combining humour and bad taste' (2015: 144). As Biltereyst argues, the BBFC was more interested in what he describes as 'pre-production consultation' rather than post-production censorship; it was about providing a 'constructive form of censorship' (144). Indeed, Trevelyan argued that Kubrick would make a responsible film given his perceived level of artistry. Trevelyan said that his initial reservations were informed by the book's 'sensational publicity', claiming that 'the most responsible film will suffer from a backlash of this' (cited in Biltereyst 2015: 148).

The film is even more problematic and disturbing than the novel for the way it treats Humbert's story. Harris and Kubrick turn one man's dark sexual obsession into a convivial and blackly humorous tale in which the audience is encouraged to laugh at Humbert's relationship with Lolita, as well as her exploitation by other powerful men in the film, including the character Clare Quilty (Peter Sellers). The producers claimed they changed the age of Lolita to around fourteen or fifteen, but this is of no real consequence. After all, the story remains the same: a middle-aged man's illegal sexual activity with a minor.

To overcome many of the potential censorship issues, Harris and Kubrick resorted to sexual innuendo in place of actually portraying on-screen sex. The sexual innuendo throughout hints at the continued abuse of Lolita by men in the world she inhabits ('She [Lolita] is having a cavity filled by Uncle Ivor', says Quilty at one point), while there are instances in which Humbert and Lolita's sexual relationship is made quite clear (the simulation, off screen, of oral sex). In contrast to how some academics have suggested, and continue to suggest, that the film is not sexually explicit and tones down the novel's sexual content, or worse blame Lolita for the sexual advances of adult men (Abrams 2018: 76; Abrams 2021: 285; McEntee 2021: 193), or how Kubrick himself suggested that he was compelled to make significant compromises ('Had I realized how severe the limitations were going to be [...] I probably wouldn't have made the film' [cited in Zimmerman 1972: 32]), both the content and style of *Lolita* are highly problematic and sexually explicit.

The film is further problematized due to recent allegations of a purported sexual relationship between Harris and Lyon at the time of the film's production and release (Weinman 2020). Archival evidence in the form of correspondence clearly indicates that there was an exploitative production culture on *Lolita* in which Lyon was manipulated and controlled by powerful men. This included Harris and Kubrick, who were responsible for contractual discussions about Lyon that treated her as a sexual commodity to be used by Hollywood as quickly as possible before she grew out of her 'Lolita image' (Fenwick 2021: 12–13; Ritzenhoff 2021: 170–2). Lyon's image and career were tightly controlled by Harris and Kubrick. Yet, Lyon herself stated publicly, 'My destruction as a person dates from that movie. *Lolita* exposed me to temptations no girl of that age should undergo' (Macdonald 1996).

Clearly *Lolita*, both the novel and film, generated excitement and condemnation, and demonstrated the gap in society and popular culture between liberal Hollywood producers like Harris and Kubrick (liberal in the sense of wanting to push against censorious bodies and regulation and to represent transgressive relationships and taboo topics on screen) and the morally conservative religious pressure groups determined to suppress both the book and prevent any film adaptation. One such group was Christian Action.

Christian Action was an inter-church organization founded in 1946 by Collins. It was an organization of laymen 'founded to further Christian beliefs and to encourage its members to take personal responsibility as Christians in the social and political life of the country' ('Libel' 1953: 2). Collins wanted to, in his words, 'root out intolerance' from national life ('Canon Collins' 1953: 10) and to 'make the church more responsive to social issues' (Herbstein 2004: 6); he intended to use Christian Action to achieve these aims. Collins was the Canon of St Paul's Cathedral in London from 1948 until 1981. He was a politically active individual, a Labour Party member, and was involved in a number of movements in the UK, from the Campaign for Nuclear Disarmament (CND), the campaign to abolish capital punishment and the establishment of the British Anti-Apartheid Movement ('The Origins' n.d.). He was a radical priest, politically progressive and a Christian Socialist.

Collins believed vehemently in his mission of Christianity and of social morality and took direct action in spreading those values. But there was a contradiction between Collins's progressive politics and his dedication to the Church, which took a strongly conservative approach to sex, marriage and relationships. Collins's sermons in the 1950s and 1960s often focused on his belief in the moral decay of youth in the UK. For instance, Collins took aim at young people in a sermon on 14 September 1959 following race riots in Nottingham and London; Collins criticized what he saw as the 'growth of violence among the young' ('Imputation' 1959: 2). Similarly, in a sermon given on 21 July 1963, Collins referred to modern British youth as 'disillusioned rebels' and said that, 'Christians and the Churches must condemn licence and selfishness in sexual behaviour' ('Churches' 1963: 2). What Collins's activities and background reveal is an individual who believed in political action motivated by his deep Christian beliefs.

Archival Traces

Utilizing correspondence held in the Lambeth Palace Archives and the Stanley Kubrick Archive, the aim is to analyse the exchange that took place from 1959 to 1962 between Collins, Kubrick and Trevelyan. The correspondence, which consists only of a handful of letters, indicates how the arguments stemmed from the representation of a sexual relationship between an adult and a minor. I have annotated the extracts to provide further context, to consider the language utilized and to place the letters within a wider argument about *Lolita*'s problematic nature.

Collins to Kubrick, 1 March 1961

The first letter from Collins to Kubrick came towards the end of *Lolita*'s production in March 1961. Collins was unaware that *Lolita* had already started filming. He immediately launches into his line of attack against the film, a position that he maintained throughout the course of his letters to Kubrick over the next two months:

> We understand that you are to produce a film based on the book Lolita. We believe that any such film must have deleterious effects upon our society, particularly in the light of the publicity already given to the book Lolita, and therefore ought not to be made. We must presume that you see the project in a different light, and I would be grateful, therefore, if you would kindly tell us what are the grounds which you believe justify you in making it.
>
> (Collins 1961a)

Collins was inviting Kubrick to share his ideas about the plot of Nabokov's book and the adaptation process. Of particular concern to Collins was the ongoing publicity the book was receiving, something that we know excited Harris and Kubrick (Fenwick 2020: 110), but which Collins considered dangerous. However, in this letter, he refrains from expounding on just what the 'deleterious effects' are to which he refers, instead wanting Kubrick to first justify his approach.

Collins to Kubrick, 15 March 1961

Collins followed up his initial letter to Kubrick in response to a *Sunday Pictorial* news report about *Lolita*. Kubrick had not yet responded to Collins, but Collins was clearly disturbed by what he had read in the newspaper, as well as coming to realise that the film was in the advanced stages of production:

> I have read a report in the 'Sunday Pictorial' this week which suggests that the filming of Lolita is already in hand. I think the Pictorial's pictures and comments are such as to arouse considerable misgivings throughout the country. I would be glad of a reply to my letter. We would not wish to launch upon any protest without first trying to discover what are the reasons which you seem to think justify the making of this film.
>
> (Collins 1961b)

The news piece referenced by Collins was published under the headline 'Startling Scenes from "Lolita" Film: Seedy, Shocking, Sensational – Lolita in Action!' (1961). The three-page spread contained six production stills that were released by the film's producers, mainly focusing on Lyon. Repeatedly, the piece describes Lyon using sexualized language. Though only a short profile, the newspaper spread seemed designed to elicit shock and controversy as focused on the sexual relationship between an adult and a minor and the appropriateness of this. As the news story stated, '"Lolita" is an unpleasant story about a middle-aged man's obsession for a twelve-year-old girl [...] With all the world of tender and innocent adolescence to draw on – WHY DID THEY HAVE TO MAKE "LOLITA?"'.

Kubrick to Collins, 23 March 1961

Kubrick's first response to Collins aimed to shift the blame away from himself and the film to the media instead, arguing that what Collins found shocking was not the film (which he had not seen) but the media reaction, what Kubrick calls an 'air of sensationalism'. Kubrick suggests that the controversy and sensationalism surrounding the film, along with the publicity, is something that was out of his hands and that he had nothing to do with:

> I appreciate your concern about the making of 'LOLITA' into a film, because of the sensational publicity which has been attached to the novel.

Knowing the sincerity of your intentions, I can only register a certain degree of surprise at your willingness to pre-judge a motion picture (which, by the way, has already been filmed) before you see it. The air of sensationalism which has surrounded 'LOLITA' from the beginning has been completely beyond our control, and we have done everything possible to avoid it and to detach ourselves from its implications. Wouldn't you say that it gives some cause for thought on your part, when you consider the calibre and reputation of the people involved in the picture, notably James Mason, Peter Sellers, and Shelley Winters.

(Kubrick 1961a)

What Kubrick does not mention is the number of actors, of a calibre and reputation akin to – if not surpassing – those mentioned above, who turned down the project because they believed it to be pornographic. This group included Kirk Douglas, Laurence Olivier and David Niven (Fenwick 2020: 109). Kubrick then emphasizes his own reputation:

I hesitate to add (but your letter enforces me to), that a quick look at the films I have made in the past, might also imply a certain dedication to filmmaking, rather than to the exploitation of 'unwholesome' subjects. I must say, that I do not think you will find the motion picture in any way deleterious to the morals of any segment of society. By the way, the photographs you referred to in the 'Sunday Pictorial', were stolen from the Laboratory and mis-captioned and, as a result, gave a completely distorted impression.

Kubrick's response to Collins, and ultimately his justification for filming *Lolita,* centred on the issue of reputation. Kubrick referred to his own esteem within the film industry and his own track record as a director as evidence that he did not pursue films about 'unwholesome' subjects. However, he conveniently overlooked many aspects of his films, each of which up to that point contained at least one murder, often brutal scenes of violence against women, and regularly caused controversy.

As for Kubrick's claim that he would never exploit the controversy surrounding Nabokov's novel, this was far from the truth. The use of controversy to promote a film was a tactic to which Kubrick was not adverse. Indeed, he previously encouraged the exploitation of the controversial reaction to *Paths of Glory* in Europe. The film had not been released in France and had been withdrawn from exhibition in several other European countries due to its perceived negative representation of the French military. However, Kubrick attempted to encourage a French distributor to release *Paths of Glory* and to take full advantage of its controversial reputation, as he urged in a letter in 1958: 'The controversy over [*Paths of Glory*] would undoubtedly cause front page headlines and public demonstrations. At the risk of sounding cynical, one could hardly hope for a better kind of movie publicity and promotion' (Kubrick 1958).

Harris and Kubrick exploited the controversy of *Lolita* in a similar way, from directly attaching Nabokov's name to the project (and thereby the pre-existing history of the novel's pornographic reputation) to playing up the book's disrepute in poster taglines such as, 'How did they ever make a movie of Lolita?' (a line that appears almost verbatim in the *Sunday Pictorial* news article). They also later emphasized in publicity material the X certificate that the film received in the UK, playing up the fact that Lyon herself, while able to attend film premiere functions, was not legally able to watch the film. The promotional campaign for the film, which began during pre-production, was carefully orchestrated by Harris and Kubrick, who cultivated what they termed the 'Lolita-image', which was entirely based around Lyon. They tightly controlled access to her and published photographs and press releases that purposely sexualized the young actor. For example, they hired photographer Bert Stern in 1960 to take a series of iconic images of Lyon. As Karen Ritzenhoff argues, 'Stern created a visual vocabulary of teenage female sensuality in which Lolita is predominantly engaging with the viewer behind the camera, satisfying voyeuristic pleasure, that is echoed in Kubrick's films. Stern's promotional photography, therefore, was more representative of male power than female empowerment' (2021: 172). Harris was particularly close to the creation of the 'Lolita-image', in the process transforming Lyon into the embodiment of a sexualized teenager and encouraging the world's media to describe her in graphic, sexualized language as he accompanied her on a press tour around the world. The 'Lolita-image' depended on turning Lyon into a sexualized commodity, a young teenage girl that audiences and critics alike were encouraged to fantasize about. In short, the publicity campaign amounted to turning Lyon into the dangerous symbol of a sexualized, permissive society that Collins and others feared. She embodied the air of sensationalism that surrounded *Lolita*.

Collins to Kubrick, 27 and 28 March 1961

Collins followed up Kubrick's response with two letters of his own in which he escalated his line of attack against *Lolita*. In his first letter, he requested that Kubrick reconsider releasing the film:

> I note that the picture of Lolita has already been made, and that you feel that it will not be in any way deleterious to the morals of any segment of society. My concern is nevertheless that the subject matter of the novel is not suitable to film. I have no doubt that the actors concerned, as well as yourself, would give the best possible consideration to the production

of an artistic film and would have no wish to produce anything which would harm public morals. The fact remains that the book has sensational publicity and the showing of the film would, in my opinion, inevitably incur the risk of being seen by people suffering from the same perversion as is the subject of the book, and might, therefore, do great harm, perhaps even leading to rape or murder, which would otherwise not have occurred. I would therefore beg you to give further consideration in the matter, before you seek to get it released.

(Collins 1961c)

Collins, for the first time, inferred that Kubrick's film could potentially incite real-life sexual violence, without any evidence to support this claim. Collins also disputed Kubrick's filmmaking reputation, arguing that it did not matter about the artistic calibre of those involved because of the very fact that the story remained that of a sexual relationship between an adult and a child. The following day, Collins sent Kubrick another letter that confirmed Christian Action was to officially lodge a case against *Lolita* with the BBFC:

I have decided that we must present to the Board of Film Censors what we believe to be the case against the film Lolita being given any kind of certificate for showing in Britain. The case we wish to present is not against the particular version of the film Lolita which you have produced – if it were, it would of course, be necessary for us to see the film before objecting to it. Our contention is that any film version of this book, unless it departs so radically from the book as to be unrecognisable, must be a provocation of the kind that might lead to rape and even murder.

Collins appears to be suggesting that Kubrick's defence about being a respectable artist did not provide him with the right to adapt the book into a film. Indeed, Collins seems to hint at a greater responsibility to prevent such material from being adapted into films. He then outlines the basic plot structure of *Lolita* and how he believes no filmmaker could deviate from this story.

Lolita, which I have read with care, is a cleverly written novel about an ugly sex perversion. It is a story of a man possessed by an insatiable desire for physical sex experience with pre-adolescent girls. He marries his landlady, a widow with a daughter aged 12, expressly to possess the daughter. When his wife is killed in an accident, he takes the little girl as his mistress, moves around with her from place so as to avoid arrest, and, in the end, kills the man who is responsible, he believes, for releasing her from his clutches. You will not, I believe, dispute that this is a fair outline of the book. As to the film version, I understand that the part of the male pervert is played by a middle-aged actor, and that of Lolita by

a girl actress. It would seem evident, therefore, that the film version does
not seek to disguise the book's essential characteristics, and indeed your
letter does not suggest that it does.

(Collins 1961d)

Collins made it clear that, no matter Kubrick's justification, Christian Action
would object to any film adaptation due to the essential storyline of the
novel. He also focused on the material and social realities of the production,
particularly Lyon's age, seeing the film as exploiting and sexualizing a young
female actor. Collins proceeded to expand upon this latter point:

We shall submit to the British Board of Film Censors that it would be
irresponsible to regard this as just another erotic film to which an X
certificate can be given. Of course, children and adolescents must be
protected against corrupting influences. But our point in regard to 'Lolita'
is that it might attract men who have this particular sex obsession and
also those in whom there is a potential obsession and in whom their
latest desires might be stirred into criminal action. In the interval between
my first writing to you and your reply, Arthur Albert Jones appeared at
the Old Bailey and was sentenced to fourteen years' imprisonment for
the rape of a girl guide. Jones' victim Barbara sat beside the Old Bailey
judge telling the story of her night of terror at the hands of one such
pervert as is described in Lolita. This case was only the most recent of
many which have horrified the public in recent years, some of which have
ended in murder. That is why we shall fight against the showing of this
film in Britain.

(Collins 1961d)

Collins and Christian Action wanted the BBFC to enact a permanent ban
of any film based on *Lolita*. Collins argued that both the novel and any
film adapted from it risked normalizing dangerous sexual behaviour. He
believed that the X certificate was inadequate. Preventing children from
seeing *Lolita* would be pointless if adult men were still permitted to view
it, while the film itself would be far from entertainment and instead a
depiction of a predatory paedophile. Collins outlined his key approach to
the case against *Lolita*: the idea that it could provoke rape and murder.
This included the case of Arthur Albert Jones, who was sentenced in March
1961 for the rape of an eleven-year-old girl. Jones, who possessed a history
of abusive behaviour, was later discovered to have also murdered a 12-year-
old girl, Brenda Nash, and was given a life sentence in June 1961 ('Jones'
1961: 5). Psychiatrists determined that Jones was motivated by a persistent
need for incestuous sexual gratification and of excitement at young girls
in Girl Guides' uniforms. Collins directly linked the Jones case to *Lolita*,
stating that Jones's crimes were as described in *Lolita*. Collins was in part

responding to a climate of sensationalism in which a number of books and films at that time – for instance D. H. Lawrence's *Lady Chatterley's Lover* (1932) or George Cukor's *The Chapman Report* (1962) were deemed to be morally reprehensible and contributing to a sexually deviant society. Indeed, letters written to *The Observer* in 1959 about Nabokov's book suggested that it would lead to a breakdown of moral standards in the country. One letter proclaimed that the publication of *Lolita* would result in an increase in 'auto-erotic fantasies of a perverted kind'; the author believed that *Lolita*'s supposed encouragement of masturbation would be detrimental not only to the individual, but also to wider society, 'by impairing [human] emotional capacity for entering fully into normal human relationships' ('Letters' 1959: 11). Another letter argued that *Lolita* would encourage the normalization of paedophilia and make sexual abuse of children acceptable within society. Collins contributed to this discourse, linking *Lolita* to deviant sexual behaviour, child abuse, and violent crime by releasing to the press a list of over twenty cases of rape involving young girls. The aim was to link in the public's mind the story of *Lolita* to actual crimes and to stress the weak barrier of moral convention that Collins was trying to defend.

Kubrick to Collins, 6 May 1961; Trevelyan to Kubrick, 11 May 1961

Christian Action submitted a case against *Lolita* to the BBFC in early May 1961. The case included the correspondence between Kubrick and Collins, alongside press cuttings. Collins gave Kubrick the opportunity to respond, explaining that he intended to make the case public. Kubrick's response once again focused on the fact that Collins was prejudging *Lolita* without having seen it and was privately attempting to unduly influence the BBFC:

> I would not think it unfair to say that even by the most objective interpretation of your own words, your opinion as to the possible effects of the motion picture, 'Lolita', is based entirely upon presumption and not upon evidence. I would therefore hope that upon re-examination of the facts at hand, you might come to the conclusion that your announced intention to attempt to prejudice the British Board of Film Censors before the film is even submitted to them is not only an extremely unfair action but one which seems to hinge upon a rather paradoxical moral principal. I sincerely regret that you and your council have found it necessary to devote so much of your worthwhile time to something which in the end I am certain you will find completely unobjectionable.
>
> (Kubrick 1961b)

Most likely unbeknown to Collins, Kubrick possessed a pre-existing relationship with the BBFC that ensured *Lolita* would be released without any cuts. This meant that, upon receiving Christian Action's case, Trevelyan immediately wrote to Kubrick:

> I am now sending you privately a copy of the document sent to me by Canon Collins. As I have told you, anything of this kind will not prejudice the Board in its discussions. Canon Collins will be informing the press. If there are any developments I will let you know.
>
> (Trevelyan 1961)

This letter suggests that Collins's campaign was futile and that the BBFC had already sided with Harris and Kubrick.

Collins to Kubrick, 9 May 1961

The final letter from Collins contained in the archives focuses on the urgent imperative to convince the BBFC to prevent *Lolita*'s release. By this point, Collins and Kubrick had already reached entrenched positions. The only indication of any compromise was Collins's request to Kubrick to provide a copy of *Lolita* for a private screening of the film for the Council of Christian Action. This, however, was a highly unlikely situation, given that it would provide Christian Action with the evidence it needed to support its claims that the film should not be released:

> Believing as we do in the possibility, or even probability, of the film version of LOLITA having the ill effects to which I have referred previously, it would be both foolish and immoral on our part to await factual evidence (which, in any case, would be extremely difficult to establish with any degree of certainty) before making our protest. It is our hope, therefore that the Board of Film Censors, will not grant it a licence. There would be little point in our waiting to present our case against any film version of LOLITA until the licence had been granted and the picture released for showing to the public. In your reply you do not respond to the suggestion of the Council of Christian Action that, should you think any good purpose would be served by our doing so, we would be willing to see a private showing of the film. It would seem to me, therefore, that any 're-examination of the facts at hand' would not justify us in staying our purpose of asking the Board of Film Censors not to grant a licence of any sort.
>
> (Collins 1961e)

Resisting Christian Action's efforts to ban *Lolita*, the BBFC ultimately gave the film an X certificate in September 1961, but this only served to further motivate Christian Action. The organization partnered with the Moral Law Defence Association to mobilize supporters in a national boycott. The groups requested that local authorities ignore the BBFC's classification of *Lolita* to form their own judgment ('Lolita' 1962: 3). However, Collins and Christian Action's campaign proved counter-intuitive by further contributing to the 'air of sensationalism' surrounding the film. Kubrick seized the opportunity to criticize Collins's actions in the press, calling his campaign 'dangerous and silly' and calling Collins 'incredibly presumptuous' due to not having seen the film ('Action Group' 1961: 12). Kubrick turned Collins's campaign back on himself, declaring him – not the film – to be dangerous to society and to free speech, telling the press that 'it is surely undesirable that unofficial organizations, who have no knowledge of a film, should attempt to put pressure on official censorial bodies' (12). According to Kubrick, it was not *Lolita* or filmmakers like himself that were a threat to the moral standards of society but rather Collins and Christian Action in their attempts to suppress films like *Lolita*.

Conclusion

Lolita's X certificate was largely pre-ordained given that Harris and Kubrick had been involved in censorship negotiations with the BBFC since the script stage. Kubrick even encouraged self-censorship and the removal of shots that he thought might encounter trouble with censors. For Collins, the key problem was not whether there was any representation or even suggestion of sex on screen but rather in the fact that Harris and Kubrick decided to adapt a story about a paedophile. Christian Action's objections with the BBFC centred on the inadequacy of the X certificate to prevent such films from being seen and the potential harm it could have in normalizing deviant sexual behaviour. Harris and Kubrick welcomed the controversy that surrounded the production, and even encouraged it, despite Kubrick's protestations to Collins that he would never do such a thing. As such, Harris and Kubrick seemed to welcome the attention that Collins's campaign brought *Lolita*, particularly following Trevelyan's private reassurance that it would have no bearing on the rating decision.

What also arises out of the study of these letters is the question of artistic reputation and how Kubrick himself possessed the self-belief (even at this early stage of his career) that he was a great artist and that in of itself was justification to allow him to adapt whatever he wanted and to resist any attempts at censorship or external control. This confidence in his own directorial image and reputation was undoubtedly bolstered by the critical and commercial success of *Spartacus* (1960), which garnered him new levels of power in the film industry. Arguably, Kubrick's attitude in his

letters to Collins also hints towards the power dynamics of the film industry
and the way white, male auteurs were treated as artists. Even Trevelyan
admitted to backing down over the censorship of *Lolita* because of his own
attitudes towards Kubrick as an artist. These letters, and this case study, can
therefore provide further insights into the myth of the auteur and the way
in which filmmakers like Kubrick felt empowered to do as they wish within
the industry.

While the letters between Collins and Kubrick are limited to a particular
time period, the discourse they contain has continued since then, reflecting
the ongoing controversial nature of *Lolita* and its story of a paedophile,
and of the impact and legacy of the 'Lolita image' that Harris and Kubrick
created – a pervasive image of teenage sexuality that has influenced fashion,
photography, culture and even pornography throughout the twentieth
and twenty-first centuries (Fenwick 2022). Adrian Lyne's 1997 adaptation
of *Lolita* encountered a variety of controversies, including initially being
rejected for release by major distributors in the United States and Australia,
as well as being labelled 'an apologia for the apparent sexual abuse of
children' (Delingpole 1998: F6). The 'Lolita image' has also been targeted
by prominent figures following the #MeToo movement. Natalie Portman
stated that she was regularly framed as a 'Lolita' figure as a child and had
feared being harassed or assaulted by men in the entertainment industries
(and beyond) as a result (Fenwick 2022). The convicted sex offender Jeffrey
Epstein was reported to have even nicknamed his private jet the 'Lolita
Express' (Eklund 2019).

With this in mind, the discussions to date of the history of *Lolita*'s
X certificate in the UK, and its difficulties with other censorious bodies
around the world, typically overlook the material, social and cultural
conditions of the film's production. It is something which Collins briefly
touched upon, when objecting to the casting of Lyon. Her exploitation
by the film's producers, the creation of the 'Lolita-image', the control
Harris and Kubrick yielded over her career and the impact it had on her
subsequent life are all indicators of how, in many ways, *Lolita* is an allegory
of its own production. Rather than focusing on the liberalizing forces of
censorship that prevailed and allowed *Lolita* to be produced and exhibited,
or on adaptation and fidelity, film historians should now examine archival
and empirical evidence of the film's material, social and cultural conditions
of production that clearly highlight the problematic production, promotion
and working relations on the film. Archival research can reframe textual
analysis of the film and show how misplaced Collins and Christian Action
were: the fears they had over the sexualization of society ignored the
exploitation taking place on the film's set. For *Lolita* is not only a film
about the sexual relationship between an adult male and a minor but a film
that is the material evidence of the film industry's power structures. While

the BBFC and Trevelyan may have excused *Lolita* in the name of art (and its producers, Harris and Kubrick, as artists), film history must reframe the debate and take account of how male 'auteur apologism' marginalizes and supresses the voice, narrative and agency of people like Lyon (Fenwick 2021; Marghitu 2018).

References

Abbreviations:

CLJCP = Canon L. J. Collins Papers, Lambeth Palace Archives, London.
SKA = Stanley Kubrick Archive, University of the Arts London.

Abrams, N. (2016), 'Kubrick's Double: *Lolita*'s Hidden Heart of Jewishness', *Cinema Journal*, 55 (3): 17–39.
Abrams, N. (2018), *Stanley Kubrick: New York Jewish Intellectual*, New Brunswick, NJ: Rutgers University Press.
Abrams, N. (2021), 'Kubrick and Childhood', in N. Abrams (ed), *The Bloomsbury Companion to Stanley Kubrick*, 281–90, London: Bloomsbury.
'Action Group Asks British Censor Board to Turn Down "Lolita" Film' (1961), *Variety*, 222 (18): 12.
Biltereyst, D. (2015), '"A Constructive Form of Censorship": Disciplining Kubrick's *Lolita*', in P. Krämer, T. Ljujic, and R. Daniels (eds), *Stanley Kubrick: New Perspectives*, 138–51, London: Black Dog Publishing.
'Canon Collins's Call to "Root Out" Intolerance' (1953), *The Manchester Guardian*, 21 September: 10.
'Churches "Proved Bankrupt for Modern Youth"' (1963), *The Guardian*, 22 July: 2.
Collins, L. J. (1961a), Letter to Stanley Kubrick, 1 March, MS 3298 f.1, CLJCP.
Collins, L. J. (1961b), Letter to Stanley Kubrick, 15 March, MS 3298 f.1, CLJCP.
Collins, L. J. (1961c), Letter to Stanley Kubrick, 27 March, MS 3298 f.2, CLJCP.
Collins, L. J. (1961d), Letter to Stanley Kubrick, 28 March, MS 3298 f.3, CLJCP.
Collins, L. J. (1961e), Letter to Stanley Kubrick, 9 May, MS 3298 f.11, CLJCP.
Corliss, R. (1994), *Lolita*, London: British Film Institute.
Cranston, M. (1957), 'Obscenity in the Eye of Only Some Beholders: Contradictions in the Case of "Lolita"', *The Guardian*, 14 May.
Delingpole, J. (1998), 'Dangerous Liaison', *The Vancouver Sun*, 30 September: F6.
Duckett, V. H. (2014), 'Letting Lolita Laugh', *Literature/Film Quarterly*, 42 (3): 528–40.
Eklund, E. (2019), 'Jeffrey Epstein's Lolita?', *Church Life Journal*. Available online: https://churchlifejournal.nd.edu/articles/jeffrey-epsteins-lolita/ (accessed 20 January 2022).
Feeney, A. (1993), '*Lolita and Censorship: A Case Study*', *Reference Services Review*, 21 (4): 67–90.

Fenwick, J. (2020), *Stanley Kubrick Produces*, New Brunswick, NJ: Rutgers University Press.

Fenwick, J. (2021), 'The Exploitation of Sue Lyon: *Lolita* (1962), Archival Research, and Questions for Film History', *Feminist Media Studies*, https://doi.org/10.1080/14680777.2021.1996422.

Fenwick, J. (2022), 'The Problems with *Lolita*', in K. Ritzenhoff and D. Metlic (eds), *Gender, Power, and Identity in the Films of Stanley Kubrick*, London and New York: Routledge.

Gordon, J. (1956), 'Current Events', *Sunday Express*, 29 January: 6.

Herbstein, D. (2004), *White Lies: Canon Collins and the Secret War against Apartheid*, Oxford: James Currey Publishers.

'Imputation against League Withdrawn by Canon Collins' (1959), *The Guardian*, 17 April.

'Jones: Life Sentence Adds to 14-Year Term' (1961), *The Guardian*, 20 June.

Kolker, R. P. (2017), *The Extraordinary Image: Orson Welles, Alfred Hitchcock, Stanley Kubrick and the Reimagining of Cinema*, New Brunswick, NJ: Rutgers University Press.

Kubrick, S. (1958), Letter to S&J Siritsky, 12 December, uncatalogued, SKA.

Kubrick, S. (1961a), Letter to Canon L. J. Collins, 23 March, MS 3298 f.2, CLJCP.

Kubrick, S. (1961b), Letter to Canon L. J. Collins, 6 May, MS 3298 f.9, CLJCP.

Ladenson, E. (2007), *Dirt for Art's Sake: Books on Trial from Madame Bovary to Lolita*, Ithaca, NY: Cornell University Press.

'Letters to the Editor: The "Lolita" Case' (1959), *Observer*, 15 February: 11.

'Libel on Canon Collins' (1953), *The Manchester Guardian*, 17 October.

'"Lolita" Starts Clean-up Row'. (1962), *Daily Mail*, 22 August.

Macdonald, M. (1996), 'Correctness Fears Keep *Lolita* Under Wraps', *The Independent*, 9 August: 7.

Marghitu, S. (2018), '"It's Just Art": Auteur Apologism in the Post-Weinstein era', *Feminist Media Studies*, 18 (3): 491–4.

McEntee, J. (2021), 'Kubrick, Marriage, and Family', in N. Abrams (ed), *The Bloomsbury Companion to Stanley Kubrick*, 191–201, London: Bloomsbury.

Metlić, D. (2019), 'Nabokov, Kubrick and Stern: Who Created *Lolita*?', *Etnoantropološki problem*, 14 (2): 435–59.

Millinship, W. (1962), '"Lolita" Publisher Sues Ministry', *Observer*, 18 March: 8.

'MPs Want Ban on "Lolita"-Type Books' (1961), *The Guardian*, 17 February.

Nabokov, V. (1955), *Lolita*, London: Penguin, 2000.

Phillips, G. D. (2016), 'Lolita', in Alison Castle (ed), *The Stanley Kubrick Archives*, 232–71, Cologne: Taschen.

'Raising Age of Consent OK'd by Senate Panels' (1995), *The Atlanta Journal*, 1 February: D4.

Ritzenhoff, K. (2021), 'Kubrick and Feminism', in N. Abrams (ed), *The Bloomsbury Companion to Stanley Kubrick*, 169–78, London: Bloomsbury.

'Startling Scenes from "Lolita" Film' (1961), *Sunday Pictorial*, 12 March: 1, 16–7.

'The Origins of the Trust' (n.d.), *Canon Collins*. Available online: https://www.canoncollins.org/about/our-story/ (accessed 23 March 2020).

'Trade Sees Condemnation Avoided Hence Metro Finalizes for "Lolita"' (1962), *Variety*, 225 (12): 11.

Trevelyan, J. (1961), Letter to Stanley Kubrick, 30 May, SK/10/8/5, SKA.

Weinman, S. (2020), 'The Dark Side of *Lolita*', *Air Mail*. Available online: https://airmail.news/issues/2020-10-24/the-dark-side-of-lolita (accessed 27 October 2020).

Zimmerman, P. D. (1972), 'Kubrick's Brilliant Vision', *Newsweek*, 3 January: 28–33.

6

Paternalism, Bohemianism and the X Certificate:

The Party's Over and the Pre-Swinging Set

Kevin M. Flanagan

London has long been a playground for young people with 'bohemian' sensibilities. Elizabeth Wilson has written about the term's romantic and somewhat tragic connotations, pointing out that since the nineteenth century, 'the bohemian has been the hero – and anti-hero – of the story the West has wanted to hear about its artists, a story of genius, glamour, outlawry and doom' (2000: 3). One avenue of escape for the artistic/free-spirited figure in times of rapid industrial change, or of social upheaval more generally, is to embrace bohemianism. As Wilson demonstrates, cinema has frequently represented and commented upon this unconventional lifestyle (64–7). Films depicting young people's bohemia have proven to be especially fruitful in hinting at the societal tensions and generational divides wrapped up in these myths.

Arguably, London bohemianism predates the widespread usage of the term in the mid-nineteenth century. Dandy figures such as socialite Beau Brummel (1778–1840) embodied a to-be-seen-ness and loudness of public presence, while Daniel Cottom explains that George Gissing, in his 1891 novel *New Grub Street*, used 'bohemian' as a term for 'poor-struggling, would-be writers' (2013: 241). London bohemianism tended to show a preoccupation with talking about work more than actually doing it. The seeming implication was that socializing and pleasure should take the place of creative output. In this sense, poet Dylan Thomas, novelist Julian MacLaren-Ross and artist Nina Hamnett were representative figures, since their consumption of drink in Soho, Chelsea and Fitzrovia overpowered their ability to work (Hewison 1977: 65–7). Autobiographical books such as Hamnett's *Laughing Torso* (1932) and McLaren-Ross's *Memoirs of the Forties* (1965) contributed to this mystique of a social frenzy that has long characterized bohemia. While literature often paid considerable attention to washed-up, middle-age bohemia and its collective lamentations over artistic work that will never quite get done, 1950s and 1960s British films instead tended to examine young people's bohemia, particularly those individuals having just left school but, at the same time, often unable or unwilling to conform to conventional ways of living. The legacy of the Bright Young Things of the 1920s, as satirized in novels like Evelyn Waugh's *Vile Bodies* (1930), is particularly important to this cycle of British youth-centred films, since its discourse is similarly obsessed with the connection between wealth/social privilege and bohemia. Moreover, the films' representation of square establishment figures and rebellion can be read as a calculated attempt to throw traditional notions of propriety into stages of shock.

This chapter focuses on a milieu of bohemian youth on the less reputable side of what fashion designer Mary Quant called the 'Chelsea Set' – an anti-establishment tendency that connected art school students, young creatives and burnouts in a world of jazz, skiffle, drugs and booze around Chelsea and the King's Road (Marwick 1998: 56–7). It investigates films about London bohemianism centred on young adults – ranging from the school leaving age of sixteen through their early twenties – in the first half of the 'long 1960s' (roughly 1958–65).[1] In addition, consideration is given to how films that dramatize a metropolitan experience of leisure, consumption, distrust of authority, partying and 'kicks' – for instance, *Beat Girl* (Edmond T. Gréville 1960), *That Kind of Girl* (Gerry O'Hara 1963) and *London in the Raw* (Arnold Louis Miller 1964) – proved a challenge to the British Board of Film Censors (BBFC), and grated against the cultural preferences of then-Board secretary John Trevelyan. As much as Trevelyan was arguably a liberalizing force who wanted cinema to explore aspects of contemporary youth culture – including music and public displays of sexuality – the cultural gatekeepers of this period seemed anxious about how these depictions would play on screen.

Further, this chapter explores how and why these films were released with X certificates, when they were eventually allowed to be released at all. In particular, I compare their content against larger cultural assumptions circulating among an older generation of professional elites both in the BBFC and the press. Throughout, I examine how a paternalistic sensibility in regard to potential responses by audiences defines the gatekeeping around these films. To do this, I will consider the films thematically, placing their sensationalist dramatizations of controversial material in their cultural context. In order to track the ways in which such films effectively signal to tensions that would determine the impending 'swinging' phase of post-war British society – a period where these tensions fully broke surface – I hone in on key film sequences that seem particularly redolent of, or indexical to, such changes. These sequences were, unsurprisingly, subject to BBFC concern and cuts. Indeed, BBFC intervention can be said to effectively call attention to sequences that are worthy of close consideration for the historian, since they often chafe against or step outside the disputed limits of what was deemed to be acceptable. I observe how these particular X certificate films often mirrored states of change in wider society and mores – albeit refracted through the idiosyncratic artistic sensibilities of the filmmakers – and anticipated an orientation of popular culture away from a staid respectability and towards youthful exuberance.

The chapter is essentially concerned with a transitional moment between several trends. On the one hand, the milieu I am analysing comes at the tail end of the 'angries' and the cycle of films representing the British New Wave: notably Woodfall's adaptations of John Osborne's plays *Look Back in Anger* (Tony Richardson 1959) and *The Entertainer* (Richardson 1960), the kind of hard-nosed social realism embodied by *Saturday Night and Sunday Morning* (Karel Reisz 1960) and the more poetic and subjective aesthetic of *The Loneliness of the Long Distance Runner* (Richardson 1962).[2] To put this in a transatlantic context, this is the milieu of the distrust of authority and the condemnation of *square* life that also manifested in the 1950s 'Beat Generation', a group to whom the so-called angry young men were often compared (Feldman and Gartenberg 1958: 12, 20). On the other, I am deliberately focusing on films that predate the overtly jubilant youth-romp sensibility of something like the A-rated *Smashing Time* (Desmond Davis 1967). In terms of scholarship, this discussion intervenes between the end of the Soho-specific youth film – narratives largely from 1959 to 1963 that examined Soho and its West End neighbours as 'a space of commercial vice, bohemian youth, and thriving cosmopolitanism' (Young 2022: 6) – but predates the Summer of Love (1967/68), which has been read as the dawn of both a more pervasive screen pornography industry and a discursive shift towards criticism of adult films from the lens of conservative commentators lamenting the 'permissive society' (Ayto 2006: 172; Halligan 2022: 9–10).

With this framing in mind, the pivotal film for demonstrating how an older generation of tastemakers confronted a burgeoning cinematic youth culture is *The Party's Over* (1965), which elicited a lengthy censorship battle between Trevelyan and director Guy Hamilton. Debates about the film also played out in the press, particularly during the period of its stalled release (filmed in 1963 and released two years later) when it was singled out as a waste of National Film Finance Corporation money ('Film Men' 1964).

Looking at larger cultural discourses around *The Party's Over*, I argue that it is not so much the specifics of the film and its delayed release that make it central to the discourse – though these are important – as the fact that it propagates a vaguely disreputable atmosphere of bohemian experience. This subcultural way of life challenges the values of an older generation, even though similar behaviour had been seen in prior bohemian movements. Approached as a convergence point between antecedent trends, discourses and mythologies, the film appears symptomatic of a whole range of cultural shifts and points of moral disagreement. In *The Party's Over*, the on-screen sadism, fetishism, implied necrophilia and lack of respect for one's elders combine with a tactical sense of languor, a refusal of industriousness and a blatant sounding of anti-austerity frivolity. *The Party's Over* is a key transitional film to the more permissive moment of the later 1960s. It also signals some of the cultural markers of an emerging Swinging London and is a sort of underseen calling card for the cultural and touristic boom of 1966–7 due to its presaging of a specifically American fascination with a London that swings.

Bohemian Youths Reach the Screen

The Party's Over is part of a cycle of British films from the mid-1950s through the mid-1960s, which depicted youth lifestyles as being always in tension. On the one hand, these representations are marketed and remain of interest in retrospect because of how they sensationalize new formations of youthful experience; on the other hand, there is usually a strand of caution or patrician-conservative disapproval in terms of how the stories are presented, either at the level of narration or in terms of the gatekeeping process that brought the stories to screen. In his analysis of post-1945 British film, Raymond Durgnat noted the prevalence of obedience to paternal figures as a lasting theme of the period, with the ideal masculine types to be submitted to ranging from the 'eternal cadet' (self-improving, boyish adults) to the 'heavy anti-father' (a bullying figure of authority) ([1970] 2011: 172–4). In films such as *Beat Girl* and *The Party's Over*, a main point of contention is how the narratives put youthful desire into competition with the culture of austerity writ large and the symbolic reasonableness of father-figures that had reigned since the war. The UK's constrained economic situation and the concurrent birth of the welfare state gave rise to a mood and set of policies around controlled consumption, restraint and scarcity, which left a mark on lived experience until, at least, the latter years of Prime Minister Harold Macmillan's Conservative administration (Kynaston 2008; Zweiniger-Bargielowska 2000).[3] A main challenge of these films about bohemian youth is how they contrast the constrained sensibilities of the immediate post-war years with a desire for excess, for consumption unrestrained by policy or control, for intangibles like art and music, and for states of bliss or oblivion through the use of alcohol and pills.

Several historical frameworks and sociocultural formations contribute to this tension. Frank Mort has revisited the notion of the 'permissive society' in the context of the 'long' 1960s, and has shown how debates around specific instances of liberalization contributed to a sea change to the social landscape as it transitioned to a place of more open agitation and unsettledness by decade's end (2011: 269–98). Richard Hoggart was emblematic of the period insofar as he simultaneously saw the value of mass education and a changing cultural landscape, but also lamented the Americanization of British habits, especially those of young people, as compared to the supposedly organic traditions remembered from his youth. In his 1957 book *The Uses of Literacy*, he writes disapprovingly of the popular amusements of young people: the 'sex in shiny packets' of jukeboxes, coffee houses, pop music and sensationalist pulp literature ([1957] 1970: 202–23). As told in the narration of Moise (Oliver Reed) in the UK theatrical version of *The Party's Over*, the film is the story of people who 'became beatniks', a subcultural formation that seemed to embody everything that Hoggart was worried about: an Americanized pack (even including some Americans in the entourage) craving booze, drugs, jazz and art. They seem to shun work in a conventional sense, preferring instead to organize life around a roving party that shuffles between spots in Chelsea.

In terms of cinematic and television genre antecedents, *The Party's Over* relates to the number of 'social problem' films that were made in the US and UK during the post-war period. These culturally significant dramatizations explored hot button issues such as racism, premarital sex and religious difference. John Hill locates *The Party's Over* into the exploitative and sensationalist treatments of youthful ennui and transgression (1986: 117–22). The film can also be understood as an attempt to engage with the phenomenon of the 'Hollywood rebel'. As Anna Ariadne Knight has shown, films such as *The Wild One* (Laslo Benedek 1953) and *Rebel Without a Cause* (Nicholas Ray 1955) introduced audiences to 'a new type of anti-hero: the charismatic juvenile delinquent or – as coined by media of the time – the "crazy mixed-up kid"' (2021: 2). Not only does *The Party's Over*'s interest in Moise as the leader of a 'pack' of bohemian partiers connect him to this world but also his lack of productive employment and disregard for laws and mores help characterize him as a rebel. This set-up connects the film to earlier waves of films combining youth and criminality, such as the social problem-noir hybrid *Cosh Boy* (Lewis Gilbert 1953), an early X certificate film focused on mugging. Lastly, a useful precursor is the films about artistic bohemia. *The Horse's Mouth* (Ronald Neame 1958) and *The Rebel* (Robert Day 1961), two popular features about painters made a few years prior to *The Party's Over*, satirized the figure of the bohemian artist. This character type was equally familiar from American imports like Roger Corman's *A Bucket of Blood* (1959), which instead focused on a sculptor who makes statues out of the corpses of his victims. Ken Russell also made several films concerning bohemian artists for the BBC's arts programme *Monitor*, including *Pop Goes the Easel* (1962, on four young pop artists) and *Watch the Birdie* (1963, on photographer David Hurn). In sum, *The Party's Over* reconciles issues relevant to the discourse around West End permissiveness, as well as other social problems such as delinquency and bohemia. The film seems to embody aspects of its precursors, thereby offering itself as an apt case study in how these trends and genres relate to the application of the X certificate.

Many of these bohemian films, which cluster around the Soho-Chelsea area and feature music, coffee bars, striptease and young protagonists, represent tensions related to the expectation of productivity versus the desire to pursue art or embrace a bohemian lifestyle. Jingan Young points to the 1955 Soho Fair as signalling a visible move towards international cosmopolitanism in the post-war moment (2022: 25–6). However, the films set in the area during the ensuing years play into its reputation for sexual adventurousness, criminality, youth subcultures and generational divides. In Edmond T. Gréville's 1960 feature *Beat Girl*, young Jennifer Linden (Gillian Hills) flees her family – older father Paul (David Farrar) and younger stepmother Nichole (Noëlle Adam) – to embrace the 'Beat' lifestyle emblematic of Soho. This decision leads to her entrée into striptease performance, from which she is eventually rescued by her father. The paternalism of *Beat Girl* fits both the bona fides of this exploitation cycle in its depiction of striptease and youth-gone-wayward, and also suggests the triumph of the Establishment (Mellor n.d.).[4] While young viewers would be interested in Jennifer's dalliances with the Soho coffee house crowd, the key element to both exploitation logic and the paternalistic frame of similar films is the way in which this older voice of reason exposes the dangers and redeems the straying child. For the *BFI Screenonline* plot synopsis, the solution to the problem posed by the film is simple and straightforward: 'Paul embraces Nichole and Jenny and, now united as a family, they walk away, turning their back on vice and Soho' ('"Beat" Girl' Synopsis' n.d.). Vic Pratt explains that despite the moralism and sense of redemption in the film, it still received an X certificate and, like *The Party's Over*, experienced censorship difficulties: '*Beat Girl* also features some seedy striptease routines – applauded by audiences of clammy old bald chaps, with bottle glass specs, monocles and moustaches – that caused consternation and immediately earned an "X" certificate' (2016: 6). Further, 'the film was banned in Italy, Israel, South Africa, Turkey, and Malaya'; ran afoul in Singapore owing to Hills being 'rude to her parents' and was banned by local censors (with no record of a lift) in Warwickshire (2016: 6). The current BBFC guidance on the film, which revised the X to a 12 for home video release in 1998, notes the use of the word 'bitch' and the visible bare breasts during a strip club performance as reasons for continued concern (*Beat Girl* n.d.).

Paternalism and exploitation also converge in additional films from this period. *That Kind of Girl*, Gerry O'Hara's film addressing the social problems of promiscuity and venereal disease, is somewhat typical. In this 1963 film, Eva (Margaret Rose Keil), a young woman from Austria, contracts venereal disease outside of wedlock. The film features a male doctor (John Wood) lecturing on the dangers of sexually transmitted diseases – mirroring early exploitation film exhibition in America, there is a weird desire to give fatherly advice to the audience as a seeming moral imperative and clever way around problems of censorship (Schaefer 1999: 180).[5] Yet, at the same time, a main draw of the film was its striptease performances. These sequences of narrative excess are often shot in close-up with gyrating bodies taking centre stage and, as a result, weening the audience from their moral imperatives. While *That Kind of Girl* elicits sympathy for Eva as she is taken advantage of by older men, it stops short of offering much of a critique of patriarchal power or established gender roles. Nevertheless, youth-inflected politics (present in a scene featuring a Campaign for Nuclear Disarmament march) and the importance of sequences of pleasure in nightclubs and other social sites link the film to anti-austerity lifestyles that were becoming more prevalent (Flanagan 2019: 166–7). Given that *That Kind of Girl* was a Compton Films production – a company known for showing sex and nudist films from elsewhere in Europe as part of a private cinema club in Soho before branching out into producing their own films in this milieu – its X certificate is no surprise, and in fact is part of the allure (Smith 2021: 354).

Both of Arnold Louis Miller's films for Compton, *London in the Raw* and *Primitive London* (1965), walked the path of paternalistic outrage by tempering it with a style offering prurient excitement – as illustrated by a sequence dramatizing the Street Offences Act in *London in the Raw*, and a glimpse into the occluded world of a striptease school in *Primitive London* (Flanagan 2011: 288–9). Like in other 'Mondo' films, there is the veneer of outrage and shock, but, at the same time, with the promise that seeing these types of sensationalistic sights (for a presumed white, male, heterosexual audience) is the main event. The gendered politics of the moment are starkly displayed in these films. While men are often depicted soliciting the presumed moral downfall of the women in question, they also assume roles as moral guardians, rescuers and course-correctors. *London in the Raw*'s X certificate rests not only with its nudity and focus on sex and the sex trade but also with its explicit association of such things with London, the city that it, in the words of its poster tagline, 'laid bare!' According to producer Stanley A. Long, *Primitive London* was nearly granted an A certificate (open to adult patrons and children under sixteen if accompanied by an adult) when it went up for certification the following year. However, in order to ensure an X, a grisly re-creation of a Jack the Ripper murder was added by the filmmakers (Long 2009: 20). As we will see of *The Party's Over*, the combination of sex and death was still clearly X territory in the early to mid-1960s.

Censorship, Paternalism and
The Party's Over

Stepping back, 1958 was the key year for the changing fortunes of the X certificate: Trevelyan, previously a schoolmaster, became BBFC Board secretary (Aldgate 1995: 15). He took over the position just as the films of the British New Wave were released, many of which were based on the novels and plays associated with the Angry Young Men, including John Osborne and John Braine. Anthony Aldgate notes that Jack Clayton's youth-themed film adaptation of Braine's 1957 novel *Room at the Top*, submitted for release in 1959, was his first major responsibility as censor (33). During his time as Board secretary, Trevelyan both liberalized what could be shown and worked to rehabilitate the X certificate, which had previously been associated more closely with horror films and sensationalist dramas (58). Admittedly, Trevelyan found himself in a tough spot in 1963. As a column by Felix Barker puts it, 'he cannot win' insofar as his leniency was never enough for those opposed to censorship. At the same time, 'if he is lenient, a thousand clergymen and ministers rise up to say he is paving the way to teenage corruption' (1963). Part of this also had to do with a sense of baked-in paternalism, which I contend was inherent to the BBFC during this period and seeped through many of the choices that Trevelyan made about films that straddled between moralism and hedonism. As Tracy Hargreaves writes in her overview of this period of the BBFC, 'in trying to adjudicate between taste and vulgarity, though, Trevelyan and the Board were also capable of making some quite patrician and normative assumptions about the cinema audience, about who could tolerate what, and of what could be tolerated at all' (2012: 54). It is worth exploring how Trevelyan's adjudications relate to a wider context of paternalistic planning relevant to 1960s culture.

Post-war Britain was a culture built on planners of various kinds. Almost uniformly male, white and in positions of influence (though representing a range of ideological stances), they enacted policies on a wide scale. Things like the Beveridge Report – a 1942 government document outlining the welfare state and later enacted by planners such as Labour minister Aneurin Bevan – provide a blueprint: centralized planning is tied both to the ability to master the levers of what Guy Ortolano has described as 'technocratic liberalism' and to the 'worldview' of figures like the donnish, professional, science and technology-oriented C. P. Snow, whose views clashed with F. R. Leavis in the famous 'two cultures' controversy (Ortolano 2011: 52). Centralized planning is especially relevant when a somewhat technological or physically complicated set of practices encounter aesthetic choices for conspicuous public view. Otto Saumarez Smith has explored how architect-planners like Graeme Shankland and Lionel Brett set about rebuilding Britain's city centres in the 1960s along progressive-modernist lines that were influenced by theories of townscape that tried to wed modern principles to picturesque views (Saumarez Smith 2019: 7). While the idea of planners in this context could be synonymous with addressing pressing social problems, there is also the sense of top-down choices, on a large scale, over how to experience the world. Here is an older generation of professionals administering its choices to the young (which is inevitable from a governance perspective), but which feeds directly into the stories of rebellion that the young seek to experience.

The Party's Over could be said to express tensions between paternalistic austerity and bohemian partying, or between cinema concerned with moralistic social messaging and films meant for pleasure and kicks, and even between films designed for the approval of older audiences and those meant to speak to the aspirations of the young. Moreover, it literalizes the larger cultural debate over the degree to which Britain was becoming Americanized, and embeds this issue into the exploration of bohemianism in the late 1950s/early 1960s to the timbre of things at mid-decade. While *Darling* (John Schlesinger 1965) still moralizes overindulgence in partying, *Blow-Up* (Michelangelo Antonioni 1966) seems to have dropped this tendency. Instead, these types of preferences are more organically integrated into the lifestyles of the characters without either the glorification or the condemnation found in previous films.

The Party's Over was filmed in 1963, first under the auspices of the Rank Organisation, with the story/screenplay credited to Marc Behm, music by John Barry and direction by future James Bond mainstay Guy Hamilton. Rank and the National Film Finance Corporation were equal partners on the film, which cost $350,000 ('Inside Stuff' 1964: 19). As a result of the censorship troubles outlined below, Hamilton and producer Anthony Perry decided to remove their names from the compromised release version (Roberts 2010: 1). The film was also dropped by Rank and eventually distributed by Monarch Film Corporation in 1965 (Petrie 2019: 39). The same year, the exploitation outfit Sherpix announced that it would be distributing the film in the United States, but, by August 1966, it was instead released by Allied Artists – a former poverty row studio then specializing in 'foreign' films ('Servisection' 1966: 1; 'Sherpix' 1965: 15). This American release, in spring and summer 1966, coincided with the height of the myth of 'Swinging London'. Nonetheless, *The Party's Over* is not emblematic of that jet-setting ethos. Rather, it borrows from social problem films, youth delinquency exposés and a more restrained kind of bohemian-beatnik refusal.

The film opens with Moise, the seeming 'alpha' of a group of revellers whose capacity for booze and physical thrills – including jumping from a second-storey balcony – knows no bounds. The sequence unfolds as many of the revellers walk back home across the Albert Bridge, Chelsea, just as the dawn is breaking. The group, consisting of Moise, Moise's sometimes girlfriend Libby (Ann Lynn), wealthy American Melina (Louise Sorel), eccentric and impoverished sculptor Geronimo (Mike Pratt), Nina (Katherine Woodville), the older and vaguely continental Tutzi (Maurice Browning) and the perpetually heartbroken Phillip (Jonathan Burn), stumbles across the bridge, as the two main instruments of generational conflict are introduced. The first, only appearing in the theatrical cut, is the retrospective narration provided by Moise, which frames the film with a note of caution and warns that it will represent dangerous behaviours and attitudes towards life. In addition to explaining that the film depicts people who fall into the bohemian lifestyle, he also quite baldly gives the audience a moral position to consider as the story unfolds: 'The film has been made to show the loneliness and the unhappiness and the eventual tragedy'. Just as the film's title appears on screen, Moise adds, 'Living on little kicks is not enough'. Conversely, the pre-release cut leaves this moralizing out and, instead, lets the music and movement show the almost somnambulant quality of the returning partiers. The second is illustrated visually: a police officer stationed at the end of the bridge is shown gazing at the ill-dressed entourage with a quizzical look, suggesting a generational divide. To punctuate the matter, in both versions of the film, Moise throws a lit cigar at the man's feet as he passes. This sequence ends with the group all going to their respective flats, which are implied to be located within mere blocks of each other near the King's Road in Chelsea.

The plot unfolds over the next day: Melina has been partying in Chelsea as she puts off her engagement to American businessman Carson (Clifford David), the protégé of her father Ben (Eddie Albert). She has fallen in with this bohemian crowd, many of whom are either somewhat suspicious of her or in love with her. These differing attitudes towards Melina have been causing tensions within the group dynamic: Libby is jealous of Moise's infatuation with Melina, Phillip is heartbroken at her rejection of him, and peripheral characters such as Fran (Annette Robertson) are annoyed at her grace and poise. Carson has been trying to reach Melina – as he is coming to London to collect her – though she wants to push back their meeting. What follows is a group effort to befuddle and trick Carson, who meets Melina's friends and neighbours, but constantly misses her. Finally, Nina and Libby provide distractions, while Melina attends a party at Carson's. By the end of the night, Melina is nowhere to be found (she has seemingly left town); Carson has fallen in with Nina (who is in on the deception); and Ben comes over to find his daughter once and for all, at which point the truth gradually comes out. Melina fell down from a loft and hit her head, the revellers at the party took her clothes and valuables while not convinced that she was really dead (Phillip even kisses what we later learn was the corpse), and then the group takes the body from the party and dumps it just off the road (naively thinking that she only needed to sober up). The film later reveals, via a technique similar to the 'unreliable narrator' from Modernist avant-garde writing, that different characters bring different points of view to what happened. The film ultimately shows that it was no one specific person's fault for her death, but the milieu of bohemian partying and the lack of responsibility come under blame. The film condemns the lifestyle more than the individuals, a notion made clear by caustic characters like Moise. The group is redeemed to an extent due to their subsequent remorse and sense of contemplation over what they allowed to happen. John Hill notes that, because of the logic of the 'social problem' film framework, 'the beats themselves must also change, adapt and "mature"' (1986: 121).

What the characters represent, and how they relate to the suggestion that such lifestyles and attitudes are emblematic of the post-war British youth, proved problematic for the BBFC as specific issues were associated with overtly transgressive material. Over eighteen minutes were cut from the film, including more graphic shots of the climactic party sequence (and more shots of characters seemingly concerned or remorseful), as well as a differently constructed ending in which Moise ends up with Libby (Barrett 2010: 10–13; Roberts 2010: 5).[6] Hargreaves recounts that Hamilton 'challenged' Trevelyan over the Board's refusal to grant a certificate, and even accused him of 'being in the pockets of the Establishment post-Profumo' (2012: 60).[7] While the film would eventually be released with cuts and the apparent addition of Moise's remorseful narration at the beginning, these were not the only perceived problems relative to BBFC standards.

Far more typical of generational disagreements and paternal sensibilities are the attitudes of the main characters, most of whom are never made fully culpable or never vow to forsake their ways – though in the theatrical cut, Carson and Nina, a couple by the end of the film, break with urban bohemianism and embark on their talked-about trip to Stow-on-the-Wold. Instead, the pleasures of the film – the partying, as well as the suggestion of pleasure in a life of urban living surrounded by art and jazz music – are a stronger draw than the moralizing material. As Laura Mayne reveals, 'Trevelyan also cited the Chelsea setting as another problem suggesting that if the film had been set in Paris, for example, there might have been fewer issues in passing it' (2019: 123).[8] The sensibilities embodied by our main characters were dangerous insofar as they were coming from inside the country, as opposed to being expressed by young people abroad. The film's means of production may have subconsciously helped promote this worry: writing in *Variety*, Dick Richards locates the film into a trend of the early 1960s, in which low and modestly budgeted British features eschewed studio-based filming altogether, in favour of 'on the spot [location] shooting'

(1965: 3). *The Party's Over* is wholly locatable in its Chelsea/Soho milieu, which perhaps gives it an uncomfortable plausibility. Hamilton's film therefore relates to *London in the Raw* and *Primitive London* and their respective X certificates in somewhat surprising ways, with the locating of its transgressions in London as *an* issue, and its visualizing of sex and death as *the* main issue.

After making suggestions for a first round of cuts in 1963, Trevelyan 'concluded that he found the story fundamentally "unpleasant, tasteless, and rather offensive", taking pains to point out that he could make no promise that the film would receive a certificate even if the requested cuts were made' (Barrett 2010: 11). The key word seems to have been 'taste': in recalling his exchanges with Hamilton in his memoir, Trevelyan 'accepted assurances that the film would be made with good taste' after expressing reservations about the script, but admitted that upon viewing the submitted film 'the distasteful elements in it had become more distasteful' (1973: 108). In an article tracking the X certificate in 1963, Michael Knight interviewed Trevelyan, who noted that his views spoke on behalf of the mainstream viewer and also the film establishment: 'a prominent figure in the film industry told me he'd rather see the industry die than live as a result of the worst type of X films' (cited in Knight 1963: 6). In concerned, fatherly fashion, Knight added, 'that, no doubt, is a view shared by a great number of ordinary filmgoers' (1963: 6). The film was eventually released, but Hamilton disowned it in its amended form. Even before its release, the filmmakers expressed their view that the film was being misrepresented in the press. In a letter to *The People* in August 1963, producer Anthony Perry denied the prior claim that they were making a 'juicy sex drama' and, instead, insisted that the film was meant to be 'a serious attempt to examine the situation of young people who have rejected normal social standards' (8).

Thematically, the film best presents the tension between the young bohemians and the Establishment through its use of the American men who enter the world of boho Chelsea in order to first 'save' and then figure out what happened to Melina. These men, Carson and Ben, provide an interesting contrast with respect to the attraction of the pleasures and dangers of this new world. Carson arrives as a consummate 'square', who is easily duped, too trusting and dressed up as a boring business-type. While momentarily sharing their lives, he falls in love with Nina and slowly becomes more bohemian, to the point where he is not going to return to America, but instead leaves London with her in a compromise between his old life and hers. By contrast, Ben is a true authority figure: an establishment businessman, he arrives on the scene to get results and his inquiries push forward the revelations that ensue. Ben overtly alludes to London as 'soft', as his hard-edged, pro-capitalist demeanour contrasts with everyone else in the film. While other wealthy characters seem to get by thanks to ancestral wealth or implications of upbringing, the older Ben is the self-made man.

Conversely, Carson, in his capacity as Melina's fiancé, seemed poised to enter that world before the results of the investigation. In Ben, there is a not-so-subtle subtext of American dynamism breaking through British inertia. This is a narrative that is important to post-1945 reconstruction – as well as seen in both the temporary improvement of funding and production prospects for the British film industry in the years following *The Party's Over*, and suspicions over America's view of Britain's decline, as a country stuck in a rut without a coherent way forward (Malchow 2001; Walker 2005). This comes across in the press coverage of the film. In 1963, the *Chelsea News* proclaimed 'Layabouts Film is Banned' in its press notice concerning the standoff between Hamilton and the BBFC with the term 'layabouts' particularly prominent ('Layabouts' 1963: 4). While Ben leaves England heartbroken as he supervises his daughter's coffin being loaded onto a train, the film provides no indication of the sustainability of the bohemian lifestyle. Yet, at the same time, it does not really provide a satisfying alternative either. The beatniks do not 'win', but then again, neither does the father figure.

Critical Reception

The American perception of London fuelled the myth of Swinging London, as demonstrated by the well-known 15 April 1966 *Time* magazine cover by Piri Halasz (Halasz 1966: 30–4). This view later reinstalled the dynamism of jet-set London, which is missing from *The Party's Over* due, in part, to the implication that Swinging London was entrepreneurial and innovative in a way that the Chelsea of *The Party's Over* is not. While Mary Quant is an example of the Chelsea Set making good and making money, and whose designs energized British fashion in the early 1960s and became globally famous later in the decade, most members of Moise's fictitious pack were rudderless. Nevertheless, *The Party's Over* was potentially exciting to domestic audiences, since it showed bohemian/beatnik culture and the squalid glamour of the Chelsea set context, despite the paternalistic warnings. Even Edgar Wright's recent psychological horror film *Last Night in Soho* (2021) mines the line between the pleasures of youthful creativity in West London with its potential to overwhelm or show the degree to which such romanticizing can only bring about pain.

But contemporary reviews of the film were not kind. In *The Daily Mirror*, Dick Richards moans that the two-year wait was not long enough: 'it beats me why they ever wanted to make this gloomy, downbeat film in the first place' (1965). Nicolas Cottis was especially blunt in *The Birmingham Post*, noting, 'I wish I could say that the film was worthy of the stand', and that 'the young cast fit into their grossly ill-written parts as awkwardly as if they were shiny black macs a couple of sizes too large for them' (1965).

For Michael Beale, in the *Evening Chronicle*, 'it is a dreary and depressing film because the people concerned are dreary and depressing' (1965). There is a paternalistic air about these reviews: young people should not spend their time partying, and the social worlds that they have created are dangerous and anti-social. To their credit, Monarch Pictures leaned into the controversy on the film's limited release, with a notice for the film's run at the Alexandra Ford Street Theatre, Coventry, accompanied by an ad whose tagline booms 'BANNED BY SOCIETY – BUT THEY LIKED IT THAT WAY!' (*The Party's Over* ad 1965: 6).

Despite praising Oliver Reed's performance, the use of locations and Larry Pizer's cinematography, *Variety*'s pseudonymous reviewer laments that the film does not quite land, instead giving 'a sense of some sort of message that's misfired' (Rich 1965: 30). Its conclusion that the film 'is a poor advertisement for British youth and not much of a boost for British pix, either' offers an apt contrast with the reception of the film's US release (Rich 1965: 30). In *Boxoffice*, the anonymous writer saw the film's distinctive commercial prospects in the United States, at what would have been a peak moment of the 'British Invasion' of UK pop culture: 'since disillusioned youth is a global element rather than primarily restricted to locales, the premise can be applied to the states as well as to England, and the appeal can be sold to young adult audiences' ('The Party's Over' 1966: a11). As this trade publication's reviewer understood, *The Party's Over* was a British film speaking to alienated young people in other cultural contexts. It could be viewed for its generational message, rather than just its London specifics.

Conclusion

The Party's Over sits perfectly between tendencies: thematically on point with other youth films and some British New Wave films, but simultaneously possessing some creative visual and editing choices that characterize alternatives to the presumed centrality of social realism; a film emerging from a decade of relative austerity, trying to start up a party but being derailed by the hedonism; and a film that shows a class-bound and quite specifically London-based brand of bohemianism that is nevertheless steeped in American popular culture, especially in terms of the pleasures sought by the revellers. This is not a Technicolor dream of Carnaby Street fashion, but instead a lost world of greyscale hangovers and cheap city living. This is a film that emerged from a culture at the height of its investment in planning and technocracy, but was unable to be contained by either.

Part of what is historically important about *The Party's Over* is how the tension between authority figures and young people remained present in shifting guises, but lessened in terms of paternal and patrician aspects. The social panics of what young people do and what they consume continue apace, with fashions, music styles and drugs of choice changing with the times. When *The Party's Over* – a film that was refused a certificate in 1963, and only belatedly received an X certificate in 1965 – was brought to Blu-ray in 2010, it was granted a 12 rating and, by contemporary standards, among the more restrained things that a teenager on the prowl for kicks could set out to watch. Whether it be the film's explicitly X certificate material in the form of its drug and sex references and implied necrophilia or its implicitly X material in the form of its bohemianism and anti-authoritarianism as expressed by partying young people, *The Party's Over* sits fascinatingly amid the era's many moral, ethical and generational contradictions.

Author Note

The research behind and writing of this essay was supported by a 2021 Summer Research Fellowship from the Center for Humanities Research at George Mason University. I wish to thank the Center for their enthusiasm for this project.

Notes

1   It should be noted that the school-leaving age was raised from fourteen to sixteen in 1964, which corresponds to the period between the film's production and its release.

2   On the 'angry young man' phenomenon, see Taylor (1963). For a survey of the range of aesthetic strategies and ideological tensions indicative of both the British New Wave and films broadly labelled 'realist', see Hill (1986).

3   David Kynaston's subsequent books in the 'Tales of a New Jerusalem' series have, to date, tracked the move from austerity to gradual plenty and cultural plurality in their coverage of the poverty and exhaustion of immediate post-war Britain to a culture of material plenty and technological and creative innovation by 1963.

4   Roger Philip Mellor writes that the film 'belongs firmly in the exploitation genre – the film's poster read "This girl could be YOUR daughter!" – alongside other contemporary British films with scenarios involving vice and/or striptease, such as *Passport to Shame* (Alvin Rakoff 1958), *The Rough and the Smooth* (Robert Siodmak 1959) and *Too Hot to Handle* (Terence Young 1960)'. This paratextual framing suggests an implied paternalistic, older and male viewer. See Mellor (n.d.).

5   A good example of this is the supplemental lecture film produced to screen
     alongside Edgar G. Ulmer's *Damaged Lives* (1933), which was designed to
     appease local censors and standards of decency when the film circulated in the
     United States. See Schaefer (1999: 180).

6   The version discussed is based on the pre-release cut of *The Party's Over*,
     unless otherwise noted. A complete list of cuts and alternative sequences can
     be found in Barrett (2010).

7   In 1963, the Profumo Affair involved John Profumo (Prime Minister Harold
     Macmillan's Secretary of State for War) and Christine Keeler, a young woman
     who was also socially linked with Yevgeny Ivanov, a Soviet naval attaché.
     The scandal exposed potential weaknesses in state security and was covered
     in the press as a moral scandal. See Davenport-Hines (2013).

8   Hill (1960: 52–62) provides an overview of the general standards of
     censorship around 1960, when Trevelyan was getting established in his role
     at the BBFC.

References

Aldgate, A. (1995), *Censorship and the Permissive Society: British Cinema and Theatre 1955–1965*, Oxford: Clarendon Press.

Ayto, J. (2006), *Movers and Shakers: A Chronology of Words that Shaped Our Age*, Oxford: Oxford University Press.

Barker, F. (1963), 'The Hot Seat of John Trevelyan', *Liverpool Echo and Evening Express*, 2 November.

Barrett, S. (2010), 'The Censorship of *The Party's Over*', *The Party's Over* Blu-ray Booklet, London: BFI.

Beale, M. (1965), 'What a Sad Way to Enjoy Yourself', *Evening Chronicle*, 26 November.

Beat Girl (n.d.), 'BBFC file'. Available online: https://www.bbfc.co.uk/release/beat-girl-q29sbgvjdglvbjpwwc0yntqxnti (accessed 9 February 2021).

'"Beat" Girl' Synopsis (n.d.), *BFI Screenonline*. Available online: http://www.screenonline.org.uk/film/id/1022053/synopsis.html (accessed 10 August 2021).

Cottis, N. (1965), 'Romantic View of Dissipation', *The Birmingham Post*, 8 May.

Cottom, D. (2013), *International Bohemia: Scenes of Nineteenth Century Life*, Philadelphia: University of Pennsylvania Press.

Davenport-Hines, R. (2013), *An English Affair: Sex, Class and Power in the Age of Profumo*, New York: Harper Press.

Durgnat, R. ([1970] 2011), *A Mirror for England: British Movies from Austerity to Affluence*, second edn, London: BFI/Palgrave.

Feldman, G. and M. Gartenberg (1958), 'Introduction', in G. Feldman and M. Gartenberg (eds), *The Beat Generation and the Angry Young Men*, 11–22, New York: Dell.

'Film Men Back Losers' (1963), *Daily Herald*, 3 July.

Flanagan, K. M. (2019), *War Representation in British Cinema and Television: From Suez to Thatcher, and Beyond*, Cham, Switzerland: Palgrave.

Halasz, P. (1966), 'You Can Walk Across It on the Grass', *Time*, 15 April: 30–4.

Halligan, B. (2022), *Hotbeds of Licentiousness: The British Glamour Film and the Permissive Society*, New York: Berghahn Books.

Hargreaves, T. (2012), 'The Trevelyan Years: British Censorship and 1960s Cinema', in E. Lamberti (ed), *Behind the Scenes at the BBFC: Film Classification from the Silver Screen to the Digital Age*, 54–68, London: BFI/Palgrave.

Hewison, R. (1977), *Under Siege: Literary Life in London, 1939–1945*, New York: Oxford University Press.

Hill, D. (1960), 'The Habit of Censorship', *Encounter*, 15 July: 52–62.

Hill, J. (1986), *Sex, Class and Realism: British Cinema 1956–1963*, London: BFI Publishing.

Hoggart, R. ([1957] 1970), *The Uses of Literacy*, New York: Oxford University Press.

'Inside Stuff – Pictures' (1964), *Variety*, 4 November: 19.

Knight, M. (1963), 'In the name of decency BAN THESE FILMS', *The People*, 14 July: 6.

Kynaston, D. (2008), *Austerity Britain, 1945–1951*, London: Bloomsbury.

'Layabouts Film is Banned' (1963), *Chelsea News*, 11 October: 4.

Long, S. (2009), '13 Notes on *Primitive London*', *Primitive London* DVD Booklet, London: BFI.

Malchow, H. L. (2001), *Special Relations: The Americanization of Britain?*, Stanford, CA: Stanford University Press.

Marwick, A. (1998), *The Sixties: Cultural Revolution in Britain, France, Italy, and the United States, 1958–1974*, Oxford: Oxford University Press.

Mayne, L. (2019), 'The Vertically Integrated Independent', in R. Farmer, L. Mayne, D. Petrie, and M. Williams (eds), *Transformation and Tradition in 1960s British Cinema*, 119–37, Edinburgh: Edinburgh University Press.

Mellor, R. P. (n.d.), '"Beat" Girl', *BFI Screenonline*. Available online: http://www.screenonline.org.uk/film/id/1022053/index.html (accessed 10 August 2021).

Mort, F. (2011), 'The Ben Pimlott Memorial Lecture 2010: The Permissive Society Revisited', *Twentieth Century British History*, 22 (2): 269–98.

Ortolano, G. (2011), *The Two Cultures Controversy: Science, Literature, and Cultural Politics in Postwar Britain*, New York: NYU Press.

Perry, A. (1963), 'The Party's Over', *The People*, 4 August: 8.

Petrie, D. (2019), 'Distribution and Production: The British Majors', in R. Farmer, L. Mayne, D. Petrie, and M. Williams (eds), *Transformation and Tradition in 1960s British Cinema*, 33–62, Edinburgh: Edinburgh University Press.

Pratt, V. (2016), '"*Beat Girl*": Dig that, daddy-o!', '*Beat Girl*' Blu-Ray Booklet, London: BFI.

Rich. [pseud.] (1965), 'The Party's Over', *Variety*, 19 May: 30.

Richards, D. (1965), 'British Production's Got Wanderlust; Some Shot Wholly Away from Studios', *Variety*, 14 July: 3, 19.

Richards, D. (1965), 'Frankly, that Two-Year Wait Was not Long Enough', *Daily Mirror*, 7 May.

Roberts, A. (2010), '*The Party's Over*', *The Party's Over* Blu-Ray Booklet, London: BFI.

Saumarez Smith, O. (2019), *Boom Cities: Architect Planners and the Politics of Radical Urban Renewal in 1960s Britain*, New York: Oxford University Press.

Schaefer, E. (1999), *Bold! Daring! Shocking! True!: A History of Exploitation Films, 1919–1959*, Durham, NC: Duke University Press.

'Servisection' (1966), *Motion Picture Distributor*, 10 August: 1.

'Sherpix Will Distribute British "Party's Over"' (1965), *Boxoffice*, 27 September: 15.

Smith, A. (2021), 'International Sexpionage! European Popular Film on Sixties British Cinema Screens', *Contemporary British History*, 35 (3): 340–64.

Taylor, J. R. (1963), *Anger and After: A Guide to the New British Drama*, London: Pelican/Penguin.

The Party's Over ad (1965), *Coventry Standard*, 11 November: 6.

'The Party's Over' (1966), *Boxoffice*, 11 July: a11.

Trevelyan, J. (1973), *What the Censor Saw*, London: Michael Joseph.

Walker, A. ([1974] 2005), *Hollywood England: The British Film Industry in the Sixties*, London: Orion.

Wilson, E. (2000), *Bohemians: The Glamorous Outcasts*, New Brunswick, NJ: Rutgers University Press.

Young, J. (2022), *Soho on Screen: Cinematic Spaces of Bohemia and Cosmopolitanism, 1948–1963*, New York: Berghahn Books.

Zweiniger-Bargielowska, I. (2000), *Austerity in Britain: Rationing, Controls, and Consumption, 1939–1955*, New York: Oxford University Press.

7

Mediatizing Modernity:

Femininity in the X-Rated Swinging London Film

Moya Luckett

Swinging London was a highly mediated phenomenon whose self-conscious modernity depended upon a particular image of young, liberated, public-facing female sexuality. As Benjamin Halligan explains, it 'was partly the … dissemination of images that brought the idea of Swinging London into being in the first place … Swinging London itself springs from such a contradiction – it lives its own myth' (2018: 70). Targeting the increasingly important young, female filmgoer/consumer, Swinging London films focused on brightly dressed, young adventurous women who travelled to the capital seeking independence. Like many girls in the audience, their protagonists followed dreams fuelled by the media cited throughout these films such as women's magazines, fashion photography, pop music and cinema itself. Many drew on their X certificates to both entice viewers and advance more critical messages about media and modern life, ones aligning with the British Board of Film Censors' (BBFC) diktats on adult content. While in no way coterminous with unfettered, explicit representation of the female body, Britain's X certificate facilitated these films' sustained investigations into young women's sexual activities, helping shape aesthetic strategies of obscurity and abstraction that corresponded with Swinging London's own hyper-modern aesthetics.

Meshing British cinema's dual heritages of documentary-influenced realism and escapist, often consumerist, fantasy, Swinging London films like *The Pleasure Girls* (Gerry O'Hara 1965), *Darling* (John Schlesinger 1965), *Joanna* (Mike Sarne 1968) and *Her Private Hell* (Norman J. Warren 1968) exploited, engaged with and critically reflected on the period's modern, media-generated world. Crystallized into a series of oft-repeated tropes culled from pop music, album covers, fashion photography, teen magazines and newspaper colour supplements, Swinging London was spectacular and newsworthy, making it an ideal subject for the period's British cinema as well as the subject of international media attention, including *Time* magazine's infamous 15 April 1966 cover story, 'London: The Swinging City' (Church Gibson 2006a, 2006b, 2017; Freeman 2014: 357; Luckett 2000; Murphy 1992). The accompanying article, 'Great Britain: You Can Walk Across It on the Grass', cemented fantasies of an exciting, spectacular city that were almost entirely media-driven. Rather than describing the 'real' London, a large part of the essay was devoted to an imagined treatment for a Richard Lester film about the city's glittering clubs, restaurants, fashion, shops, parties and stars that referenced films like *Darling*, magazines like *Vogue* and groups like the Rolling Stones (Halasz 1966: 30–4). A year earlier, 'The *Daily Telegraph* colour supplement had run a feature on "London: The Most Exciting City" ... focusing on its attractive young women with their supposedly relaxed attitude towards sexual morality and self-presentation .... Whether the visions they offered were a reflection of real changes or part of the myth-making process is perhaps less important than their pervasiveness' (Breward 2006: 14).

Today, female-centred Swinging London films are considered more iconic than their male-driven counterparts and thus receive more cultural and critical attention, despite this short-lived cycle typically favouring male-focused narratives. Echoing *Alfie* (Lewis Gilbert 1966), perhaps the sub-cycle's ur-text, X certificate films like *Mini Weekend* (Georges Robin 1967), *Here We Go Round the Mulberry Bush* (Clive Donner 1967) and *Loving Feeling* (Warren 1969) trace their young male protagonists' (real and imagined) erotic encounters with available young women, parsing how the new, liberated femininity affected *his* sexuality and sense of self. Most of these films accordingly work to normalize heterosexual male sexual activity in the 'real world'. Evincing the different stakes of sexual liberation for men and women, their feminine counterparts both advance and critique an exciting, deceptive, image-laden modernity while framing their incarnations of modern femininity as media constructs. In purportedly offering critiques of these images' attractive duplicity, films like *The Pleasure Girls*, *Her Private Hell*, *Darling*, *Joanna* and *The Knack ... and How to Get It* (Lester 1965) served to both circumvent and bolster censorship.

Swinging London: Mediatizing Modern Femininity

Mediatization critically analyses the increasingly complex and multifaceted relationships that exist between media, culture, society and politics, pointing to media's key role as a powerful social, cultural and semantic structuring agent. As Nick Couldry and Andreas Hepp observe, the concept focuses on ways that the proliferation of media (since the nineteenth century, but particularly since the late 1990s) shaped understandings of life and culture to the point where society increasingly functions according to a 'media logic'. According to this argument, media's parameters and intersections mould events and remake public perceptions of the world in terms of the media's own image, something inherent to Swinging London (2013: 195–6). As Agnes Rocamora notes, mediatization reveals how 'society cannot be thought of outside of its intertwining with … media [which] have become "an irreducible dimension of all social processes"' (2017: 507). Effectively collapsing 'the staid triangle of production–text–audience', mediatization develops Roger Silverstone's 2005 concept of '"mediation" as a dialectical term for the continuous interchange whereby media shaped or were shaped by broader life and culture' (Couldry and Hepp 2013: 193). Influenced by Michel Foucault's theories of discourse and governmentality, mediatization traces media's role in creating networks of power and meaning, thereby engaging with 'the wider consequences of media's embedding in everyday life' (Couldry and Hepp 2013: 195). A concept deeply rooted in change and transformation, mediatization hones in on media's role in producing cultural change, parsing how people take on increasingly mediated relationships to the self and the 'real'. As individuals internalize media, its images and processes shape identity production, particularly for those who seek visibility in order to accede to society's centre – an inner circle itself defined by the presence of 'media people' (Couldry 2003: 2–17). Throughout both these studies and Swinging London films, mediatization's close links with the feminine become apparent.

Swinging London underscored the sharp increase in mediatization during the mid-1960s, demonstrating how proliferating images helped structure the real. A transmedia phenomenon, it brought together young women's magazines, Britain's pop music explosion (saturated in its own visual culture including album covers, photography and dress) and youth film genres while testifying to concomitant surges in advertising and the increased use of still and moving images in public spaces, like boutiques and nightclubs. Conflating images and the real, Swinging London signalled the power of a fabricated, media world grafted onto a physical space, particularly for women. While retaining their currency, these tropes were quickly satirized in films like *Smashing Time* (Desmond Davis 1967), whose crass narrative used its naive and inept protagonists, Yvonne (Lynn Redgrave) and Brenda (Rita Tushingham) to undermine the cycle's characteristic glamour. Given that both actresses usually played physically unremarkable foils or awkward protagonists in films like *Georgy Girl* (Silvio Narizzano 1966) and *The Knack*, their characters' unlikely, if short-lived, success as models and pop stars represented a highly cynical take on the whole cycle and the culture of Swinging London more generally.

Via their emphasis on young women's media consumption, female-centred Swinging London films simultaneously flaunt feminine possibilities and urge restraint. For example, *Darling*'s opening scene foregrounds the importance of media and critiques the feminine frivolity it both caters to and produces.[1] As Diana Scott's (Julie Christie) unreliable voice-over recounts how she became an Italian princess, a magazine ad featuring her face is pasted over a billboard that formerly alerted the public to victims of African famine. *The Knack* and *The Pleasure Girls* target the new fashion magazines that lure their protagonists and other young women to London: both characters read *Honey* on the train, a magazine that emblematized Swinging London's feminine promise. Connected to pleasure and the desire for self-advancement, the act of reading a fashion magazine takes these girls into another mediatized space, one purportedly governed by independent femininity. Consumption of these titles is also used to signal these young women's compromised media literacy: just like their putative female viewers, these protagonists are attracted to modern media but cannot discern the difference between images and reality, failing to grasp the stakes of these industries and the representations they produce. More dystopian works, like *Her Private Hell* and *Darling*, systematically indicate media's seductive and duplicitous power, its status as a business and its role in advanced forms of modern capitalism. Luring young women into sexual situations that ultimately disadvantage or disempower them, media industries are here shown as preying on girls' desire for their life-affirming power. Their avowedly liberatory modernity therefore comes at considerable cost to the feminine psyche, morality and/or social standing. By framing the relationship between young female sexuality and modern media in such ambiguous ways, these films positioned themselves as serious 'adult' content warranting an X certificate while capitalizing on Swinging London's seductive energy.

Deeply embedded in mediated promises of female agency, transformation and excitement, mediatization shaped the production of feminine identity, albeit in problematic ways that foregrounded the difficulties of disentangling the self from media. Historically, similar concerns motivated film censorship, an institution rooted in cinema's purportedly profound influence on the young, vulnerable and easily led. Often conservative, censorship has historically responded to concerns about changing social mores and the greater inclusion of women, minorities and lower-class publics in a new body politic (Grieveson 2004: 12–26; Luckett 2014: 28–46, 171–5, 185–97; Stamp 2000: 41–70). Echoes of these discourses permeate Swinging London films, both in terms of their representation of young women and the broader mediatized world they sought to inhabit.

Coupling self-evident modernity with a broader conservatism, seen below in their discourse on race, many female-centred Swinging London films were innately contradictory, a quality seen in their evocation of other period media forms like fashion magazines, pop music and photography. Media were both exploited and subject to critical interrogation across this cycle, parsing both their veracity/authenticity and their links to unsavoury and entrenched forms of power. In showcasing and bringing together various forms of contemporary media, X certificate Swinging London films opened up multiple discourses on contemporary female sexuality while offering their own appraisals of media's influence on young women, not all of it progressive.

For Church Gibson female-centred Swinging London films are repressive and often cautionary works whose utopian, emancipatory reputations largely stem from the ways past viewers and contemporary critics conflated protagonists (living often difficult and circumscribed lives) with their youthful, charismatic and magnetic stars like Julie Christie and Michael Caine (2006a, 2006b, 2017). Of particular importance here were the period's new publications such as the stylish, urbane and advertiser-friendly Sunday newspaper colour supplements and young women's magazines like *Honey, Petticoat* and *Nova*, which celebrated these actors as fashionable embodiments of the same emancipatory and progressive British culture that they claimed to represent (2006a: 86–7, 90, 92–3; 2006b: 134). While her points are well made, it remains the case that these films were precisely designed to be consumed within this highly mediatized climate. By engaging with the media's more optimistic hyper-modernity, these films were able to bypass some censorship strictures – they were, after all, investigating and critiquing a frivolous and duplicitous zeitgeist. As such, they could capitalize on the affect stirred by their use of fashion, music and images of the London scene that nurtured young women's idealized fantasies of independence.

Race and Modernity

Although often occluded, race shadows, traces and at times threatens Swinging London's urban modernity, complicating its representations of an almost-universally white lifestyle. These films' flickering images of Blackness alternately emerge as exotic (*Joanna* and *Darling*), vaguely threatening/deeply impoverished (for instance, the Jamaican immigrants who exist in the shadows, victims of a Rachman-esque landlord in *The Pleasure Girls*) or function as cyphers for broader, unaddressed inequalities (as in *Darling*'s opening scene and its later ironic placement of Black boys in eighteenth-century servants' garb at a charity ball).[2] Encounters with Blackness are typically framed in terms of white girls' experiences, alternately signifying progressive modernity and danger, both highlighting the possibilities endemic in urban life and pointing to the city's exclusions and its lawless underbelly. Sometimes they represent all of the above, seen in these films' wild parties featuring Black guests or performers, like *Darling*'s decadent Parisian soirée – a trope repeated in *Withnail & I* (Bruce Robinson 1987), a film set in 1969 but released in 1987. These reductive and deeply problematic visions of race further underscore young, white women's inability to read and control the urban spaces to which they are so deeply attracted.

More racially diverse than its peers, *Joanna* uses Blackness to foreground its namesake protagonist's extreme open-mindedness and modernity rather than engaging with racial difference and diversity on their own terms. Her beautiful and stylish best friend and sidekick Beryl (Glenna Forster-Jones) is a Jamaican immigrant, a pairing that lets Sarne create novel and colourful mod juxtapositions using his blonde lead and her Black friend, much in the style of high fashion photography. Beryl acts as a guide for Joanna (Geneviève Waïte), leading her into the heart of Swinging London, introducing her both to high society and the delights of shoplifting at the period's iconic Bus Stop boutiques. Via her affair with the dying Lord Peter Sanderson (Donald Sutherland), Beryl draws Joanna into the aristocrat's inner circle, where she finds her own rich lovers. While Sanderson is presented as a genuinely good, if eccentric, person (perhaps the only one in the film), Beryl is aware that her presence in this aristocratic milieu is not commensurate with broader social change. Instead, she understands that she is seen as an entertaining and beautiful novelty, used by this most traditional group to reframe themselves as modern. In turn, Beryl and her brother signify Joanna's modern open-mindedness; she quickly falls in love with handsome club-owner Gordon (Calvin Lockhart) and becomes pregnant with his baby. Both siblings point to fragile possibilities for Black social mobility, but their positions are precarious and exceptional, dependent on the good will of others. The film briefly addresses systematic discrimination, mainly via scenes featuring Gordon's rough treatment at the hands of racist police officers: countering explicit racism with knowledge of his legal rights, he refuses to let officers search his apartment without a warrant. Such scenes, however, ultimately underscore Joanna's fears about them being parted. Although Joanna is framed by Blackness as she transitions from permissive, single girl with Beryl to future motherhood with Gordon, this shift merely uses Black British culture to telegraph the limits of Swinging London's expansive sensibilities.

The X Certificate: Ambivalent Modernity

Swinging London films' representations of female agency and sexuality may not have received censorial approval if presented more directly, with directors frequently using spectacular images to abstract or obscure potentially sexual content. The BBFC's parameters for the X certificate notably proscribed sensation, mandating serious treatment of adult material like sexual activity outside marriage, homosexuality, single motherhood and abortion – all topics found throughout the cycle (Aldgate 1995; Brett 2017; Forshaw 2015; Robertson 1989). In presenting these discourses via already mediated images, Swinging London films managed to walk a fine line between exploitation and critique.

Launched in 1951 the X certificate was far from a free-for-all as the BBFC's records attest. Designed to permit non-exploitative or sensationalist treatment of adult content on British screens, Board secretary John Trevelyan (1958–71), later admitted, 'it has not always worked out this way', with many X certificates awarded to horror films following the abolition of the H certificate (1932–51) (Aldgate 1995: 51, 78, 112, 150–2; Brett 2017: 236). X certificates also went to respectable Hollywood works like *Rebel Without a Cause* (Nicholas Ray 1955), although standards became more lenient by the early 1960s with 'a rapid liberalisation' at the end of the decade, resulting in 'landmarks including the first full female nudity in *Blow Up* (1967), full male nudity in *Theorem* (1969) and an erection in *Flesh* (1971) [*sic*]' (Brett 2017: 236–7).[3] As the X certificate legally restricted admissions to patrons sixteen and older, most large distributors and cinema chains initially balked, refusing films they considered less lucrative and potentially controversial (Aldgate 1995: 14). *Room at the Top* (Jack Clayton 1959) alleviated some of these concerns: a critical and commercial hit, it parsed adult/sexual issues within a carefully drawn moral framework (Aldgate 1995: 35, 86). Like the British New Wave films that followed, most awarded X certificates, its serious treatment of contemporary issues highlighted the BBFC's initial lofty intentions, ones the choice of the letter X had already somewhat obscured due to its close associations with exploitation (Brett 2017: 236).

While most Swinging London films received X certificates, few were explicitly erotic. The rating instead responded to the structural importance of sexual narratives/themes, manifested in franker dialogue, more bedroom scenes (although sex was barely depicted) and a general representation of a bohemian, libertine, media-centric world. More a subject for candid discussion than visual representation, sex features prominently in Swinging London films' dialogue, not least among women, embedding them in a somewhat risqué environment. For instance, *The Pleasure Girls'* Sally (Francesca Annis) repeatedly tells her avowedly sex-addicted boyfriend, Keith (Ian McShane), that it is important for her to remain a virgin, while her flatmate

Marion (Rosemary Nicols) discusses her unplanned pregnancy, abortion and single-motherhood with her no-good boyfriend, Prinny (Mark Eden). Such conversations raise issues of possibility and knowledge, positioning even the most virginal heroines in close proximity to sexual awakening even if, like Sally, they refuse to be seduced. Representing a peculiarly innocent modernity, Sally believes she can find success through hard work, study and integrity, not sexual liaisons or other favours, telling her new boyfriend, Keith, 'I don't want to rush to the altar, I want to try for a career'.

Responding both to censorship diktats and broader cultural pressures, excitement, professional advancement and love are all upheld as more important than sex for most Swinging London heroines, unlike their male counterparts in films like *Alfie*. *Darling*'s libertine Diana even admits she doesn't 'really like sex'. *Her Private Hell*'s Marisa (Lucia Modugno) is ensnared in a naked photo scandal precisely because her nefarious employers set her up to fall in love with duplicitous photographer Bernie (Terence Skelton), who preys on her innocence and loneliness. Her more open 'European' attitude to sex and nudity nevertheless distinguishes her from unredeemable British models like Paula (Jeannette Wild), who revel in depravity (Smith 2021: 358–9). *The Pleasure Girls* links female sexual activity not to an inherent appetite for a modern liberated life but to more traditional motivations such as misplaced infatuation or desires for glamour, success and wealth. While Marion is seduced and manipulated by a compulsive gambler, Prinny, her flatmate Dee (Suzanna Leigh) is attracted to the danger and wealth that come with being the mistress of Rachman-esque gangster, Nikko (Klaus Kinski). The most sexually active of the five girls, they are, tellingly, the most traditional and the least career-minded. Although neither is condemned, their clichéd fates suggest the persistence of a time-honoured social contract – Dee leaves Nikko after he is badly beaten and his wife comes to visit him in hospital, while Marion throws Prinny out and decides to keep her baby.

Marion's choice was not inevitable. Other Swinging London films feature girls who made different decisions, initially presented in ways that befit the BBFC's preference for serious coverage of social issues. In 1965, *Darling* implicitly critiques Diana for aborting her baby once the novelty of pregnancy wanes, casting her brief return home to mourn her loss as immature self-indulgence not genuine grief. Initially thrilled to be expecting, Diana rushes out to buy maternity clothes, underscoring her compulsive consumption and her modern belief that new purchases presage new, exciting identities. Images of Christie excitedly twirling around the shop in a maternity dress and playing with baby toys frame her character's rapid change of mind as an irresponsible whim. Just three years later, censorship changes would permit *Joanna* to handle abortion more playfully and surrealistically via Joanna's friend Margot (Michele Cooke), who experiences a failed termination, ponders keeping the baby and then decides to become 'un-pregnant' again. A minor character, Margot's sole rationale is to turn abortion into a surreal joke. Like the film's interracial casting, her scenes signify the outrageous possibilities of the new, embodied in girls whose open-mindedness seems designed to shock rather than to make serious statements about modern sexuality. Mirroring *Darling*, abortion emerges as a symptom of disturbed femininity.

Female nudity is rare, found at the tail end of the cycle (*Joanna*) or in lower-budget exploitation films (*The Pleasure Girls* and *Her Private Hell*) (Forshaw 2015: 150; Smith 2021: 359–60).[4] When shown, near-naked women were usually framed from the rear, the waist up or from the side with frontal shots almost non-existent until the late 1960s. Appearing after censorship standards were relaxed, *Joanna* telegraphs its modernity through female nudity, including brief glimpses of its eponymous lead skinny-dipping in a fountain, seen from the side and front but veiled by foliage and soft-focus cinematography. Tellingly, the film's posters featured a nude image of Joanna, which was identical to the large photo adorning her boyfriend's flat. These images simultaneously invite a prurient gaze and reframe female nudity in terms of fashionable, modern bohemianism.

The parties, modelling sequences and love scenes that addressed female fantasies of agency throughout this cycle also offered opportunities to expose female flesh. *The Pleasure Girls* took this the furthest, with Marisa modelling a translucent dress without a bra and briefly appearing topless. Sequences of girl models dressing and undressing punctuate *Joanna*, *Darling*, *Georgy Girl* and *The Pleasure Girls*, addressing both the masculine-prurient and feminine-fashion-oriented gazes. Linked to the worlds of fashion, photography and acting, these scenes signify exciting and deeply mediatized professional and personal lives that put women literally in the centre of the frame. They also offered opportunities for directors to insert more explicit content for international markets. Overseas release prints of *The Pleasure Girls* feature two topless girls: an unnamed extra who plays a laughing artist's model at a party and, more significantly, Dee, who is briefly seen naked from the waist up in Nikko's bedroom. The UK version shoots her from behind but this scene prominently appears on the film's poster art, albeit with Leigh lying on a bed so her breasts are hidden. Similar examples abound in *Her Private Hell*, most notably at Bernie's hyper-mediated soirée where Marisa's libertine love-rival, Paula, performs a hedonistic striptease. International versions show her dancing from the front while all nudity is shot from behind in the UK cut, which depicts a tamer, shorter dance and eliminates a scene where she rolls on the floor topless in a libidinal frenzy. An argument can be made that this censorship reduces female agency while not lessening objectification: both partygoers lose their full capacity for physical and emotional expression, while Dee remains a pristine, if foolish, bodily presence, arguably framed more for the camera in the less naturalistic rear framing than for herself and her own pleasure.

When it came to depicting nudity, modelling was arguably more prominent than sex, highlighting both the profession's centrality to Swinging London iconography and its new visions of less overly sexualized fashionable, 'artistic' female bodies. Besides motivating scenes of dressing/undressing, modelling linked female bodies to fantasies of empowerment and creativity, inviting the female gaze, addressing young women's ambition and their desire to be part of a highly mediated scene.

Central to these films and the mythology and iconography of Swinging London more generally, modelling is often presented as a dream that could turn into a nightmare. While successful, *Her Private Hell*'s Marisa is completely controlled by her agent, Margaret (Pearl Catlin) and media-conglomerate owner, Neville Heatherington (Robert Crewdson). They house her in Bernie's flat, give her no access to her money and leak nude photos of her to maintain their power. She has little opportunity to see London (the film is almost entirely shot inside), let alone benefit from its attractions, finally escaping with kindly photo assistant Matt (Daniel Ollier). *Darling*'s Diana discovers that she cannot out-manipulate media executives like Miles Brand (Laurence Harvey) nor prolong her 'It' girl moment. Throughout, these films establish the ephemerality of these girls' careers, framing them as eminently replaceable: in *Her Private Hell* Paula's professional decline anticipates Marisa's future, *Darling*'s Diana exchanges her waning career for a gilded royal cage, while *The Pleasure Girls'* Dee seeks a rich husband for the next stage of her life. Meanwhile posters for 'Model of the Year' decorate photography studios and apartment walls throughout these films, further attesting to these girls' short shelf-lives.

In his foreword to photographer John d Green's 1967 coffee-table book, *Birds of Britain*, Anthony Haden-Guest describes the London girl in similar terms – of the moment, ephemeral, mobile, chasing fleeting, random or non-existent success. As he observed, modelling's appeal was rooted in its seeming accessibility coupled with the allure of immediate transformation into a dazzling and hyper-visible mediated self, but the reality was not so straightforward:

> the model is the Instant Girl. And modern history coruscates with the tales of the girls, normal girls, unnoticeably blending into the London traffic … ordinary girls, with that tiny secret Zip! … Model superstars. And, even afterwards, nobody can really explain why it happened. Why this girl, and not a hundred-others?
>
> (Haden-Guest 1967)

Few managed to attain these heights, however, with most models finding the work precarious and gruelling. Simultaneously irrational, accessible, transformative, dazzling and deeply seductive, the model became one of Swinging London's key mediatized myths, simultaneously celebrated and undermined in the films via their own cautionary tales. Dazzling spectators, models catered both to an erotic male gaze and its ambitious, comparative female counterpart. Central to these films' mediatization, representations of modelling helped shape young women's visions of a successful self – hyper-visible, embedded in media and ostensibly a free agent at the centre of the modern world.

Publicity and Promotions

Although exploitation fare like *Her Private Hell* and *The Pleasure Girls* flaunted their X certificates for marketing purposes, posters and print advertising for most Swinging London films handled their ratings carefully. The X was typically placed in a less-than-prominent space or incorporated into the overall design, rendering it less noticeable, as with *The Knack*. Corresponding to the film's stylized aesthetics, this minimalist black-and-white poster featured lots of white space, punctuated with largely disembodied photos of the girls from its surrealist opening sequence. Placed below the film's title, the X almost floated in its own space, becoming part of an overall mod pattern. Posters for *Darling* rendered the X unobtrusive, placing it after the title at the bottom left hand of a design dominated by a large pink-tinted black-and-white photo of Christie lying on a bed covered in a sheet, bookended by images of Dirk Bogarde and Laurence Harvey. A tagline promised, 'When she was good she was very, very good and when she was bad she was Darling'.

Marketing for lower budget films like *The Pleasure Girls* was (understandably) more exploitative, attesting to their funding and release in more sex-oriented cinemas. In a nod to her topless scene in the film, posters featured a large colour drawing of a smiling Leigh lying on her front on a dishevelled bed wearing only a pair of panties, painting her nails as a besuited Nikko looks on. At the bottom left, there is a small black-and-white photo of Annis jumping over a bollard that does not appear in the film and, at the bottom right, an image of Nikko and a Black extra fighting. Both the title (printed in yellow) and the white X stand out as they are enclosed in a black box. The tagline reads, 'They came for the kicks, these bitter-sweet beauties of bedsit land'. The pressbook provides more explicit and highly misleading marketing, ramping up the film's limited sexual content with a new tagline: 'They made love their way ... ANY WAY!' The topless image of Leigh dominates, here captioned, 'Kept in a plush Pad for his Desires ... She played the game and payed [*sic*] the Price!' Large posters included four smaller images, replete with salacious descriptions. Sally and Keith embrace under the tag 'Profane Love was their Pleasure!' An image of Marion and Prinny in bed becomes 'The Tryst with a Twist ... It stopped when She stopped paying!' A picture of Paddy (Tony Tanner) and Cobber is headed 'The boy they all liked … BUT he liked BOYS!', while another photo shows the artist's model draped in a sheet sitting next to a guitarist, hailing, 'The wild Bohemian Parties … where ANYTHING goes!!!' The X figures prominently in *Her Private Hell*'s limited marketing campaign: its sole poster featured a dark image of Marisa and Terry in bed, a prominent X and the tagline 'In the Glamorous Model World, There's Fun and Excitement, Lust and Deceit'.

Trailers consistently promised more sex and nudity than these films could have possibly delivered: unlike posters which could be seen outside cinemas by the underage public, they would have been consumed in theatres by adult audiences. As in many Swinging London films, censorship-evading strategies of obscurity and abstraction were widespread, combined with jazz or rhythm-heavy music to signify eroticism. Accompanied by the African-style theme from its wild party, *Darling*'s trailer focuses on Diana's sexual exploits, using graphics of the word 'Darling' to filter out and simultaneously flag (non-existent) salacious content. Its final sequence shows Diana undressing as she walks through her palace in despair. Vertically printed, the word 'Darling' moves up from the bottom of the screen to obscure her body, suggesting nudity where none exists. *The Knack* intercuts its hallucinatory seduction scene with moments of surreal playfulness and more sexualized images such as Tolen (Ray Brooks) kissing Nancy (Rita Tushingham) or the photobooth scene where a girl hands her bra to a bowler-hatted gent. Accompanied by John Barry's jazzy score, the trailer promises insight into a kooky, sexualized, mediatized London. *Georgy Girl* receives perhaps the most overtly sexualized preview, presenting its awkward heroine as a masterful lover, adored by men, as its voice-over declares: 'She's a whole lot of woman!' *Joanna*'s teaser merges nudity, fashion and exoticism, showing its star skinny dipping (although only her head and shoulders are seen) and its interracial kiss. The male-focused *Mini Weekend* is arguably the most explicit trailer in terms of nudity. Amid a montage of protagonist Tom's (Anthony Trent) sexual conquests (including one putative menage à trois), it includes a scene of a topless stripper dancing on stage, complete with prolonged close-ups of her somewhat disembodied breasts, an image that hints at further sexual licence. Heralded as the latest thing from Swinging London, Tom is physically unremarkable and somewhat impassive as women alternately caress, undress and mob him, including while he performs with his pop group. Here, women are the sexual aggressors, with Tom claiming he feels their eyes 'burning into my back, watching every step I take'. By comparison, trailers for both *The Pleasure Girls* and *Her Private Hell* are surprisingly tame. The former repeats the poster's taglines but its only slightly salacious image is that of an extra kissing at a party, her mini-skirted legs on full display.

Mediatized Fantasies of Femininity

Rather than accepting the convergence of media and real life, some Swinging London films try to separate these domains, seeking to restore order to a media-disrupted society that has transformed femininity. Like *Joanna*, *The Knack* employs striking imagery to interrogate differences between reality and fantasy in a hyper-mediatized world, with both films using unmotivated/ unannounced dream/fantasy sequences that prompt viewers to reflect on the status of what they have just seen. Such abstraction also serves the needs of censorship, combining the new, exciting and modern with difficult-to-read and obscure images that both hint at sexuality and mask it. In *The Knack*, images capturing Swinging London's hallucinatory, modern and often sexual promise contrast with the more mundane streets, flats, shops and schools that constitute the 'real' city, where 'real' girls like Nancy live and work. Opening with its most eye-catching such scene where large number of identically dressed model-esque young women queue to enter playboy Tolen's bedroom, *The Knack* initially confirms viewers' impressions of a swinging, surreal city. Resonant of period fashion photography by William Klein and John D. Green, this iconic scene is quickly revealed to be a fantasy expressing landlord Colin's (Michael Crawford) frustrations with a Swinging London lifestyle that he cannot access, likely because it only exists in the realm of images. Its visual difference from the rest of the film further underscores the potential duplicity of hyper-modern imagery, something that also marks Nancy's immediate experience in London. After arriving in the city, our *Honey*-reading heroine shops for new clothes and is quickly dissatisfied when she realizes she cannot approximate the look of the Swinging London girl, regardless of her attire. Although she pragmatically shrugs off her disappointment and moves on, embracing her ordinariness, her actions invite wise girls in the audience to dispense with their dreams and follow suit, a message echoed in *Georgy Girl*.

Besides framing their most iconic Swinging London images as misleading, some films situate them as unreadable and obscure. Here *Joanna* is perhaps the limit case with its dream sequences and mod/psychedelic stylization rendering its narrative both opaque and secondary to its displays of late Swinging London fashion and iconography. Recommended by the BBFC to avoid direct representations of perversion, obscurity is a tactic favoured throughout this cycle: tellingly, it also problematizes young women's ability to read images, challenging their relationship to modern mediatization (Aldgate 1995: 150). As Aldgate and Forshaw observe, obscurity typically structures the daring parties these films use to both represent the heart of urbane, youthful modernity and signify their female protagonists' confusion and disempowerment (Aldgate 1995: 150; Forshaw 2015: 150). Incapable of making sense of often image-laden events, these girls are positioned as outsiders who cannot integrate into this form of modernity – a reading that extends to similarly confused spectators. In some cases, this is to the characters' advantage, as with *The Pleasure Girls*' level-headed Sally, whose pragmatism suggests her capacity to survive and retain her morality. In others, visual obscurity indicates young women's naïve absorption of media-generated fantasies, their incapacity to understand the forces behind these spectacular events and their inability to return to 'normal' life.

Her Private Hell is notable here, particularly via one of its centrepieces – photographer Bernie's hyper-modern image-laden party – which telegraphs model Marisa's inability to navigate the mediatized world in which she lives and works. It places her in a nightmarish situation analogous to the one she experiences early in the film where, as a newcomer to London, the mansion and the modelling world, she explores the uncanny and creaky building that houses multiple flats before being shocked back into her apartment by a flash from photographer, Matt's camera. Both scenes position her as a vulnerable outsider in a mediatized world of uncertain boundaries and hidden traps that she cannot comprehend but nevertheless deeply desires. During the party, a cavalcade of images from multiple projectors renders the flat she shares with Bernie alien and difficult to read amid walls decorated with murals, mobiles made from models' photos and girls' test shots. Meanwhile, her more worldly fellow model (and love rival), Paula, embraces this palimpsest as images flood over her as she dances, prompting her to peel off her bra while the words 'vanishing cream' flicker across her skin. Linked to sexual abandon and potential betrayal, the party causes Marisa to collapse, distinguishing her from Paula and the other media types in attendance, all while associating the contemporary media scene with nonchalant, untrammelled (female) sexuality.

Such events further reinforce the insider/outsider ethos central to mediatization, a sensibility that positions media people as central to society and culture, seen in Couldry's 'myth of the mediated centre' (2003: 2). At the deeply mediated heart of this hyper-mediatized world, these parties signify how media might trigger this new female sexuality while placing these young women in an ambiguous relationship to it. Like Marisa, either they are unable to comprehend anything beyond the dazzling surfaces that shape their dreams, or they become the evanescent symbols of mediatized fantasies they have fully absorbed, just like Paula.

Mediatization and Feminine Media Literacy

Media's centrality to Swinging London, its films and its visions of femininity directly and indirectly raised issues of feminine media literacy. Besides addressing the image-based culture that inspired and thrilled ordinary girls in the audience as well as their on-screen counterparts, these films explored broader socio-economic relationships between young women and media industries. Titles like *Her Private Hell, Darling* and *The Pleasure Girls* parsed issues of insider/outsider access, pointing to the (very) traditional patriarchal operations of power at the centre of dazzling modernity. In *Darling*, Diana's life spins out of control when she abandons one media professional lover, erudite TV reporter Robert Gold (Dirk Bogarde), for another more powerful insider, advertising executive, Miles. While Robert straddles both sides of the image industries as a writer-presenter, Miles possesses greater power as the behind-the-scenes dealmaker, securing a contract for Diana as the face of an international haircare brand and then a small part in a Hammer-style film. He quickly tires of her, causing her to lose her spark, her career and some of her power over eligible men. The advertising industry's cynicism is illustrated in a scene where Miles presents Diana's headshots to a group of conservative besuited male executives who discuss her qualities over a table strewn with other models' discarded photos. After joking that her Teutonic looks will go down well in the German market, Miles pops a balloon with his cigar, its brief ascent foreshadowing the brevity of careers like Scott's while gesturing to these men's power over young women – ones who are not as free as they look but rather embedded in corporate culture.

In keeping with its sexploitation roots, *Her Private Hell* envisions the modelling world as innately shady, with its model protagonist, Marisa, struggling to make sense of the environment in which she is placed despite feeling fully alive during her modelling shoots and love scenes. The operations of the labyrinthian enterprise that employs her remain opaque to viewers and Marisa alike, gesturing to the complexity and corruption of corporate capitalism, particularly enterprises that trade in images of women. Neville's (unnamed) business has multiple media holdings, including photography, advertising, model agencies, fashion magazines and pornography, the latter bringing in much of its income. Strictly a corporate figure, Neville is depicted discussing deals during wild parties or asking for stock prices in his office while discussing new acquisitions. Margaret, a somewhat older pneumatic blonde, is one of his more visible deputies, working as a fashion magazine editor in order to lure the likes of Marisa with commercial and editorial work before embedding these girls in the pornographic end of the business.

Although they appear on magazine covers, in films and on TV, mix with media insiders and inhabit spaces decorated with ad art, modelling shots and works of contemporary art, girls like Diana and Marisa are depicted as having no real understanding of the media *industries*. Disregarding what they have experienced, they continue to absorb fashion magazines, films and TV, clinging to visions of themselves as part of a spectacular mediatized centre linked to duplicitous promises of feminine self-fulfilment.

Conclusion

In presenting utopian images of female liberation as media constructs, Swinging London films addressed a far more conservative social and cultural lived reality that continued to problematize young, single women's participation in sexual activity outside marriage. These liberated images may have appealed to young women precisely because they were counter-factual and represented an alternate, liberatory space, albeit one that was deconstructed and compromised by the end of these films. In framing Swinging London as a form of mediatization, these X certificate films point to multiple 'realities' – the world of images and representation and the (often more conservative) world of lived experience, the affective pleasures of media consumption and the often callow business of media industries. Ultimately, these films need to be considered within the moralistic confines of a film industry regulated by a censorship board, albeit one looking to modernize amid a rapidly changing social zeitgeist.

Swinging London's very mediacentric, image-oriented nature ultimately presented filmmakers with a solution that both accommodated censorship and allowed them to exploit its spectacular, cutting-edge, sexual and visual qualities. By upholding themselves as critical investigations, these films could both interrogate and exploit connections between the spectacular, the mediatized and the modern feminine. In the process, they could tout their own modernity by employing abstract and obscure aesthetics to evoke and mask the sexual while simultaneously engaging in censorship's historical mission to protect the public from salacious and absorbing imagery that might lead the vulnerable astray. As such, these films mediated the period's modernity, albeit in a contradictory way that signified broader confusions about the morality of a new and spectacular culture then delivering the nation's belated post-war rebirth.

Notes

1   Here, *Darling* points to a broader foreclosed racial subtext that shadows Swinging London media and its visions of femininity, something addressed further in *The Pleasure Girls* and *Joanna*.

2   Peter Rachman was a corrupt landlord operating in West London around Notting Hill during the 1950s and early 1960s. Exploiting recent Caribbean immigrants who struggled to find places to live in then deeply racist cities, he rented out slum flats for highly elevated prices. He was reputedly involved in prostitution and connected to Mandy Rice-Davies, Christine Keeler and the Kray brothers (Sinclair 1998).

3   The correct years of general theatrical release are: *Blow-Up* (1966), *Theorem* (1968) and *Flesh* (1968).

4   According to Adrian Smith, 'The continued presence of erotic European films eventually wore down the steely reserve of the BBFC, and they could no longer withhold the same freedoms from British filmmakers. This meant that the blackmail drama *Her Private Hell* (1968, Norman J. Warren, Piccadilly Pictures: UK) was able to present British audiences with sex and nudity happening right here on home soil, and this relaxation of restrictions contributed towards an eventual change in the way BBFC certification worked in 1970, when the minimum age for someone attending an "X" film was raised to eighteen' (2021: 359–60).

References

Aldgate, A. (1995), *Censorship and the Permissive Society: British Cinema and Theatre, 1955–1965*, Oxford: Clarendon Press.

Brett, L. (2017), 'The BBFC and the Apparatus of Censorship', in I. Q. Hunter, L. Porter, and J. Smith (eds), *The Routledge Companion to British Cinema History*, 231–41, London: Routledge.

Breward, C. (2006), 'Introduction', in C. Breward, D. Gilbert, and J. Lister (eds), *Swinging London: Fashion in London and Beyond, 1955–1970*, 8–21, London: V&A Publications.

Church Gibson, P. (2006a), 'From Up North to Up West? London on Screen 1965–67', *The London Journal*, 31 (1): 85–107.

Church Gibson, P. (2006b), 'Myths of the Swinging City: The Media in the Sixties', in C. Breward, D. Gilbert, and J. Lister (eds), *Swinging London: Fashion in London and Beyond, 1955–1970*, 80–101, London: V&A Publications.

Church Gibson, P. (2017), 'The Fashioning of Julie Christie and the Mythologizing of "Swinging London": Changing Images in Sixties Britain', in E. Paulicelli, D. Stutesman, and L. Wallenberg (eds), *Film, Fashion and the 1960s*, 135–48, Bloomington: Indiana University Press.

Couldry, N. (2003), *Media Rituals: A Critical Approach*, London: Routledge.

Couldry, N. and A. Hepp (2013), 'Conceptualizing Mediatization: Contexts, Traditions, Arguments', *Communication Theory*, 23 (3): 191–202.

Forshaw, B. (2015), *Sex and Film: The Erotic in British, American and World Cinema*, London: Palgrave Macmillan.

Freeman, N. (2014), 'Permissive Paradise: The Fiction of Swinging London', in P. Fox (ed), *Decadences – Morality and Aesthetics in British Literature*, 349–73, Hannover: Ibidem Verlag.

Grieveson, L. (2004), *Policing Cinema: Movies and Censorship in Early-Twentieth Century America*, Berkeley: University of California Press.

Haden-Guest, A. (1967), 'Introduction', in J. d Green, *Birds of Britain*, n.p., New York: Macmillan.

Halasz, P. (1966), 'Great Britain: You Can Walk Across It on the Grass', *Time*, 15 August: 30–4.

Halligan, B. (2018), *Desires for Reality: Radicalism and Revolution in Western European Film*, New York: Berghahn Books.

Luckett, M. (2000), 'Travel and Mobility: Femininity and National Identity in Swinging London Films', in A. Higson and J. Ashby (eds), *British Cinema: Past and Present*, 233–45, London: Routledge.

Luckett, M. (2014), *Cinema and Community: Progressivism, Exhibition and Film Culture in Chicago, 1907–1917*, Detroit: Wayne State University Press.

Murphy, R. (1992), *Sixties British Cinema*, London: BFI Publishing.

Robertson, J. C. (1989), *The Hidden Cinema: British Film Censorship in Action, 1913–1972*, London: Routledge.

Rocamora, A. (2017), 'Mediatization and Digital Media in the Field of Fashion', *Fashion Theory*, 21 (5): 505–22.

Sinclair, I. (1998), *Lights Out for the Territory: 9 Excursions in the Secret History of London*, London: Granta.

Smith, A. (2021), 'International Sexpionage! European Popular Film on Sixties British Cinema Screens', *Contemporary British History*, 35 (3): 340–64.

Stamp, S. (2000), *Movie Struck Girls: Women and Motion Pictures Culture After the Nickelodeon*, Princeton: Princeton University Press.

PLATE 1 *The film censors of the long 1960s: John Trevelyan (left) and Stephen Murphy (right).*

PLATE 2 *The deadly spiked binoculars in* Horrors of the Black Museum *(Arthur Crabtree 1959).*

PLATE 3 *The transformation of Rick (Graham Curnow) as he rides through the Tunnel of Love with Angela (Shirley Anne Field) in* Horrors of the Black Museum *(Arthur Crabtree 1959).*

PLATE 4 *Helen (Anna Massey) bathed in red light in* Peeping Tom *(Michael Powell 1960).*

PLATE 5 *Mark (Carl Boehm) setting up a shot with Milly (Pamela Green) in the photographic studio in* Peeping Tom *(Michael Powell 1960).*

PLATE 6 *Alice (Simone Signoret) appraises Joe (Laurence Harvey) with understanding and interest in* Room at the Top *(Jack Clayton 1959).*

PLATE 7 *Karen (Vivien Leigh) cries with joy at Paolo's (Warren Beatty) 'love' in* The Roman Spring of Mrs Stone *(José Quintero 1961).*

PLATE 8 *Stella (Susannah York) gets the measure of Zee (Elizabeth Taylor) in* Zee & Co. *(Brian G. Hutton 1972).*

PLATE 9 *Ruby (Shelley Winters) gives Alfie (Michael Caine) his marching orders in* Alfie *(Lewis Gilbert 1966).*

PLATE 10 *Carmilla (Ingrid Pitt) caressing and kissing Emma (Madeline Smith) in* The Vampire Lovers *(Roy Ward Baker 1970).*

PLATE 11 *The Count (Damien Thomas) as onscreen male voyeur for the 'lesbian' moment in* Twins of Evil *(John Hough 1971).*

PLATE 12 *Identical twins Madeleine and Mary Collinson in matching translucent nightgowns in* Twins of Evil *(John Hough 1971).*

PLATE 13 *Beryl Evans (Judy Geeson) and Timothy Evans (John Hurt) negotiating the terms of their lease from John Christie (Richard Attenborough) in a scene exemplifying the 'Grand Guignol kitchen sink' style of* 10 Rillington Place *(Richard Fleischer 1971).*

PLATE 14 *The illiberal bookshelf: Anti-permissive British literature from the early 1970s.*

PLATE 15 *Hammer Horror's reputable credentials: The company receives the Queen's Award for Industry in 1968, on the Pinewood Studios set of* Dracula Has Risen from the Grave *(Freddie Francis 1968); visible in this news footage are Arthur Banks (Construction Manager, and longest serving Hammer employee), actors Peter Cushing, Christopher Lee, Veronica Carlson and Barbara Ewing. (Footage source unknown; screengrabs from Reuters ScreenOcean news archive.)*

8

What Are the X-Rated Secrets of the Windmill Girls?

Adrian Smith

In 1964 the Windmill Theatre, whose wartime slogan had been 'We Never Closed',[1] brought down the curtain for the last time. Having survived as a theatre serving up a constant stream of 'fan dances, comic revue and nude tableaus' (Young 2022: 181) for more than thirty years, it was sold to the film producers Michael Klinger and Tony Tenser, who intended for it to be converted into a cinema for their rapidly expanding Compton chain. But before the builders moved in, filmmakers Stanley Long and Arnold Louis Miller were sent along to shoot a film commemorating the Windmill girls, their fellow performers and the legacy of this legendary Soho institution.

On 5 October 2019 I sat onstage at the Regent Street Cinema to chair a Q&A with film writer, critic and historian David McGillivray following a well-received screening of *Secrets of a Windmill Girl* (Arnold Louis Miller 1966), shown as part of the Soho a Go Go Film Festival. McGillivray's book *Doing Rude Things: The History of the British Sex Film, 1957–1981* (1992, reissued in 2017), as well as his participation in writing British sex comedies and horror films in the 1970s,[2] has made him both an insider and an authority on exploitation cinema. We discussed the significance of the Windmill Theatre in British cultural history then and now. The first question from the audience was unexpected: 'What gives you the right to come here and represent the Windmill Theatre with this film, which is an inaccurate portrayal of what the Windmill was like?'[3] True, former Windmill girls have frequently been disparaging of *Secrets of a Windmill Girl* (Delargy 2020); yet the film makes it very clear just how well the girls were looked after. In *Secrets of a Windmill Girl* the problems only set in when the main character leaves its safe, maternal environs. The question prompted me to wonder: just what is it about this film that can still be causing upset and outrage more than fifty years after it first appeared on London's cinema screens? How can a cheap and occasionally shoddy film like *Secrets of a Windmill Girl* retain this power? What secrets does it still hold?

By drawing primarily on extant archival material connected to *Secrets of a Windmill Girl,* this chapter will go beyond a filmic analysis. As such I will explore promotional material such as posters and front-of-house stills alongside newspaper and magazine archives collected by the Compton film office, discovered in a battered old suitcase in a Pinewood Studios office. These sources will enable me to capture the wider context and issues relevant to a study of distribution and exhibition. In the context of the swinging sixties and the backdrop of censorship, this extensive archival material allows insights into the wider culture of promoting and exploiting independent films in the 1960s. The film's journey through the British Board of Film Censors (BBFC), an organization which, it can be argued, makes decisions 'based on a tradition of government and politics as the prerogatives of an elitist, educated, privileged and trustworthy few who know best what is appropriate for the common, ill-educated, inarticulate, and untrustworthy many' (Robertson 1989: 158), sheds some light on the relationship between the film industry and its censors. The chapter will also offer points of comparison with other British X certificate films made in and about London's nightlife and lowlifes – including the documentaries *London in the Raw* (1964) and *Primitive London* (1965), both, like *Secrets of a Windmill Girl,* shot and directed by the production partnership of director Arnold Louis Miller and cinematographer Stanley Long. Instead of exploring just how and why the film received its X certificate, this chapter will make a connection between the people involved, the legendary Windmill Theatre and the British public.

The Burlesque

The work of Eric Schaefer provides a useful approach when looking at how we read and understand exploitation cinema, and at the act of viewing the striptease show from both the audience and performative perspectives. Watching a burlesque show, or a striptease show (stripping on stage was not part of the Windmill's repertoire, as the girls were already disrobed before the curtains opened), places the audience as observers. Therefore, when watching a filmed performance, one is observing from one step removed, watching the audience watching a show. In reference to this performative element as seen in French films of the 1960s, Schaefer emphasizes that a filmed performance operates within an 'observational/retrospective' mode (2014: 210). The 'observational' element comes through the voyeuristic gaze of the audience as they watch performative acts onstage. The 'retrospective' element in his analysis is through the nostalgia for a former time evoked through the films which feature France as a setting, given that they recall 'images of France in the popular imagination as a setting for sexual adventure' (2014: 211).

The Windmill, although a British institution, was clearly trying to make a connection in the minds of their customers with France through elements such as frequent performances of the Can-Can, and even calling their show the 'Revudeville', combining 'Revue' and 'Vaudeville' and coming up with something that sounds positively Parisian. By the mid-1960s the Windmill was trading almost as much on nostalgia for its heyday in the 1940s as anything else, and in one further remove, *Secrets of a Windmill Girl* is presenting a nostalgia for the lost Windmill experience itself. British audiences, both those who attended the Windmill and those who watched the film, which was already looking back on a piece of history, were themselves rooted in that 'observational/retrospective' mode of viewing.

Compton and the Windmill

Compton was founded by Klinger and Tenser in 1960 when they opened a private cinema club on Old Compton Street in Soho. Tenser's background was in publicity for Miracle Films and Klinger was the successful owner-manager of the Nell Gwynn and the Gargoyle Club, both popular strip clubs in the middle of Soho that were often frequented by film industry types. Klinger and Tenser were both Jewish, from the East End of London, and got to know each other through a mutual love of film.[4] To begin with they concentrated on screening films refused a BBFC certificate, such as *The Wild One* (László Benedek 1953) or *Triumph des Willens* (*Triumph of the Will*, Leni Riefenstahl 1935): these examples show that initially sex films were not the prime interest of the club. However, it did not take long before they were importing European sex films like *Anonima Cocottes* (*The Call Girl Business*, Camillo Mastrocinque 1960), and then producing their own films. Just a few years after their first production, *Naked – As Nature Intended* (George Harrison Marks 1961), they were a vertically integrated company with cinemas across the country and film offices around the world, as Klinger's son Tony explained:

> First the cinema chain grew and then they became distributors, and that just exploded. I remember it went from nothing to a large number of employees, a building full of employees in, I think, less than a year. It was incredibly quick. I think they became the biggest independent British

film distributor in Europe in one year. Also, because they had a big cash flow coming from the cinemas, they were able to pay up front. Whereas everybody was paying on a promise or a minimum guarantee, they could actually pay, so when I went on a buying trip for the company, I had a budget and we could just pay it. Sometimes that was good, and sometimes, because we were rushing and growing so quickly, sometimes you'd make mistakes. It didn't really matter because the reach of the company was becoming so big, and then they started making stuff and could sell them. They were literally making films out of cash flow. They didn't have to borrow anything, and that's a huge advantage.

(Klinger 2017)

To say that Compton were successful is an understatement; they were arguably at the height of their success in 1965 when *Secrets of a Windmill Girl* was under production.

A full-page advert in the American trade publication *Boxoffice* features pictures of Klinger and Tenser alongside the statement that Compton have 'Pictures with the BIG BOX-OFFICE FORMULA' (emphasis in original). The ad reminded readers that in 1964 Compton had big successes not only with *London in the Raw* but also with three films directed by Robert Hartford-Davis – *The Black Torment, Saturday Night Out* and *The Thrill Seekers* (the US retitling of *The Yellow Teddybears*,[5] actually released in the UK in 1963). The ad also provided recent updates: Compton had recently completed *Repulsion* (Roman Polanski 1965), *Primitive London* and *The Pleasure Girls* (Gerry O'Hara 1965); future productions would include Roman Polanski's 'Katelbach' (which would become *Cul-de-Sac*, 1966), 'Fog' (which would become James Hill's *A Study in Terror*, 1965), and two 70 mm films which never moved beyond the title stage – 'The Loch Ness Monster' and 'The Lunapark Horrors', the latter ambitiously planned to be in 3D. 'The Windmill Girls Story' was also announced, yet to find its more salacious and misleading final title (Compton Group ad 1965: b55). This advert is an indication of the growing confidence Compton had, and it is worth noting that while sex and horror, the company's bread and butter, are well represented across these titles, Klinger was also keen to develop arthouse credentials, and the hiring of Polanski was something he was deeply committed to – with *Repulsion* he would get sex, horror and art. In February the following year another *Boxoffice* ad, complete with photos of both Klinger and Tenser, claims that Compton are at the 'Centre of the World Market … WITH PRODUCT OF INTERNATIONAL APPEAL' (Compton Group ad 1966: b53). One of Compton's strengths lay in their absolute belief that they knew how to beat their competition.

Part of Compton's exponential growth included acquiring the Windmill Theatre on Great Windmill Street, a short walk from the Compton offices above the cinema club on Old Compton Street. Vivian Van Damm, who created the non-stop revue at the Windmill when he became manager in 1932, had died in December 1960 ('Memorial' 1961: 5). His daughter Sheila took on the day-to-day running of the theatre, but its glory days were long behind it. The theatre was losing customers to X certificate film cinemas and the more explicit Soho strip clubs nearby.

These clubs, those owned by Klinger included, did not have to conform to the Lord Chamberlain's theatre censorship restrictions in which nudity was tolerated on the understanding that the performers did not move and that the lighting was dimmed – a 'bare statues' clause that the Windmill revue shows had been famously exploiting for years with their *poses plastiques*. A contemporary exploration of Soho described the Windmill as

> One of the most respectable places you could ever wish to find. True, the girls stood around six parts naked, but should they move so much as an eyelash the chances were they would get slung out on their ears, for it is laid down by the Lord Chamberlain that while it is all right for the girls to appear before the public naked they must not move a muscle. The shows at The Windmill were continuous from about lunch time, and many men wearing rather nasty raincoats used to line up outside the box office waiting for the first house, and sometimes did not leave until the end of the last!
>
> (Norman 1966: 51)

Somewhat complicating this account, which perpetuates the myth that the girls were never able to reveal too much during the dance sequences, are some of the memories of former dancers, such as Ann Hamilton, who recalled:

> [Vivian Van Damm] would always say that we were in showbusiness – with the accent on show. Because of censorship he never told the girls to show everything, but, as far as the Fan Dance was concerned, he certainly wasn't averse to the fans being lowered to reveal the breasts, which could always be explained away as an unfortunate slip.
>
> (cited in McCann 1998: 73)

Soho's reputation for being London's seedy underbelly had previously been capitalized upon in 1940s 'bottom of the barrel' British quota-quickies, films made quickly and cheaply to capitalize on tax breaks through what was known as the Eady Levy subsidy (Chibnall and McFarlane 2009: 35). Films such as the talky and predictable murder mystery *It Happened in Soho* (Frank Chisnell 1948), which focuses on all-night cafés and bars but strangely misses the revue shows, or the 'creaky whodunnit' *Murder at the Windmill* (Val Guest 1949) (McGillivray n.d.) – both traded on the already sensationalized reputation Soho had for sleaze, glamour and crime.

The Windmill Girls and Censorship

Following the final review performance on 31 October 1964 the Windmill was extensively refurbished and converted into the Cameo Moulin, a cinema and casino owned by Compton, whose publicity department took up residence in the offices above the theatre (Boorne 1964). Stanley Long had shot footage of the final revue's rehearsals for the Compton-distributed documentary *Primitive London*, but it had not been used, presumably because they already had enough material for one film, what with all the wife-swapping parties and beatniks. Tenser suggested that a film could be created utilizing this unused footage alongside new material to be shot in the theatre before the builders moved in. This is what would eventually become *Secrets of a Windmill Girl*. Long later described the film as a shocking tale of 'backstreet strip clubs, marijuana, kinky masked orgies and stag parties' (2008: 109). From this description, either the film was a reactionary illustration of all that was wrong with 'the permissive society'[6] or it could be interpreted as an intriguing reimagination (and satire?) of the press accounts associated with the Profumo Affair. Long admitted, 'It was probably just as well that the Windmill had already closed, as it didn't exactly paint the venue in a particularly favourable light!' (2008: 109). This kind of sensationalist talk about the film has not helped its reputation.[7] When I met Miller at a Cinema Museum event in 2013, his memories of the film aligned with Long's assessment.

The narrative of *Secrets of a Windmill Girl* unfolds around two childhood friends, Pat (Pauline Collins, in her first major film role) and Linda (April Wilding). Wanting to make it as dancers in the West End, they audition at the Windmill Theatre. Stage manager Mike (Martin Jarvis) has a soft spot for the shy and sensible Linda, who is happy in her surroundings. Pat seems desperate for fame and success, so she leaves the safety net of the Windmill, and this results in her eventual drug-fuelled downfall and untimely death in a drunken car crash. The tragic tale is related in flashback by Linda to the police, as the film interweaves backstage action with musical numbers and comedic turns from the Windmill stage.

Long and Miller's lack of experience in creating coherent narrative is evident in *Secrets of a Windmill Girl*. As described by McGillivray, the film is 'documentary evidence of the kind of tat that inflamed the senses of a million voyeurs during the three decades the Windmill operated non-stop revue' (1992: 35). The film has a disconnect between the backstage portions and the actual revue segments owing to the way the two elements were shot some years apart. These structural discrepancies are not helped by the fact that the main protagonists never appear on stage, or even in the same costumes, as the girls in the show segments. The film is also prone to repetition, particularly of the Windmill's legendary fan dance: most likely to fill out the running time, but one may also suggest that this was the emblematic dance of the Windmill, and they knew audiences would want to see it again. And again.

The completed film was submitted to the BBFC in early April 1966. To receive the X certificate for the film very few cuts were required, and those were concerned with the performance segments of the film rather than anything from the story itself. Films were usually viewed by two BBFC examiners. Their notes for *Secrets of a Windmill Girl* suggest that their concerns had already been discussed informally with the director:

> [Reel] 4 – In the Mexican dance a woman throws aside a veil, her sole garment, and is seen virtually naked several times.
>
> [Reel] 7 – In the blonde dancer's fan dance there is one shot where the camera is focused on her as she stands naked, front view during the main part of the dance. This is a particularly light shot.
>
> Mr Miller said that he could easily fade this down ... in fact he thought it might be a gain artistically.
>
> There are other shots of partial nudity in the film, but they are all either very brief or of the Windmill 'static' type and we thought that they will pass in an X film.
>
> (Examiners' notes 1966)

As seen in previous Compton films, such as their nudist documentary *Naked – As Nature Intended*, a certain degree of topless female nudity had previously been permitted within the X certificate by the BBFC, particularly if it was in a documentary or performed context, like a striptease in front of an audience. Nudity within a romantic or erotic scene was still subject to tighter censorship, although all that was about to change shortly with the passing of European films including *Blow-Up* (Michelangelo Antonioni 1966) in 1967 and *Puss & kram* (*Hugs and Kisses*, Jonas Cornell 1967) in 1968. At this time, unlike the current organization, there were no set BBFC guidelines available to filmmakers or the public. It was felt that this allowed for greater flexibility, as Trevelyan explained in 1970: 'If there were rules, they would have to be applied equally to films of quality and to films of commercial exploitation, and both the film-maker and the public would suffer' (cited in Hargreaves 2012: 54) – effectively meaning that the above-mentioned European art films would be granted far more leniency, based on their perceived intellectual qualities, than something like *Secrets of a Windmill Girl*.

There is no documentation in the archive to suggest that anyone at Compton tried to quibble with the BBFC over their concerns with the naked fan dancer or the other requested cuts, whereas Compton argued back and forth with Board secretary John Trevelyan over decisions with which they were unhappy on other occasions (Smith 2018). One may suggest two reasons for Compton's immediate approval of the censor's request: they might have been relieved to get away with as much of the material as they did, or perhaps the suggested early intervention of the film's director might have solved issues with aesthetic negotiation rather than hard cuts. Miller's suggestion to darken the print was a logical response, and one already used by the Windmill's lighting scheme in attempts to pacify the Lord Chamberlain. However, the note that he could apparently see an artistic gain in darkening that last shot of the naked dancer is intriguing. There are no references that any attempt was made towards artistic expression in any of the film's existing documentation or interviews, and Long's contribution to the cinematography on Polanski's *Repulsion* represented the closest either of them got towards what could be described as an art film. In this instance, *Secrets of a Windmill Girl* stands as a rare example of the intervention of the BBFC being considered a positive step by the film director.

The X certificate was awarded to the film on the 22 April 1966. It was not until late May that a trailer was submitted to the BBFC, with the request that it receive a U, meaning that it could be shown in front of any film in general circulation. This time, several cuts to the trailer were requested by the censors:

> Remove fan dance.
> Remove incident in which man says to girl 'I'll see you all right for the rent.'
> Remove man's question 'What about the rent?'
> Remove men's cries of 'Come on, get it off.'
> Remove 'I'm short of money, that's why I'm doing this.'
> Remove C.U.'s of woman's face in car crash and sound of her screams.
> <u>These are minimum cuts. Resubmit in colour.</u>
>
> (Exceptions form 1966)

These requested cuts suggest that Compton's trailer was attempting to amplify the drama of the film rather than the more salacious aspects, and the fact that these lines of dialogue were rejected for the U certificate shows just how sensitive the BBFC could be. Compton initially offered to remove 'What about the rent?' if they could keep everything else, but this was rejected. The trailer must have been disappointingly tame for audiences excited at the prospect of a Windmill exposé.

Publicity and Popular Appeal

A variety of approaches were taken to promote *Secrets of a Windmill Girl*, from the poster and front-of-house stills created by Compton to newspaper coverage, some of which was archived by Compton through a press clippings agency. The fact that clippings agencies were employed by people like Compton to track the effectiveness of their publicity clearly shows the value these materials had at the time, and they are now able to shed light on the process of low budget independent film promotion. Compton produced a full colour quad poster and a set of eight black and white front-of-house stills for *Secrets of a Windmill Girl*. Alongside the large title, depicted as if in lights, is a traumatized-looking young woman in a bra and suspender belt clutching her head in pain. The tagline screams: 'The thrill, the excitement, the passion, of a WINDMILL GIRL!' As a reminder of the Windmill, their original slogan, 'We Never Closed!', is also included. In some cinemas, including the Astoria, Finsbury Park and the Essoldo, Chelsea, *Secrets of a Windmill Girl* was on a double bill with the Eurospy film *Agente 077 missione Bloody Mary* (*Mission Bloody Mary*, Sergio Grieco 1965), which had been acquired for UK distribution by Compton. An unusual pairing thematically, but both had been awarded X certificates, which make it appear to be a double bill of convenience.

The front-of-house stills are from photos taken during the main production itself, rather than of the actual Windmill rehearsal sessions shot on film by Long. As such none of these eight images includes shots of the revue; in fact, only two of the stills give any suggestion of the Windmill itself being part of the film. In one the stage manager Mike smiles longingly at Linda, who appreciates his attention while Pat watches approvingly – both Linda and Pat wear full Windmill costumes, complete with fishnet stockings and feathers. In another the choreographer Peter (Peter Gordeno, the real Windmill choreographer) is shouting instructions to some of the girls in rehearsal, who are all in leotards and stockings.

The remaining six images could be taken from any youth film of the early 1960s; they include Pat with one of her older gentlemen admirers, Pat smoking in an open-top sports car and Pat clamouring for attention in a coffee bar, striking a pose against a wall of photos. As the film follows Pat's tragic downfall, we also see Linda with Detective Inspector Thomas (Derek Bond), and arguing with her parents. Perhaps most surprisingly, one photo shows the moment Linda is required to identify the charred remains of her lifelong friend Pat. A morgue attendant lifts a sheet covering the corpse, Linda looks on in distress, and Inspector Thomas looks at Linda with paternal concern. These last three images seem like an odd choice when Compton were trying to promote a film based on the Windmill, with its scantily clad girls and the legendary fan dance. Perhaps Compton felt they had to lean into the 'warning' angle of the film in order to appease local councils who could take issue with advertising materials as well as the film, although there is no evidence of this in the existing documentation. Promotional imagery could certainly become an issue with local councils, although in practice any objections were usually regarding imagery on display to the street rather than inside the lobby. Perhaps the more prosaic reason was that a photographer had not been present when Long and Miller had shot the actual Windmill revue scenes so they had no imagery of those to use.

I have been unable to locate an original campaign book for *Secrets of a Windmill Girl*; however, comparison with publicity materials for Compton's previous Miller and Long collaborations *London in the Raw* and *Primitive London* do yield insights. The eight-page campaign book for *London in the Raw* features several images of glamourous dancing girls in various stages of undress. Highlighting the risqué and salacious nature of *Primitive London*, the smaller foldout campaign book suggests that cinema owners could hold a 'key party' on opening night: 'Invite patrons to take a numbered key from a goldfish bowl in the foyer. Make the draw for the lucky number prior to the screening of PRIMITIVE LONDON and present prizes on stage'.[8] Though the exact tone of the promotional activities for the film cannot be confirmed, one can assume with some confidence that similar levels of showmanship would have been employed for *Secrets of a Windmill Girl*, even if the available advertising imagery for the film is somewhat downbeat.

Both the General Press Cutting Association of Chancery Lane, London, and Durrant's Press Cuttings of London compiled a large collection of clippings for Compton, finding many references to *Secrets of a Windmill Girl* in local, national and international newspapers. These card-mounted cuttings mostly feature reviews, but more revealing are the examples of Compton's pre-publicity. Even during production, the film was making the papers. In a December 1965 issue of the *Evening Standard* a large photo shows six young actresses who play Windmill girls in the film – Janet Hall, Wendy Cotellee, Jill Rose, Frances Pidgeon, Aimi MacDonald and Nita Howard – in miniskirts and winter coats during their coffee break from filming 'The Windmill Girl Story' ('Windmill girls' 1965). None of these girls would be credited in the film, so this newspaper article was most likely the only time their names would be in print connected with *Secrets of a Windmill Girl*. Nonetheless, featuring an image of these six women would serve to alert a potential audience to look forward to seeing more of them when the film was eventually released.

Some newspapers featured articles that explicitly pointed towards the tension and drama that came from Pat's decline, and this is perhaps where *Secrets of a Windmill Girl* began to trouble former Windmill girls, who saw such reports and incorrectly assumed that this was supposed to reflect the behind-the-scenes antics at their beloved theatre. One of the bigger cuttings is taken from a full-page spread in the *Scottish Daily Express*, featuring three large photos of Collins and Linda Page fighting and pulling hair, with Page in lingerie. Dubbed '"Claws" Collins' and '"Panther" Page', the pictures are said to come from a 'Vicious hair-pulling, eye-gouging, flesh-tearing dressing room fight between two Windmill beauties' ('Heated Girls' 1966), a description which reads like it was from the pen of Tenser himself. An almost identical photograph and caption in the 3 April 1966 edition of the *Sunday Citizen* suggests this purple prose was at least lifted from a Compton press release.

Secrets of a Windmill Girl was one of the only starring roles April Wilding enjoyed during her career, being more accustomed to working on television in the 1960s. One of the better-known names at that time, she naturally took centre stage in some of the publicity. Wilding posed for a promotional photo in *London Life* magazine (circa 1965) modelling a Terylene crepe navy dress, as well as appeared in a publicity still in the *Sunday Mercury* (Birmingham) that plugged the film's local screening at the Scala Superama Cinema in June 1966. The *Nottingham Guardian Journal* chose to run a story about the revolving glass stage at the Windmill Theatre: '"It's a small world", says actress April Wilding'. This glass had been installed in 1932 by the Pilkington glass company, and her father was a director of the firm. Perhaps it was felt that Nottingham readers would be more interested in this aspect of the production over the Windmill girls themselves, given its manufacturing heritage ('Dad's stage' 1966).

There are two unexpected clippings from India in this collection. Published in the newspapers *Hitavada* and *Northern India Patrika*, both are undated and share the common title 'London's "Folies" Recaptured'. The two clippings provide similar content, possibly from a press release, in which the Windmill theatre is described for their readers:

> For 30 years the little Windmill theatre of Piccadilly Circus dispensed London's nearest equal to the Parisian Folies Bergère. Tourists and tired businessmen alike found relaxation and escape in the fantasy world its stage created. Non-stop revue glorifying young femininity largely unadorned ran from before lunch to near midnight.

The article gives a relatively in-depth overview of the history of the theatre, its creator – the legendary Mrs Henderson – and the censorship restrictions which led to the popular jest, 'If it moves, it's rude'. There is also that comparison to the Folies Bergère, demonstrating that parallels with Paris came easily to the minds of audiences.

Music is central to *Secrets of a Windmill Girl*, both through the musical performances and the additional songs produced for the narrative film, and this enabled some publicity through the burgeoning pop scene. In a pop news column in *Disc Weekly*, Valerie Mitchell and Dana Gillespie are both mentioned for their singing in the film ('Scene' 1966). This was an early film appearance for Gillespie, who sings and plays guitar in a scene shot when she was only seventeen. She later tells the story that Tenser invited her to his office after the filming was over to 'talk about her career' (Mawston 2017: 20).[9] Mitchell was a budding singer and former cabaret girl who's single 'The Windmill Girls' was used as the theme song for the film. According to one press-cutting, 'She's making a big name for herself', detailing her busy schedule in Glasgow, London and Blackpool.[10] Again by using up-and-coming young women in the publicity, it ensures that Compton continue to appeal towards the film's prospective predominantly male audience. Yet by marketing to the teen pop market they appear to be attempting to expand their appeal to a younger, potentially female audience.

Attempting to appeal to the pop scene was an essential element for many 1960s British films, demonstrating an influence of the American model as frequently exemplified in the films of Elvis Presley. It was common in British youth-oriented films, such as *Beat Girl* (Edmond T. Gréville 1960), that the story would stop to allow a singer or band to perform. In *Secrets of a Windmill Girl* not only were Gillespie, Mitchell and even Collins herself given their moments to perform but a band called The Pro Form also play in a Soho club decorated to look like a cave.[11] Rey Anton, lead vocalist of The Pro Form, took part in a publicity stunt alongside former Windmill dancer Deirdre O'Dea to help promote the film: in one newspaper cutting, they are pictured suspended from a scaffolder's cradle at the top of the theatre, touching one of the famous windmill sails. Anton, a scaffolder as well as a budding pop star, was working on the theatre's conversion at the time ('Young Couple' 1966).

According to John Hamilton, photos of unnamed starlets, most likely actual dancers or girls playing background roles, were also supplied by Compton to 'girlie magazines' (2005: 82). *Secrets of a Windmill Girl* was a nostalgic film marketed here in an almost nostalgic fashion, with these 'girlie magazine' photos being not dissimilar from what the Windmill itself used to publish in its own souvenir programmes.[12] With these photos and the various articles covering everything from the stars and their lives, the plot, the music, the history of the Windmill and the conversion of the building itself, Compton were clearly casting as wide a net as possible to attract an audience for a film about an entertainment venue that real-life audiences had already drifted away from. Perhaps an awareness that the Windmill Theatre was out of date contributed to fears that their new film might be as well.

Press Reaction

Only eighteen months after they bought the Windmill Theatre and converted it, Compton sold the building to the Classic Cinemas chain before *Secrets of a Windmill Girl* was even ready for release ('Classic' 1966: 31) – although other sources have it being sold to Capital and Provincial Cinema Chain (Hamilton 2005: 82). Despite having now changed hands, it was agreed by the new owners that the film should premiere at the venue now called the Cameo Moulin, which it did in the last week of April 1966. O'Dea and Vicky Scott, who both played dancers in the film, attended in skimpy outfits to attract press attention (Hamilton 2005: 82). One reviewer commented, 'It's an odd feeling, sitting in a theatre turned cinema watching a film about the building's old stage days' ('Miscellany' 1966). With tongue in cheek, but revealing some essential truths about the real Windmill girls, the review continues: '"Windmill girls" secrets, according to this epic, consisted of knitting socks for soldiers during the war ... going goose-pimply when posing in a strong wind and having feet which killed them' ('Miscellany' 1966).

The venue was clearly intending to specialize in films for an adult audience: a listing for the Cameo Moulin the week before the premiere promised the audience that they would be screening films featuring: 'Girls, Girls! Luscious, delicious, will send you delirious' ('Classified ad 116' 1966). The films in question were *The Naked World of Harrison Marks* (Marks 1965) and *La donna nel mondo* (*Women of the World*, Gualtiero Jacopetti/ Franco Prosperi/Paulo Cavara 1963). A double bill of documentaries from Gala Film Distributors, the former was distributed with an A certificate from the Greater London Council and does not appear to have been submitted to the BBFC. The latter was given an X certificate by the BBFC on its initial release in 1963.

An undated, unidentified cutting featuring a review of *Secrets of a Windmill Girl* is titled 'Naughty, yes, but it was never like this corn', and features an image of an unnamed Windmill girl in full dance attire with a caption reading, 'This is how we remember the Windmill lovelies', alongside a photo of a demure, fully clothed Wilding. Under this is the somewhat protesting caption: 'One of the Windmill girls – this time with her clothes on'. Unsurprisingly, given its title, the review offers an acerbic summation that the film possesses 'a plot no amateur dramatic group would touch with a barge-pole'. Tenser and Klinger were no doubt amused when they read that the writer 'knew it was only a matter of time before the moguls put their cash-register minds to work' on a film about this 'revered Mecca-among men'. With this comment the writer gets cynically to the truth of the whole venture. *Secrets of a Windmill Girl* was never intended to be anything other than a 'programmer' (Hamilton 2005: 82), and as such provided a steady return on their small investment.

Monthly Film Bulletin's review was disparaging: 'There is virtually nothing one can say about this film except that one has seen it all before. Ethically it is as dubious and naïve as most; the hygienic, hard-working happiness of the average Windmill girl is one of the film's more tiresome propositions; the direction is non-existent. Pauline Collins is an attractive, spirited Pat' ('Secrets' 1966: 97). It comes as no surprise that critics were for the most part unimpressed with the film, as they usually were with what were perceived as cheap sex films. As audience data is unavailable, it is only this critical response that we have to draw on, and as is often the case, negative reviews do not guarantee poor box office. It is therefore impossible to gauge just how commercially successful the film was. Hamilton claims the film made a 'steady return' (2005: 82) but does not give a source for this information. However, Compton did put the film on the front page of the 18 May 1966 issue of the trade publication *Kine Weekly*, with an image of Pat arguing with other girls next to the tagline 'No punches are pulled in ... *Secrets of a Windmill Girl*'. This would have attracted the attention of cinema managers and boosted bookings, and a serialized photo-story of the film in the men's magazine *Parade* also apparently helped increase the number of rentals (Hamilton 2005: 83). It can be inferred from this that the film would have found its target audience and provided Compton with another commercial success.

Whatever Happened to the Windmill Girls?

Secrets of a Windmill Girl's barrage of negative reviews most likely further fuelled the real Windmill girls' ongoing negativity and antagonism towards the film. The archival material offers us some insight into the Windmill and the girls themselves: at least four former Windmill girls became croupiers in the new casino in the basement of the building after its conversion ('Chatter' 1966). Some of the girls married former customers and others went on to form a revue show with Sheila Van Damm which toured the world, one reviewer in Melbourne pointing out that 'patrons expecting to see the celebrated Windmill nudes are likely to be disappointed. Only one girl appears topless, between fluttering fans' (Stan 1965: 59). By 1973 the Windmill was owned by property tycoon (and renowned philanthropist) Laurie Marsh,[13] and a group of former Windmill girls including Polly Perkins, who was posing nude on the Windmill stage from the age of fifteen, launched a campaign to return the building to its Folies-style revue days: 'We would like to recreate the Windmill just as it was in wartime. Nostalgia is very fashionable and if we recreate it just as it was we think it would be a very saleable commodity' ('Down with' 1973: 6). The 'retrospective' mode again demonstrating that the Windmill was primarily about looking backwards, framing their shows as being from a rose-tinted past. This plan never came to fruition, and the building was purchased by Soho property magnate and pornographer Paul Raymond, who converted it back to a theatre specializing in risqué and erotic productions. This final opportunity to reclaim the Windmill having failed, it is left to *Secrets of a Windmill Girl* to be the final word on its days (and nights) as a revue venue.

The future for the Compton Group was also to be short-lived: Klinger and Tenser parted ways in 1966. Compton were bought out by shareholders and became Cinecenta, an exhibition chain responsible for the first purpose-built multi-screen cinemas in the UK. Tenser formed Tigon, which focused primarily on productions made in the sex and horror formula developed at Compton, while Klinger became an independent film producer making ambitious projects such as *Baby Love* (Alastair Reid 1969) and *Get Carter* (Mike Hodges 1971). Tenser always was a showman at heart who loved exploitable properties guaranteed to turn a profit, so it seemed natural that he would continue to make the kinds of films that helped build Compton's empire in the early part of the decade. Klinger on the other hand had pretentions towards respectability and loved the plaudits that came with artistic success, especially the Silver Bear for *Repulsion* at the Berlin International Film Festival in 1965. It was inevitable that he would want to follow the independent producer route, looking for interesting projects without having to answer to a business partner like Tenser.

Conclusion

What can the connoisseur or historian of scandalous cinema of yesteryear conclude regarding the legacy of *Secrets of a Windmill Girl*? This humble little film, cheaply produced to make the most of a free location and pre-existing footage, is still causing trouble over fifty years later. The only colour film showing the inside of the Windmill Theatre, featuring footage of the last revue ever performed there, the film is a valuable historical document of a long-lost pillar of the London entertainment scene, yet it remains contentious, a victim of its own marketing scheme which focused on the suffering of Pat rather than on the happy Windmill girls themselves. And just what were the secrets of the Windmill girls? They remain tantalizingly out of reach, perhaps hidden behind carefully positioned fans.

Notes

1   This slogan was popularly altered by comedians of the day to 'We Never Clothed'.

2   This includes *House of Whipcord* (Pete Walker 1974), *I'm Not Feeling Myself Tonight* (Joseph McGrath 1976) and *Satan's Slave* (Norman J. Warren 1976).

3   The question was preceded by a disclaimer that they were asking on behalf of someone else, presumably a former Windmill girl.

4   See Spicer and Mckenna (2013) or Hamilton (2005) for a detailed history.

5   *The Yellow Teddybears* was based on the supposed true story about schoolgirls who wore golliwog badges to indicate that they had lost their virginity.

6   See Halligan (2022) for an in-depth discussion of the 'permissive society' and the fears of the conservative right, as embodied in the campaigns spearheaded by Mary Whitehouse.

7   This might explain why *Secrets of a Windmill Girl*'s male lead Martin Jarvis was not available for comment when I contacted his agent.

8   This extract from Compton's *Primitive London* campaign book is part of my personal collection, as are many of the other archival sources from here to the end of the chapter. Often, the loose clippings from the Compton film office are incomplete and occasionally the full reference is unknown. In such cases I have detailed all the available elements within the text itself.

9   According to Gillespie, Tenser gave her a drink and then pulled a lever causing her chair to collapse backwards, at which point she threw the drink in his face and he chased her around his desk (Mawston 2017: 20).

10   'Valerie ... flies in, and as I predicted, she's making a big name for herself', states the unknown press cutting. The article also points out that Valerie is the younger sister of Janie Jones, who had a hit record with 'Witches Brew' in 1965. In 1964 the two were charged with obscenity for appearing in topless dresses outside the premiere of *London in the Raw*: another publicity stunt from the mind of Tenser (see Macrae 1964).

11   This was possibly because of the popularity of Chislehurst Caves, a frequently used venue for live music during the 1950s and 1960s. The caves featured heavily in *Beat Girl*.

12   See the online gallery by Flickr user Windmill3 for examples: https://www.flickr.com/photos/40604141@N02/ (accessed 20 July 2021).

13   Laurie Marsh had put up some of the capital for Compton to acquire the Windmill Theatre in 1964, and later became involved with Tenser's company Tigon, helping fund films such as *Witchfinder General* (Michael Reeves 1968).

References

Boorne, B. (1964), 'Curtain' at the Windmill and It's Goodbye to the Windmill Girls', *The Evening News and Star*, 1 October.

Branaghan, S. (2006), *British Film Posters: An Illustrated History*, London: BFI Publishing.

'Chatter: London' (1966), *Variety*, 27 April: 76.

Chibnall, S. and B. McFarlane (2009), *The British 'B' Film*, London: Palgrave Macmillan/BFI.

'Classic Cinemas Adds Windmill to Its Chain' (1966), *Variety*, 20 April: 31.

'Classified ad 116' (1966), *Observer*, 24 April: 26.

Compton Group ad (1965), *Boxoffice*, 5 April: b55.

Compton Group ad (1966), *Boxoffice*, 28 February: b53.

'Dad's Stage – in Glass' (1966), *Nottingham Guardian Journal*, 1 April.

Delargy, D. (2020), *Soho Bites Podcast*, 21 July. Available online: https://sohobitespodcast.libsyn.com/soho-bites-episode-fifteen (accessed 20 July 2021).

'Down with Strip …' (1973), *Guardian*, 11 August.
Examiners' Notes (1966), *Secrets of a Windmill Girl* file, 2 April, London: BBFC Archive.
Exceptions form (1966), 'Trailer: Secrets of a Windmill Girl', *Secrets of a Windmill Girl* file, 27 May, London: BBFC Archive.
Halligan, B. (2022), *Hotbeds of Licentiousness: The British Glamour Film and the Permissive Society*, Oxford: Berghahn.
Hamilton, J. (2005), *Beasts in the Cellar: The Exploitation Film Career of Tony Tenser*, Godalming: FAB Press.
Hargreaves, T. (2012), 'The Trevelyan Years: British Censorship and 1960s Cinema', in E. Lamberti (ed), *Behind the Scenes at the BBFC: Film Classification from the Silver Screen to the Digital Age*, 53–71, London: BFI Publishing.
'… Heated Girls' (1966), *Scottish Daily Express*, 18 March.
Klinger, T. (2017), unpublished interview with the author, 30 May.
Long, S. with S. Sheridan (2008), *X-Rated: Adventures of an Exploitation Filmmaker*, London: Reynolds & Hearn.
Macrae, R. (1964), 'Bare-Bosom Girls Are Found Guilty', *Daily Mail*, 22 August.
Mawston, M. (2017), 'Dana Gillespie: Hammer Red, White Dukes and Cool Blues', *Cinema Retro*, 13 (38): 20.
McCann, G. (1998), *Morecambe & Wise*, London: Fourth Estate.
McGillivray, D. (1992), *Doing Rude Things: The History of the British Sex Film, 1957–1981*, London: Sun Tavern Fields.
McGillivray, D. (n.d.), 'Murder at the Windmill', *Radio Times*. Available online: http://www.radiotimes.com/film/cyvj5/murder-at-the-windmill/ (accessed 4 July 2017).
'Memorial Service For Man Who Made Stars' (1961), *The Stage*, 5 July: 5.
'Miscellany at Large: The Thrill of It All' (1966), *Guardian*, 28 April.
Norman, J. (1966), *Soho Night and Day*, London: Corgi.
Robertson, J. (1989), *The Hidden Cinema: British Film Censorship in Action, 1913–1975*, London: Routledge.
'Scene' (1966), *Disc Weekly*, 7 May.
Schaefer, E. (2014), '"I'll Take Sweden": The Shifting Discourse of the "Sexy Nation" in Sexploitation Films', in E. Schaefer (ed), *Sex Scene: Media and the Sexual Revolution*, 207–34, Durham, NC: Duke University Press.
'Secrets of a Windmill Girl' (1966), *Monthly Film Bulletin*, June: 97.
Smith, A. (2018), 'The Distribution and Exploitation of Popular European Film in British Cinemas, 1960–1975', PhD thesis, University of Sussex, Brighton.
Spicer, A. and A. McKenna (2013), *The Man Who Got Carter: Michael Klinger, Independent Production and the British Film Industry, 1960–1980*, London: I.B. Tauris.
Stan. [pseud.] (1965), 'Windmill Review, Melbourne, Nov. 9', *Variety*, 17 November: 59.
'"Windmill Girls" Take a Break' (1965), *Evening Standard*, 21 December.
'Young Couple Who Share the Secrets of a Theatre' (1966), *Daily Express*, 13 April.
Young, J. (2022), *Soho on Screen: Cinematic Spaces of Bohemia and Cosmopolitanism, 1948–1963*, Oxford: Berghahn.

9

The Potent Sexuality of the Middle-Aged Woman:

Alice Aisgill, Karen Stone, Zee Blakeley and Ruby

Lucy Bolton

Of all the elements to focus on as a feature of X certificate cinema, the sexual desire of middle-aged women might seem innocuous. The sexual appetites of the older women characters in *Room at the Top* (Jack Clayton 1959), *The Roman Spring of Mrs Stone* (José Quintero 1961) and *Zee & Co.* (Brian G. Hutton 1972) are, however, presented as transgressive and scandalous, and the characters strongly resonate with the stars who played them. Each of these films centres the desires and physical yearnings of a middle-aged woman as potent and enduring, yet viewed with ambivalence by others in the film: Alice Aisgill (Simone Signoret) is both adored and reviled by social-climber Joe Lampton (Laurence Harvey); Karen Stone (Vivien Leigh) is viewed with pathos by her friends, and ridiculed by her young lover Paolo di Leo (Warren Beatty); and Zee Blakeley's (Elizabeth Taylor) husband Robert (Michael Caine) finds her outrageous and vindictive, yet sexually daring and provocative. Each is positioned in comparison to a younger woman – enabling callous dismissal of the older woman's sexual desirability – and stereotypical traits, such as vanity and neediness, are exaggerated so as to emphasize the embarrassment aroused by their sexual endeavours. But this chapter will also consider Ruby (Shelley Winters) from *Alfie* (Lewis Gilbert

1966), a character who defies these conventions and joyfully asserts her ribald confidence. Through analysing these sexual dynamics, and considering the ways in which they contributed to the concerns of the British Board of Film Censors (BBFC) and chime with the star images of the actors, this chapter will enhance the understanding of the complexity of the women as characters and stars, and the perceived transgressiveness of the sexuality of the middle-aged woman.

'Alice is all woman': Simone Signoret as Alice Aisgill

Room at the Top inaugurated the 'kitchen sink' period of British cinema and was also the first British film to deal frankly with sex. The film's press book suggests the film 'merits an X certificate because of its candid approach to an adult subject', and cites reviews to be included in publicity, such as 'The saltiest, frankest, most adult British picture for years ... some of the most realistic sex episodes, the most unminced dialogue yet seen and heard in a cinema' (*Daily Sketch*); 'Very remarkable. The most adult picture on sex ever to be made in this country' (*News Chronicle*); and 'This week the British cinema grew up ... For the first time in a British film, sex is given the status of an adult occupation' (*Sunday Dispatch*).[1] Sexual content was plainly a major part of the film's publicity, then, but there was more to worry the BBFC than sex alone. Tracy Hargreaves describes how the film gave John Trevelyan 'one of his earliest challenges in his new role as secretary' (2012: 54). The cuts that were negotiated by Trevelyan and director Jack Clayton 'were few in number but they offer a revealing insight into the kinds of sensitivities at play at this turning point in the BBFC's history' (2012). In terms of language, Charles Soames (Donald Houston) was allowed to keep 'you lust after her' in relation to Alice, but his fiancée June Samson (Mary Peach) was not allowed to keep: 'don't waste your lust on her', and 'bitch' was changed to 'witch' (Hargreaves 2012: 55). Another concern was over Alice's death in a car crash which, although not explicitly seen, is graphically described by a character in the film. The line 'she was scalped' was deleted by the BBFC, but the description of how Alice was crawling around on the road before she died remains as a distressing evocation of her final hours (Dewe Mathews 1994: 144). Alice's body is therefore central to the censorable content of *Room at the Top*: her age, sexuality and death.

The role of Alice is poignant and provocative, and Signoret's Oscar-winning performance imbues the character with heartbreaking vulnerability. We first meet Alice as a leading actress in the local amateur dramatic group, on stage playing a scene with Susan Brown (Heather

Sears). Alice is a relaxed and confident performer, with a curvaceous figure shown off in a silk shirtdress, and an enticing French accent.[2] We next see her at her dressing table, in the backstage milieu of post-performance excitement. Joe is introduced to Alice, and she shakes his hand, appraising him with a slight smile and a lingering glance in her mirror as he climbs the stairs. Alice is rubbing her face with the excessive amounts of cold cream associated with the removal of stage make-up, and appears as a star in this small town – on stage, at a mirrored dressing table, surrounded by admirers and the accoutrements of backstage environs. Joe joins the acting group in order to get closer to Susan, who, as his wealthy boss's daughter, has caught his eye as his ticket to the top. He causes the cast to burst out laughing when he says 'brassiere' instead of 'brazier', and is infuriated by their laughter. Alice spots his sensitivity and finds his anger amusing. Outside, by her car, he apologizes to her and offers her a coffee, and she says no, but he can buy her a drink. She throws her car key at him, which means she can watch him as he drives. She observes, 'You're very touchy aren't you'. When Joe and Alice are in the pub, Alice faces the camera, so we can see how she watches him with amusement (see Plate 6); she understands that he's jealous of Susan's boyfriend and feels inferior to him. Joe says that she must think he's terribly conceited, to which she replies, 'young and terribly inexperienced, but not conceited'. Alice is thereby established as a woman who can read Joe's hunger and ambition, and who is interested in him.

Joe tells Alice that he likes her, although he says he doesn't mean sexually. Alice says that he looks about eighteen sometimes, and that he reminds her of a boy she used to know at university in Paris. These parameters establish their initial perceptions of each other: for Joe, Alice is a sympathetic, kindred spirit, but beyond the purview of sexual attraction. For Alice, Joe is an angry and exciting young man, who reminds her of a younger love from her past. Her wistfulness is evident, and Joe asks her whether she is very unhappy. 'No', she replies, 'not very'. This painful response, conveying that she is indeed unhappy, inspires pity in Joe, her fellow Warnley neighbours and indeed in us. And yet, Alice also continues to express strength and confidence in herself, such as when she kisses Joe on the cheek, and waves behind her, over her shoulder, as she walks off, knowing he'll be looking at her. When discussing their scene in the play, Alice tells Joe he has to grab hold of her as if he means it, and says, 'I'm not fragile, I won't break, you must take hold of me as if you meant it'. When Joe says he'll try, she responds, 'Is it so difficult?', conveying her self-consciousness about her undesirability. Eva (Delena Kidd) insinuates that Joe will be seduced by Alice, to which Teddy Merrick (Richard Pasco) responds, 'Don't be catty, she's a very nice and long suffering woman'. Then, in an apt description, Eva proclaims, 'Alice is all woman'. This is not an insult but rather insinuates sexual experience and irresistibility. Alice is perceived as a sexy woman, with a philandering husband, who represents a dangerous temptation to Joe, to which he inevitably succumbs.

Susan is sent away by her parents to get her out of Joe's clutches, but he does not appear to be missing her, not least, because, as he says to Charles, while bouncing on his bed, 'I've got compensations'. The film cuts from Joe's boyish enthusiasm for his lover to the sight of Joe and Alice in bed together. Alice gets up and begins to dress, wearing a basque, stockings and suspenders, under a silk robe. She looks curvaceous and sexy, with blonde hair in a bouffant but casual bob. Joe says he hates it when she puts her clothes on, to which Alice replies, 'It's very sweet of you honey but I'm too old to walk around in my girdle'. Alice's self-consciousness is echoed by the camera, as we see only a glimpse of her stocking top, and she moves modestly behind a screen to dress. She tells Joe that no one has ever been so good to her, and that all of her feels alive, saying, 'It hurts sometimes but I don't care'. He says to her, 'It's so good for me, is it good for you too – I didn't know it could be so good'. Alice's sexual knowledge has introduced Joe to an experience of sex he has not known before, and clearly does not have with Susan, when he finally persuades her to lose her virginity (even though Susan describes the experience as 'super'). These scenes convey the discussion of sex, which marked the film out as a game-changer. As Dewe Mathews explains, 'it was *Room at the Top*'s dialogue that struck home with audiences in the late fifties' (1994: 194). Certainly the conversations get right to the heart of the sexual dynamics in play.

When they are next in bed together, Alice asks Joe, 'Supposing you had met me when I was ten years younger, would you have taken me seriously. Would you have loved me and wanted to marry me?' Alice may consider herself to be out of Joe's realm, but he replies, 'I like you the way you are now'. Joe is falling in love with Alice, and he says he wants to 'really sleep with you, and wake up beside you in the morning'. But his inexperience and jealousy are then triggered when they get into a heated discussion about the fact that Alice posed nude for an artist when she was at university. Joe is infuriated by this and consumed with disapproval of her actions. Alice says she didn't sleep with the artist, but somehow that makes Joe even more angry, as it conveys a sense of her varied sexual history with other men. He becomes violent, grabbing her around her neck. Alice rebuffs this fury by chiding him that he is 'very brave and very moral all of a sudden'. Their argument becomes highly personal and vicious, and descends into insults, culminating with Joe asking her what she did in the Great War, fifty years ago. Finally, he has resorted to using her age as an insult. This furious fight seems to break up their relationship, but they cannot keep apart. Joe manages to borrow a cottage for a few days, where they can live together as a couple in love. They walk on the beach barefoot, sleep and wake up together, declaring their love for each other. And yet, as they part at the railway station, Alice fears they will not be together again. And she's right.

Joe has 'got Susan in the family way', and is to marry her. Susan knows about Alice, and is outraged, mainly because Alice is 'so old'. Others call Alice 'an old whore', criticizing both her age and sexuality. Alice drinks herself to drunkenness in the pub, and surveys herself in the mirror, her reflected image staring back at her from multiple mirrored surfaces. She looks away, resigned at the state of the image she sees, and we later learn – at the same time as Joe – that she got into her car and drove to Sparrow Hill, where she and Joe first made love. A terrible accident occurred, leaving Alice mutilated and dying, crawling about the road, before succumbing to her fatal injuries. Joe is devastated but can do nothing, and proceeds with his marriage to Susan, ending the film with tears in his eyes, mistaken by his young bride as tears of joy. Joe's future as a misunderstood, misplaced outcast seems assured, and Alice is the casualty of his determination to marry into wealth and privilege.

Hargreaves describes how Alice's gruesome death was seen by the film's producer as 'right': 'Concerned that Alice's gruesome death should not be too understated, John Woolf suggested to Trevelyan that "[d]ramatically, it is of course terribly important and I should have thought too that the fact she met a violent end is morally right from the censorship point of view"' (2012: 55). The film punishes Alice for her adultery with death, and her sexuality by describing the horrific and humiliating circumstances, but her character remains a striking challenge to convention.

Sue Harper writes how this film 'is about the declining marketability of older women', and yet, '[t]he film is transformed by Signoret' (2000: 96). Alice's sexuality is at the heart of the film's tension and trajectory. As Alice, Signoret is erotic, amused, intelligent and playful. Harper notes, the film 'evokes a profound pity; pity for Alice's willingness to confer her love on an unworthy object, and pity for Joe's inability to disregard her age and lack of status' (2000). In her memoirs, Signoret records what a special character Alice was:

Alice was intelligent, generous, understanding, maternal, sexually liberated and socially without prejudice. Alice was a character who had everything going for her, including her death before the end of the novel. Alice was a piece of cake to play [...] Did I say a piece of cake? A wedding cake is more like it: a part whose like one seldom encounters in the course of a career.

(1979: 247)

Signoret brings sophistication and vulnerability to Alice, and looks glamorous and beautiful, standing apart from her fellow citizens with the openness of her face, her sleepily seductive hooded eyes and her 'Gallic cool' (Sandlin 2020: 69). For Susan Hayward, Signoret 'in her performances is ineluctably the subject of her own desire – not the object. She is a woman in her own

sexual right' (1995: 65). This is clearly the case with Alice, who appraises Joe
as a sexual possibility from the first time she sees him and approaches him
actively as a desiring subject. Hayward writes that 'in the 1950s, Signoret
was a stunning looking woman who exuded sexuality' (1995: 65).

By the late 1960s, however, Signoret had transformed into an image
of ageing and suffering. Guy Austin draws a direct link between Alice
Aisgill and the change in Signoret's image. He suggests that although the
affair between her husband Yves Montand and Marilyn Monroe in 1960
is usually identified as the beginning of the loss of her looks, the 'shift
in star image (from youth and beauty to age and suffering)' begins in
Room at the Top: 'As Signoret herself acknowledged, this performance
(given at the age of thirty-seven, but representing a woman well into her
forties) marked a watershed in her career' (2003: 29). Austin points out
that Signoret is lit and shot in a variety of ways throughout the film, from
line-erasing brightness, making her hair and complexion glow, to tired
and shadowed, reflecting a downcast turn in her mood and vigour. He also
correctly observes that Alice's reflection in a variety of mirrors indicates
how she appraises her image, as she surveys her neck, eyes and general
appearance. However, the film's concern to show the pressure that her
age exerts on Alice does not reflect upon Alice's desirability as a sexual
being but rather as a marriageable prospect. At no point is Susan a more
appealing lover than Alice, but is simply a rung on the ladder of Joe's social
climbing. As Hayward writes, 'One wonders how Joe could ever relinquish
her rich voluptuousness for the gangly and prudish awkwardness of
Susan's immature body' (2004: 123). The fact that Alice's age is perceived
as negative by herself and others is a source of sadness in the film mainly
because it so evidently should not be. When Susan expresses shock at Joe's
interest in Alice because of her age, it confirms that she is part of the
hierarchical system of age, class and gender to which Joe is now committed
but which Alice was not part of. As Joe reveals his envy for Susan's family
when they drive past the Brown family house, saying, 'They've got just
about everything', Alice's response, 'I wouldn't say that', suggests that she
knows the limitations of life, love and passion in the Brown household.

It is certainly true that Signoret came to stand for negative connotations
of ageing, such as marital infidelity, weight gain and loss of beauty. However,
Signoret assumed a stance of acceptance in relation to her appearance.
She stated, 'I'm fat and ugly, and I'm going to put that to use' (Hayward
1995: 65, n. 7). She claimed to have chosen not to fight the ageing process
and rather to embrace it as a way to obtain more interesting roles and to
be like usual people, rather than actresses who fought time with plastic
surgery. This resistance to gendered industry norms is a significant element
of Signoret's star image, and is entirely consistent with the resistant figure
cut by Alice Aisgill.

'She still wears very beautiful clothes': Vivien Leigh as Karen Stone

In *The Roman Spring of Mrs Stone*, Vivien Leigh plays Karen Stone, 'an actress advancing in years and failing in reputation' (Vickers 1988: 313). As shown in the press book, the Warner-Pathé Press Campaign described the film as 'The daring and explosive story of a woman's hopeless drift towards moral deterioration, set amidst the glittering decadence of modern Rome'. Made up to look older than her forty-eight years (Karen is said to be 'approaching fifty'), with the addition of crow's feet wrinkles and a silvery-beige wig, Leigh embodies what Tennessee Williams describes as 'grace and tragic style' (Williams 1976: 314). The film's voiceover declares that 'self-knowledge was something Mrs Stone had always managed to avoid': she is a woman who has failed to engage honestly with her emotions and her sexual desires. Married to an older man who is bankrolling her career, we meet Karen backstage when she is playing Rosalind in Shakespeare's *As You Like It*. The costumes she wears are those of the cross-dressing Rosalind disguised as a young man, and then a gleaming white bridal outfit replete with veil and headdress. Both of these incongruous outfits accentuate Karen's age and the fact, noted by audience members and her friends alike, that she is far too old for the role.

At this stage in her career, Leigh had embarked upon a trajectory of playing women confronting the ravages of time on their looks, sexuality and career. Her Oscar-winning performance as Blanche DuBois in *A Streetcar Named Desire* (Elia Kazan 1951) is a visceral depiction of a woman lost in her younger years and in denial of her faded sexual appeal, and her performance as Hester Collyer in *The Deep Blue Sea* (Anatole Litvak 1955) painfully evokes the tragedy of the middle-aged woman desperate for the love of her younger beau. Her tempestuous marriage to Laurence Olivier had ended in divorce in 1960, and Leigh's mental and physical illnesses made her life challenging. However, Leigh certainly never lacked courage as an actor, and her unflinching performance as Karen Stone embraces the fears and humiliations of an actress deemed to be past her prime (Bolton 2018: 109).

Critic Felix Barker wrote, in a review titled 'A Warning to Women':

They should put up a notice in the foyer of the Warner Cinema saying their new film as a 'W' Certificate – 'More suitable for exhibition when no women between 40 and 50 are present.' I have it on the highest authority that *The Roman Spring of Mrs Stone* (X) will scare the hell out of women in this age group.

(1962)

Expressing surprise that Vivien Leigh was prepared to appear in 'this study of despairing middle-aged sexuality', Barker claims that she has 'closed her ears to dangerous echoes' with her own life and career. Barker believes that women between 40 and 50 'will reel to the exits muttering: "there but for the grace of God ..."' (1962). This portentous attitude reveals a perception that middle-aged women are at risk from becoming 'the biological door-mat of a no-good Italian gigolo', as scathingly described in *Harrison's Reports* at the time ('The Roman' 1961). Alexander Walker, however, believed that Leigh had made 'probably the most courageous choice she could make after seven years away from the screen', and praised how she embodies the 'terrifying degradation of Mrs Stone' (1962).

In the pre-credit sequence, when Karen faces up to the fact that she is too old to play Rosalind, she looks tiny, ashen and anxious. But in her spectacular apartment in Rome, she is smartly dressed, with set hair, full make-up, pearls and manicure. She is confident and assured, and, as a wealthy widow, ideal prey for the scheming Contessa Magda Terribili-Gonzales (Lotte Lenya) and her 'marchetta', or hustler, Paolo. Initially, Karen resists Paolo's attentions, aware that she is being set up. But when Paolo tracks her down in the Borghese gardens, Karen is more receptive. Paolo's invitation to dinner unnerves her, and she suddenly looks wary and vulnerable. At dinner, she appears slightly shy, but she is charmed by the possibility of being understood by Paolo. Paolo observes that 'your hand is a fist', drawing attention to Karen's tension; even though her hand is gloved, she is still shy to open the hand at Paolo's touch, indicating her repression and physical isolation. Paolo breaks through her veneer, and, once exposed, we see Karen's susceptibility to his fickle attentions. She becomes slightly more joyful as she entertains the possibility he might be attracted to her. When he suggests that she is 'frightened of her feelings', and leaves her tantalizingly on her doorstep, she gazes longingly after him. Following Paolo's attempt to trick her into giving him 10 million lira for an invented 'friend', Karen reveals that she knows it is a lie, and says, 'When the time comes when nobody desires me for myself, I'd rather not be desired at all'. She goes into her bedroom, removes her luxurious accessories, undresses and gets into bed, still wearing her slip. He enters her bedroom, closes the curtains and caresses her hand with the practised and charming lovemaking of an experienced gigolo. After they have spent the night together, we see Karen excited and giddy having had her hair cut into a shorter style, wearing a bright tangerine suit and accompanied by light, hopeful, non-diegetic music. She cries when she holds Paolo, as she confesses, 'I'm so happy'. In these scenes she appears rejuvenated and is more emotionally aroused than at any point in the film so far (see Plate 7).

Paolo and Karen repeatedly clash, however, as his preening behaviour amuses Karen, and he cannot bear to be laughed at. Never on an even keel, the relationship is threatened by the arrival of Hollywood starlet Miss Bingham (Jill St John), orchestrated by the Contessa. Tension erupts when they invite people over to see their home movies, including Miss Bingham. Karen overhears the Contessa describing her as a chicken hawk – a bird that feeds on the flesh of young birds – and she and Miss Bingham make a series of bitchy comments about her past beauty and 'the length, the extent of her career'. They begin to watch the home movies, and as Karen is on screen playfully throwing a cushion at Paolo behind the camera, he is out on the terrace flirting with Miss Bingham. Karen explodes, has a fight with Paolo and asks everyone to leave. Her furious emotion overwhelms any sense of pride or decorum she may have had left. Karen sits in the darkness, deserted and tear-stricken, as the film reel has come to an end, but her final humiliation is yet to come, as she follows Paolo and sees him go into Miss Bingham's hotel. This is enough for her to throw her keys to the vagabond boy who has been following her throughout the film. She waits for him in her apartment, her chest rising and falling rather heavily as she sits opposite the door and lights a cigarette. She has previously said to Paolo, when he tells her about a middle-aged woman murdered by a young lover in the French Riviera, that she only needs three or four years after which a cut throat would be a convenience. The suggestion is that Karen has decided the time for the cut throat is now. Paolo's rejection has been the final blow, as without the flattery of this love affair she feels she has nothing to live for.

The most notable element of Leigh's performance as Karen is her sexual vulnerability. In a 1962 review titled 'The Roman', Harrison claims that Paolo's 'lovemaking has made her his captive' (1919–62). Unlike the other characters discussed in this chapter, Karen is not a woman of sexual experience, comfortable in her skin, but rather a woman distanced from sexual pleasure. She experiences a fragile rejuvenation aroused by sexual attention, but then rejection, and abandonment. Karen is humiliated by Paolo because she is essentially a 'pawn' in his trade of avarice and laziness. He repeatedly tells her that she makes a spectacle of herself, and ridicules her for her vanities. That sex with Paolo is transformative for her could not be clearer, and for this sexual attention, she is prepared to endure his insults and the mockery of others. Paolo suggests she is approaching fifty, which Walker claims is 'the bitterest way that man can taunt woman' (1962); and yet Walker's observations are sharply attuned to the piercing commentary of the film, as he observes how, for a British film, 'it creates brilliantly an atmosphere of cosmopolitan iniquity' (1962). His conclusion echoes Barker: that the film will be salutary to other women, claiming 'her final self-disgust and guilt will rivet the sympathy of every woman facing up to the middle-age of the emotions' (1962).

'Yes I am a bitch, open and straight':
Elizabeth Taylor as Zee Blakeley

Walker identified a uniquely relevant element of the Elizabeth Taylor star image when he observed:

> Elizabeth Taylor is one star whose off-screen life and temperament have many similarities with the roles she plays. When the public sense this, it confers a mythical quality on even her worst films. But of course she is a modern star, bound to no studio, who has profited by the permissiveness prevalent in films and society.
>
> (1974: 188–9)

The supercilious comment about Taylor 'profiting by permissiveness' overshadows the pertinent point he makes about the integral value of her star image and her appearance in films from the mid-1960s. From *Who's Afraid of Virginia Woolf?* (Mike Nichols 1966), where Taylor played older than her thirty-four years, her roles became increasingly exhibitionist. Susan White (2010: 182) describes her as the 'lusty heterosexual' Leonora Penderton in *Reflections in a Golden Eye* (John Huston 1967), and in *Boom!* (Joseph Losey 1968) she plays the reclusive movie star Flora Goforth, attracting the attentions of a younger man who preys on dying older women, played by her then husband Richard Burton.

By the time of *Zee & Co.* in 1972 (also known as *X, Y & Zee*), her film career was 'withering to the point of annihilation' (Spoto 1995: 335). As the vindictive Zee Blakeley, she is happy to awaken the latent lesbian tendencies of her rival in love, Stella, in order to corrupt the affair between Stella and Zee's husband, Robert. Donald Spoto calls it 'one of the worst films of her career' (1995: 334).

Taylor as Zee performs hysterically, veering from spoilt party animal to sapphic predator, with a suicide attempt and deliberate car crash along the way. Maintaining a pitch of emotion and intensity that Taylor herself seems to be amused by, her energy exists in a self-centred tornado, failing to connect with any other character or contribute to any narrative meaning. Spoto observes that '[f]or the role, the now frankly zaftig Elizabeth exaggerated her make-up, wore mammoth fright wigs, and generally created a parody of Martha' (1995: 334). Spoto is right to identify the excesses of Taylor's hairstyles and make-up in the film, where she is adorned with teased, backcombed hair and lilac eyeshadow from her eyelashes to her eyebrows, but the word 'zaftig' is most significant. Taylor is clearly heavier than in the 1950s and early 1960s, when her voluptuous breasts and tiny waist epitomized the 1950s silhouette, as highlighted by the famous Edith Head white ballgown in *A Place in the Sun* (George Stevens 1951). By the time the late 1960s silhouette became mini-skirts and long boots, Elizabeth's small stature and large chest made her appear top-heavy and unsuited to high fashion. Taylor's battles with her weight are well documented, and one of the most unflattering photographs of her adorns the cover of Kenneth Anger's salacious 1984 book *Hollywood Babylon II*. The era of her life where she made *Boom!* and *Zee & Co.* is certainly one where her excesses with Burton, in terms of alcohol, jewellery and jet-set lifestyle, were dominating her star image. As Walker writes, '[i]n her case life does not ape art, but transfuses it. She magnifies any film she makes simply by being in it' (1966: 132). The qualities that most transfuse Taylor's performance in *Zee & Co.* are that of excess and primal ferocity: 'Conditioned by the marriage-divorce syndrome of stardom, the public saw her as a woman of instinct, without any driving passion to put her life in order: the messes must just be cleared up as she goes along' (137). An attempt to apply John O. Thompson's commutation test to the performance of Taylor as Zee, where we might try to imagine another actor playing the role, proves an insurmountable challenge (1991: 186). The press book for the film states, 'When producer Elliott Kastner and his partners Alan Ladd Jr and Jay Kanter read Edna O'Brien's original screenplay, "Zee & Co.", they recognised the role of Zee as perfect for Elizabeth Taylor'. Taylor brings passion, instability and indefatigable desperation to cling on to her husband by doing anything to come between him and his lover. This pitch of romantic ferocity resonates with Walker's comment about Taylor's 'messes': there is no evidence that Zee is concerned to deal with the problems in her marriage, but simply to prevent anyone else from having her husband.

The film begins with credits showing Zee and Robert playing table tennis which, in slow motion, show Taylor looking wildly excited, and running and jumping enthusiastically. Zee announces gleefully that she has beaten Robert, and he chases her around the flat and into the bedroom, as she squeals with hilarity. The next shot is of her surveying her wardrobe, with loud 1970s rock music playing and Zee moving vaguely in time with the rhythm. Everything looks off-kilter for Taylor: the clothes are seventies mini-skirts and bohemian silks, her body moves are stilted and not suited to the music, and she twirls her scarf as if aping the moves of someone more casual or cool. Zee refuses to turn down the volume of her music, and insists that Robert wear the shirt she bought for him because she loves him in bright colours. She is demonstrating her intense feelings for him as well as her need to control him. At the party that night, however, Robert sees Stella, a cool, reserved blonde in a refined silver sheath dress. Observing them, Zee says she thinks Stella looks like a bag of bones, and her competitive instincts are aroused. The host tells Zee that Stella has said she tends to cry when something nice happens, and Zee pulls a face as if she is vomiting and exclaims, 'yurk'. The next day she visits Stella in her dress shop, staging a confrontation with her rival. She picks at Stella's lunch box, saying, 'I love to eat between meals', and says she's proud of her figure because 'men don't like skinny women'. She insists on buying a dress that has been promised to somebody else, even though it does not fit her, and asserts how wonderful she and Robert get along in a far-from-subtle warning to Stella: 'we mustn't take what isn't ours, must we' (see Plate 8).

Zee puts on little girl voices and paws Robert like a child. Robert and Zee fight and taunt each other: he calls her a slut, and she says he loves it; he says she can't keep the love of a man, and she calls him a son of a bitch. Returning home early from a trip to Spain so that she can surprise Robert and Stella together, Zee orchestrates an excruciating confrontation where, upon hearing that Stella has twin boys, she conjures up the image of a woman breastfeeding twins, discussing milk and maternity in order to undermine Stella's sexual appeal to Robert. The dinner becomes so unbearable that Robert leaves, and Zee and Stella actually begin to talk to each other and have a laugh. They confide that they were each expelled from school, and so begins the insinuation that Stella has a bisexual past.

Zee describes Stella as 'soulful slob' as she oozes contempt, and imitates her perfectly when she says that 'she's always a little out of breath and sees beauty in everything … especially in shit'. The contrast between Zee and Stella is extreme. Stella weeps, saying she is frightened, while Zee provokes Robert to hit her to get her to confess where she has hidden his car. Zee predicts how his future with Stella will go: she will want more children, and he'll notice her smelly armpits, and, as she says to Stella herself in an abusive phone call, 'listening is dull in the sack'. She refers to Stella's 'chicken-leg arms' and calls her a bitch. This is Taylor portraying a messy, vindictive and manipulative wife, who is crashing cars one minute and weeping into her whisky the next. She even does an impersonation of Michael Caine to his character's face! It is unsurprising when Zee attempts suicide in their bathroom, slashing her wrists in the bath, but more surprising when she asks Stella to come and visit her in hospital. She becomes an unconvincing philosopher of life, remarking to Stella that it is funny how one's happiness comes at the expense of someone else. And, following this apparent intimacy, Stella confides that she was expelled from school because she fell in love with one of the nuns, and Zee explains that she was expelled for eating the 'altar breads' before they had been blessed. Zee then begins a litany of tearful revelations, which appeals to Stella, and their relationship appears to shift to one of mutual understanding and sympathy. Zee has begun her next campaign, to steal Stella away from Robert for herself – albeit temporarily. She succeeds in driving a wedge between Stella and Robert, and while Robert is in bed with his secretary, Zee seduces Stella based on the confession of her love for the nun, and by coaxing her into thinking about other women she might have been attracted to, before embracing her. We never actually see them kiss: this may have been a step too far for the 'lustily heterosexual' Taylor. Robert eventually arrives at the apartment he and Stella have rented, to be let in by Zee, who makes it clear that she has slept with Stella. As Zee instructs Robert to leave with her, saying, 'it has been one hell of a day', the film ends with still shots of the three players frozen in this moment. Unclear of who Robert is going to stay with, Zee has proven herself to be how she described: 'I may be the worst thing in the world but I carry it in front where you can see it'.

Experiencing Taylor as Zee is like seeing Maggie the Cat twenty years after *Cat on a Hot Tin Roof* (Richard Brooks 1958), having managed to 'just stay on' the roof as she planned. The Taylor persona does indeed 'transfuse' every utterance and mannerism, as Walker suggests. There is a combination of vitriol, excess and vulgarity. Her childish squeals and bouncy enthusiasms do not convey a childlike innocence but rather an infantile petulance: a 'little girl' act, as Robert calls it, which is entirely consistent with the 'spoilt princess' facet of her star persona, present from her days as a child of the studios, educated on the MGM lot (Theroux 2005: 24). J. Randy Taraborrelli writes how, at a private screening of the film, while watching herself, Elizabeth howled with laughter, 'sometimes putting her hands up to her face or whispering something to Richard' (2006: 264). This image, of Taylor howling at Zee behaving monstrously, is a perfect confluence of star and character, and indicative of the resilience and extravagance that characterized Taylor's stardom at that time. Comparison with Stella does not diminish Zee, but rather enables her to draw on all her resources and limitless energies to ensure that she emerges the victor.

'A ruddy great lust-box': Shelley Winters as Ruby

Although only appearing in three scenes, Ruby is the standout character in *Alfie*: her interest in Alfie Elkins (Michael Caine) is sex, and she is in the driving seat. She's wealthy, she calls him baby, and he's overwhelmed by her 'lovely condition'. As he holds her firmly and runs his hands over her, this 'condition' is plainly one of being 'well covered', and he shows great appreciation for her voluptuous body. Alfie says, 'She's a mature woman – when she gets hold of ya, you can feel a lifetime of experience in her hands'; and with a salacious close-up on her cleavage, Alfie opines that he has a good idea of what her two husbands died of. He calls her 'a little sex pot'; she clicks her fingers and commands 'bedroom!' When he decides to settle down with Ruby, however, and have no more of 'these young birds', Alfie finds that he has been thrown over for another man, whom he finds in Ruby's bed. When he challenges Ruby to say what he's got that Alfie hasn't, 'apart from long hair', Ruby looks him dead in the eye and says, 'He's younger than you are, you got it?' (see Plate 9).

Ruby's body and sexuality feature prominently in the publicity for the film, and were one of the two main preoccupations of the censors, the other being the film's abortion scene. Having already battled with the censors as a play, Anthony Aldgate and James Robertson describe how 'By the time, then, that the film script for *Alfie* landed in the BBFC's lap, in April 1965, it had been through the censorship treadmill already and shorn of several vital elements' (2005: 149). A BBFC script reader thought it had to carry an X certificate 'because of the abortion and the grossness of some of the sex talk'. The reader asserted that 'we really do not feel that the sex is dragged in to titillate the idle mind' and concluded that 'there is a case for being as lenient as possible' (cited in Aldgate and Robertson 2005: 149). Trevelyan still had some specific comments: 'Ruby's costumes should be adequate and not transparent', Alfie and Ruby's love-making 'should not be too extravagant', and 'We are not too happy about the phrase "lust-box". If you make use of this I think that you should have an alternative available' (cited in Aldgate and Robertson 2005: 150–1).

The press book features a photograph of Ruby, with the byline 'A Spicy Seduction and the question is who is seducing whom?' and an article focusing on the 'adult' nature of Winters's filmography, titled 'Academy Award Winner Shelley Winters makes films her daughter can't see'. Winters claims that, in *Alfie*, 'All I do is wear a nightgown and hop in and out of bed'.

Ruby is a highlight of feminine power in the film, which is otherwise a relentless litany of women's grim experiences. Ruby's rebuff makes Alfie think: 'Who'd have thought a ruddy great lust-box like her would find her way into anybody's feelings?' (The phrase clearly did survive.) Alfie is affected by Ruby's 'beautiful condition', suggesting that she has a great physique, personality and energy. The character of Ruby was consistent with Winters's star persona, but also an important step in its development. As Charlotte Haze in *Lolita* (Stanley Kubrick 1962), Winters plays a woman who is, in Winters's words, 'dumb and cunning, silly, sad, sexy, and bizarre, and totally American and human' (Winters 1989: 342). Without the resignation of Alice Aisgill, or the pride of Karen Stone, Charlotte displays her yearning for love as well as her availability. Winters was a highly successful star of Hollywood and Broadway, as well as a dedicated character actress and student of the Method. Nominated for Best Actress for her role as Alice Tripp in *A Place in the Sun*, and winning Best Supporting Actress for Petronella Van Daan in *The Diary of Anne Frank* (George Stevens 1959), in many ways Winters was in her prime at the time of *Lolita*, aged forty-two. Unlike Signoret and Leigh, who came to stand for the challenges and decline of pleasure in middle-age, or Taylor, who lived a dangerous slalom between indulgence and recovery, Winters's image developed into a site of unexpected and unruly pleasures. As James Morrison describes, in the 1970s, in roles like Belle Rosen in *The Poseidon Adventure* (Ronald Neame 1972), 'Winters takes on a new Dionysian energy, revelling joyously in camp performance and eschewing any taint of shame' (2010: 121). The redoubtably amorous Ruby was a character for Winters to relish as a blueprint for those to come. Winters embodied a full-figured woman who loved and lived, and who enjoyed eating, drinking and sex, as set out in her two substantial memoirs.

Conclusion

Sue Harper writes how 'the raw material of women's bodies and experiences can be variously shaped by the film industry', as she considers 'the relative strengths and weaknesses of women as players in the cultural game' (2000: 1). The women in this chapter – the characters and the stars – are winners and losers in the cultural game of gendered ageing. The discourses of stardom, beauty and sexual desirability for women have always been linked to youth and, in the 1960s and 1970s, these mature stars were having to negotiate their advancing years both on and off screen. In some ways, their very presence as middle-aged women demystifies the celestial beings that were the young Signoret, Leigh and Taylor, but Winters only got better with age. If Signoret stands for ageing as neglect, and Leigh as suffering, then Taylor is indulgence and Winters is celebration. This selection of films, taken together, offers an array of the challenges presented by women who are no longer young but not yet old, and the characters played by these actors mesh with their star personas in revealing and indisputable ways.

Notes

1   The press books referred to in this chapter are stored on microfiche at the British Film Institute.

2   Geoffrey Macnab writes, 'In British films of the period, the sophisticated older woman was invariably continental' (2000: 153).

References

Aldgate, A. and J. C. Robertson (2005), *Censorship in Theatre and Cinema*, Edinburgh: Edinburgh University Press.
Anger, K. (1984), *Hollywood Babylon II*, New York: Dutton.
Austin, G. (2003), *Stars in Modern French Film*, London: Arnold.

Barker, F. (1962), 'A Warning to Women … and a Triumph for Vivien Leigh', *The Evening News and Star Review*, 16 February.

Bolton, L. (2018), 'Film Performance and Vivien Leigh: From Starlet to Scarlett, and Blanche Dubois to Mrs Stone', in K. Dorney and M. Gale (eds), *Vivien Leigh: Actress and Icon*, 94–117, Manchester: Manchester University Press.

Dewe Mathews, T. (1994), *Censored*, London: Chatto & Windus.

Hargreaves, T. (2012), 'The Trevelyan Years: British Censorship and 1960s Cinema', in E. Lamberti (ed), with J. Green, D. Hyman, C. Lapper, and K. Myers, *Behind the Scenes at the BBFC: Film Classification from the Silver Screen to the Digital Age*, 53–68, London: Palgrave Macmillan, British Film Institute.

Harper, S. (2000), *Women in British Cinema: Mad, Bad and Dangerous to Know*, London: Continuum.

Harrison, P. S. (1919–1962), *Harrison's Reports and Film Reviews*.

Hayward, S. (1995), 'Simone Signoret 1921–1985: the Star as Sign – the Sign as Scar', in D. Knight and J. Still (eds), *Women and Representation*, Nottingham: WIF Publications.

Hayward, S. (2004), *Simone Signoret: The Star as Cultural Sign*, London: Continuum.

Macnab, G. (2000), *Searching for Stars: Stardom and Screen Acting in British Cinema*, London: Cassell.

Morrison, J. (2010), 'Shelley Winters: Camp, Abjection, and the Ageing Star', in J. Morrison (ed), *Hollywood Reborn: Movie Stars of the 1970s*, 120–37, New Brunswick, New Jersey: Rutgers University Press.

'The Roman Spring of Mrs Stone' (1961), *Harrison's Reports*, 25 November: 186.

Sandlin, M. (2020), '*Room at the Top*', *Cineaste*, Summer: 68–9.

Signoret, S. (1979), *Nostalgia Isn't What It Used to Be*, London: Grafton.

Spoto, D. (1995), *Elizabeth Taylor*, New York: HarperCollins.

Taraborrelli, J. R. (2006), *Elizabeth*, London: Pan Books.

Theroux, P. (2005), *Two Stars*, London: Penguin.

Thompson, J. O. (1991), 'Screen Acting and the Commutation Test', in C. Gledhill (ed), *Stardom: Industry of Desire*, 183–97, Abingdon, Oxon: Routledge.

Vickers, H. (1988), *Vivien Leigh*, London: Pan Books.

Walker, A. (1962), 'Such Courage, Miss Leigh, – and What a Triumph!', *London Evening Standard*, 16 February.

Walker, A. (1966), *The Celluloid Sacrifice: Aspects of Sex in the Movies*, London: Michael Joseph.

Walker, A. (1974), *Stardom: The Hollywood Phenomenon*, Middlesex, England: Penguin.

White, S. (2010), 'Marlon Brando: Actor, Star, Liar', in R. Barton Palmer (ed), *Larger Than Life: Movie Stars of the 1950s*, 165–83, New Brunswick, New Jersey: Rutgers University Press.

Williams, T. (1976), *Memoirs*, London: W.H. Allen.

Winters, S. (1989), *Shelley II: The Middle of My Century*, New York: Simon & Schuster.

10

Censoring Carmilla:

Lesbian Vampires in Hammer Horror

Claire Henry

On 1 July 1970, the British Board of Film Censors (BBFC) moved to accommodate the stronger film content of the era by increasing the age limit for the X certificate from 16 to 18 ('Cineguide' 1970). Hammer had long exploited the X certificate, illustrated by the titles and marketing for their mid-1950s hits, *The Quatermass Xperiment* (Val Guest 1955) and *X the Unknown* (Leslie Norman 1956). Indeed, Hammer's place in the market – particularly their reputation and success in the horror genre – was built on the shifts in censorship, exhibition and the composition of British film audiences that were signalled by the introduction of the original X certificate (Hutchings 1993: 40). A new level of exploitation in British horror cinema 'unimaginable only five years before' was encouraged by the new X certificate (Rigby 2004: 197), and Hammer again capitalized on this change. The first film in their 'lesbian vampire' cycle, *The Vampire Lovers* (Roy Ward Baker), led the way in September 1970, initiating the so-called Karnstein trilogy (named for the family of vampire characters). The trilogy was completed in 1971 with *Lust for a Vampire* (Jimmy Sangster) and *Twins of Evil* (John Hough). Known for introducing lesbianism and increased nudity and sexual content to Hammer's vampire films, these films took advantage of censorial permissiveness and the broader 'permissive moment' of the long 1960s (Weeks 2017: 272–301) to make their mark and temporarily revitalize Hammer's horror slate before the studio's decline mid-decade.

This chapter explores how Hammer horror, and specifically their lesbian vampire cycle, was impacted by the new X certificate at the start of the 1970s. I trace how the abovementioned films were shaped by their encounters with the British censors at script stage or after completion, examining the notes and correspondence of the censors and the cuts or changes required for the granting of an X certificate. The BBFC raised typical concerns about the combination of sex and violence in their treatment of these Hammer films, but a closer look reveals it was lesbianism that truly crossed the line. While accounts of British censorship and horror cinema tend to highlight the censors' efforts to block or dilute the genre's horrific nature (e.g. Kermode 2002: 13; Petley 2014: 142), what was at stake in these Hammer horrors was the lesbian content. I argue that the British censors limited such content in tandem with the studio tempering the foregrounded performative lesbian elements with heterosexual sex and romance, which together curtailed the lesbianism of the 'lesbian vampire' subgenre.[1] Barbara Creed asserts that 'it is the sexual desires of the lesbian vampire that render her the most abject of all vampire monsters' (1993: 72), and this is confirmed in the treatment of those films by Hammer and the BBFC. The convergence of this censorship moment with this point in Hammer's history shaped the lesbian vampire film subgenre in an immediate and long-term way, towards an eroticized yet campy aesthetic, overlaying narratives of heteropatriarchal anxiety in which lesbianism is punished and constrained.

Histories of British cinema often highlight censorship's restrictive or destructive impact on the horror genre. Without denying censorship's repressive impact on horror and its audiences, it is worth considering how the ongoing negotiations between horror producers and the BBFC shaped the genre's peaks, troughs and trends. In this chapter, the censorship process is recognized as a key force in determining the existence and specific characteristics of Hammer's influential lesbian vampire cycle. While acknowledging the importance of the period's broader cultural context – in particular, the tipping point between the 1960s 'sexual revolution' and the rise of second-wave feminism – I look more closely at how these films are a product of their censorship context. Censorship has had a historically significant role in shaping public understanding of lesbianism, from the legend that Queen Victoria claimed lesbianism could not exist (when indeed the legislative omission pointed to a broader denial of its existence) to how '[t]he publicity surrounding the 1928 obscenity trial of [Radclyffe Hall's novel] *The Well of Loneliness* has been regarded as crucial in generating a new public awareness of lesbianism' (Jennings 2007: 7). In cinema, the BBFC had encountered the occasional foreign title with lesbian themes, such as the literary/play adaptations *Olivia* (Jacqueline Audry 1952), *The Loudest Whisper* (*The Children's Hour*, William Wyler 1961), *The Fox* (Mark Rydell

1967), *The Killing of Sister George* (Robert Aldrich 1968) and *Therese and Isabelle* (Radley Metzger 1968), which tended to punish their lesbian characters with suicide or other tragic ends. Each of these titles received an X certificate, setting a precedent for the cycle of lesbian vampire films that shortly followed, but the more explicit representation of lesbianism that also combined nudity and vampirism presented new challenges for the BBFC. Hammer's direction in the early 1970s (including the increased nudity, lesbian themes and campy humour) was channelled through the censorship system, its values and its negotiations over each of their productions.

Hammer and the BBFC

Hammer's horror films frequently faced resistance from the BBFC throughout their relationship from the mid-1950s. For David Pirie, the BBFC files reveal that during John Trevelyan's tenure as Board secretary (1958–71), the British censor's office was 'utterly disgusted and enraged by the British horror films, constantly waging a frantic and hysterical campaign against them, with most of the examiners secretly trying to stop them being made at all' (2008: 37). John Springhall highlights the BBFC's remarks on Jimmy Sangster's script for *The Curse of Frankenstein* (Terence Fisher 1957) as indicative of the censors' broader attitude to horror in the period, such as an examiner's comment:

> This is infinitely more disgusting than the first script [by Milton Subotsky], in fact, *really evil*. A lip-smacking relish for mutilated corpses, repulsive dismembered hands and eyeballs removed from the head, alternates with gratuitous examples of sadism and lust. While the general outline of the story cannot be rejected for 'X', a great many details will have to be modified or eliminated.
>
> (Cited in Springhall 2009: 17)

Another BBFC examiner similarly objected to the script, suggesting that 'we should hold out no hope of passing a film based on this script' and that Hammer should have it re-written and re-submitted (cited in Springhall 2009: 17). A third examiner commented that 'the writer of this script seems to think that the X category is a depository for sewage' (cited in Pirie 2008: 38). Despite this condemnation at script stage, the film eventually received an X certificate and remained largely intact, which Springhall credits to 'Anthony Hinds' diplomatic and negotiating skills as a Hammer producer' (2009: 17).

One of the recurring points of tension between Hammer and the BBFC was the taboo against combining eroticism and violence. Although the broader renaissance of the horror genre from the late 1950s (in Italian, Spanish, American and British cinema) 'exploited a general relaxation of censorship through an increased explicitness in their representations of sex and violence' (Hutchings 1993: 20), Hammer still needed to walk a fine line through the 1960s. For example:

> when presented with the script of *Dracula Has Risen from the Grave* (1968), Trevelyan informed Hammer that the Board would be concerned about 'any close association between blood-sucking and sex' (cited in Kinsey, 2007: 73), while of *Taste the Blood of Dracula* (1970) he observed that 'I have always advised keeping vampirism and sex apart' (cited in Kinsey, 2007: 192).
>
> (Petley 2014: 143)

As the BBFC's subsequent treatment of lesbian vampire films indicates, this taboo on the combination of sex and violence continued into the 1970s and beyond, as did the taboo on explicit representations of lesbian desire.

Vamping up Hammer's Horror Slate

Hammer's lesbian vampire cycle coincided with the beginning of a general decline of British horror in the period and a perceived downturn in the quality of Hammer's productions (Barnett 2022: 23; Rigby 2004: 201). Throughout the long 1960s, 'British horror was one of the most commercially successful areas of British cinema' and Hammer Films was the most prolific of horror producers (Hutchings 1993: 1). However, in his 1973 book, Pirie's criticism of Hammer productions suggested that horror was coming to the end of a generic cycle, and he bemoaned the shift away from traditional Hammer fare: 'The dark, over-laden allusiveness is being replaced more and more by banal sexual antics, the charged hermetic atmosphere by heavy-handed humour, the solid narrative structure by half-understood experimentation' (165). Hammer producer Anthony Hinds was similarly not in favour of Hammer exploiting the relaxed censorship of the 1970s:

> I did not like the change that came after I left when it was thought that the films would have increased audience appeal by making them soft-porn shows. I thought the originals were sexy enough by implication without having to resort to tired music hall tricks ... Jim Carreras thought this was great. He was a showman. He told me, 'God, you can do anything now.' I thought, 'Well, I'm not sure that doing everything is what it's all about'.
> (Cited in Hearn and Barnes [1997] 2007: 132)

David Sanjek similarly suggests that the permissiveness of the censorship context contributed the horror genre's decline because filmmakers took a 'heavy-handed' approach: 'Rather than reanimating the horror genre, many individuals merely grafted overt sexual material with liberal doses of gore to a preexistant framework' (1991–92: 115). Sanjek characterizes the state of British horror cinema in the post-1968 period as 'moribund' and the attempts to resuscitate it as 'increasingly anxious and often frantic' (1991–92: 112). In what might be considered the final chapter of this scramble to sustain their approach, executive Michael Carreras was trying to raise finance for the unrealized Hammer film *Vampirella* as the company's last horror film, *To the Devil a Daughter* (Peter Sykes 1976), was being made (Springhall 2009: 19). The title's portmanteau of 'vampire' and 'Barbarella' is indicative of the genre intersection and the market that Hammer was targeting in their sunset period, and the casting of underage Nastassja Kinski in a heavily eroticized role in *To the Devil a Daughter* similarly points to the lengths of their exploitation strategies.

While the quality of Hammer horror may have deteriorated, the quantity had not yet declined; 1971 was Hammer's peak year of production with ten films completed in twelve months (Eyles, Adkinson, and Fry [1973] 1984: 11). The vampire, 'the most consistently filmed and financially remunerative character in Hammer's horror pantheon' (Sanjek 1991–92: 116), continued to be popular, appearing in at least ten films from 1968 to 1975. By the end of the 1960s, Dracula had almost been drained and new ideas were needed. Known as a 'trilogy', the 'Karnstein trilogy' films in fact followed the model of a cycle. In generating its prolific output, Hammer relied on this model of the horror film genre used by Universal in the 1930s: 'the company established various monsters (Dracula, Frankenstein, the Wolfman, the Mummy) within cycles of films, with their destruction and subsequent reconstitution built into a particular generic pattern that commanded the movement from one film to another' (Hutchings 1993: 98).

The first film of the cycle, *The Vampire Lovers*, sees the Countess Karnstein 'beheaded in a chapel', thereby 'reestablishing the authority of the church and state threatened by a lesbian vampire' (Holte 1999: 165–6); in *Lust for a Vampire*, she is revived forty years later only to be punished for her vampiric and sexual transgressions by a mob of villagers who set the castle on fire; and in *Twins of Evil*, the revived Countess Karnstein is again destroyed, this time by a group of male witch hunters called the Brotherhood. Along with the way that 'Hammer proceeded gratuitously to augment the sexual dimension of the vampire's powers' in the later films of the Dracula cycle, and updated the setting of its final two instalments to the twentieth century, Sanjek describes the introduction of lesbian and female antagonists in the Karnstein trilogy as an 'equally unsatisfying attempt to renovate the vampire narrative' (1991–2: 117). However, *The Vampire*

Lovers was commercially successful and kicked off a new cycle of 'lesbian vampire' films at Hammer and beyond.

Joseph Sheridan Le Fanu's 1871 novella *Carmilla* was the source text for a series of screenplays by Tudor Gates that Hammer used to reinvigorate their vampire slate. Film adaptations of *Carmilla* commonly 'emphasize the seductive eroticism of the original, often making the lesbian elements of the novella the films' focus' (Holte 1999: 166). However, the extent to which this can be shown onscreen has varied. There were limitations on the representation of lesbianism in the 1930s that affected *Dracula's Daughter* (Lambert Hillyer 1936), even as the eroticism of the female vampire was being exploited, as the screenwriter John L. Balderston was aware: 'The use of a female Vampire instead of male gives us the chance to play up SEX and CRUELTY legitimately ... We profit by making Dracula's Daughter amorous of her victims ... The seduction of young men will be tolerated, whereas we had to eliminate seduction of girls from the original as obviously censorable' (cited in Skal 1993: 197). The model Lili (Nan Gray) could not be naked in her lesbian scene with Countess Zaleska (Gloria Holden) in 1936, but nudity was a hallmark of Hammer's later Carmilla adaptations as more liberal censorship in the 1970s gave filmmakers licence to further 'play up SEX and CRUELTY legitimately'. Lesbian sexuality featured in vampire films from the early 1960s – in films such as *Et Mourir de Plaisir* (*Blood and Roses*, Roger Vadim 1961) and *Il mostro dell'opera* (*The Vampire of the Opera*, Renato Polselli 1964) – but the combination became more explicit in the early 1970s' golden era of lesbian vampire films. As Barry Forshaw points out, for *Et Mourir de Plaisir*: 'censorship had not yet relaxed to the extent that the erotic interaction between Vadim's beautiful stars Elsa Martinelli and his then-wife Annette Vadim (née Stroyberg) could be presented in the graphic fashion that Baker was to utilise in his unblushing version [*The Vampire Lovers*]' (2013: 70). Each Carmilla film is a product of its production and censorship context (as well as its broader social and cultural conditions), and while the Karnstein trilogy was facilitated by the permissiveness of the era, the lesbian content was still significantly constrained, as an examination of each film attests.

The Vampire Lovers

As befitting the vampire genre, *The Vampire Lovers* contains key moments of violence: it is bookended by decapitations of female vampires and features General von Spielsdorf (Peter Cushing) putting a wooden stake in Carmilla/ Marcilla's (Ingrid Pitt) heart. However, the film was distinguished less by its violence than by its lesbian content and nudity, which includes a scene between Carmilla and Laura (Pippa Steel) in which she kisses her cheek, lips and breast. For co-producer Michael Style, 'lots of pretty girls, a certain amount of sex' were key ingredients of a good horror film alongside 'a lot of murders, a lot of blood', and a good hero and villain (cited in Maxford 2019: 519). Star Ingrid Pitt recognized the 'strong sexual element' in Le Fanu's *Carmilla* too and felt that 'the director, Roy Ward Baker, really made it work – although the producers were two lascivious little chaps' (cited in Forshaw 2013: 187). Gates capitalized on the shifting censorship context by foregrounding lesbian content and nudity: 'Censorship was in rapid decline ... [and this] allowed me to create the first nude, lesbian vampires, and a picture I little thought at the time would be another cult success' (cited in Maxford 2019: 825). Director Roy Ward Baker was cautious about the script's amplification of lesbianism:

> The producers, Harry Fine and Michael Style, were fired with enthusiasm for the script which Tudor Gates had written .... It gradually became apparent that they were even more excited by the possibilities generated by having female vampires and claimed they had uncovered an underlying theme in the original story, which Le Fanu had either discreetly suppressed or perhaps didn't even realize was there. By tradition, when a vampire bites someone, the victim automatically becomes a vampire too. When Carmilla bites a female victim she not only becomes a vampire – but also a lesbian. This one was full of traps for the unwary.
>
> (Cited in Maxford 2019: 825)

The BBFC vetted the submitted script and expressed concerns about the lesbian content and what Trevelyan described as its 'dangerous cocktail' of sex and horror. In a five-page letter to Fine (dated 26 January 1970), Trevelyan warned: 'it contains a lot of material that we would be unhappy about even with an X at eighteen ... I want you to take my comments seriously since if you do not we are likely to have on our hands a film that we cannot pass for exhibition in this country' (cited in Hearn and Barnes [1997] 2007: 136; see also Maxford 2019: 826). He reminded Hammer that '[o]ur policy is that we have always been strongly against a close association between horror and sex, especially when horror includes sadism and brutality' (cited in Kinsey 2007: 169). Of particular concern were scenes depicting 'punctured breasts' and 'a dream orgasm ending in a scream': 'I do not like this at all' (Trevelyan cited in Hearn and Barnes [1997] 2007: 137).

The BBFC's treatment of *The Vampire Lovers* echoed – and was informed by – their recent decision about lesbians and their orgasms in *The Killing of Sister George*.[2] In his letter to Fine, Trevelyan also 'reminded Hammer to be cautious about their portrayal of lesbianism in light of the Board's "firm treatment" of Robert Aldrich's *The Killing of Sister George* the previous year' (Hearn and Barnes [1997] 2007: 137). The BBFC had decided that *The Killing of Sister George*'s 'lesbian love scene must be entirely removed' (Examiner's note 1969), and when distributor Cinerama queried the

BBFC on the removal of facial expressions (Cinerama 1969), Trevelyan's reply noted, 'Huge fuss about this film, BBFC very worried about orgasm' (Trevelyan 1969). Interestingly, when *Therese and Isabelle* – 'which showed more explicit lesbian sex-scenes than we had seen before, more explicit even than the scene in *The Killing of Sister George*' (Trevelyan 1973: 118) – received an X certificate later that year (in July 1969), Trevelyan recalls: 'We felt obliged to cut the more explicit sex-scenes but we passed more than we had in previous films'. Trevelyan's account notes that the Board 'thought it a film of some quality and sincerity', which perhaps explains their more generous treatment of this film in comparison to films that struck them as more exploitative, or which combined sex with horror. *The Vampire Lovers*' boundary-pushing nature is underscored by the fact that Trevelyan sent a confidential note to James Carreras three days after his letter to Fine, asking Carreras to use his 'personal influence' over producers Fine and Style to 'keep this film within reasonable grounds' (cited in Hearn and Barnes [1997] 2007: 137). Despite the concerns raised about the script (after the film had already started production on 19 January 1970), the film was ultimately released with an X certificate.

The BBFC's file notes on *The Vampire Lovers* indicate a double standard in how British film censors dealt with male and female sexual pleasure, and with gay and lesbian behaviour, in the 1970s (Barber 2009: 356). There were debates about the decapitation scene, but as an examiner reflected in 1984 (when the rating was reviewed for video release), 'What was perhaps the concern behind the 18 decision in 1970 was the regular unveiling of female breasts and here particularly the strong lesbian undercurrent' (Examiner's note 1984). As Barber observes, the examiner's notes from 1970 display a striking level of disgust at the film's lesbian content (2009: 356).

> Admittedly, we must allow stronger meat in horror films for the new X. But the very overt emphasis on lesbianism here goes far beyond anything we have allowed, except the uncut version of *Sister George*. We are very concerned with the combination of nudity into horror. There are some very sick things here – Bathing scene where Carmilla is obviously about to make love to her [Emma] … we very much dislike this unnecessary episode. Carmilla bares Emma's breasts, lowers her face, breast and her head towards and down her body (off/screen). We see a close up of Emma's face with a very strange sensual expression. We do not think we can possibly accept this sequence. We do feel that this film without considerable cuts will set a very bad precedent. It has a very horrible atmosphere in parts. New X.
>
> (Examiner's note 1970a)

The examiner's comments in the 1984 video release forms present further evidence that '[i]t was clearly felt that material depicting female sexual pleasure went beyond the boundaries of acceptability' (Barber 2009: 356), particularly if such pleasure involved another woman: 'The relationship of Vampire to victim – given that it is based on biting, sucking and blood – how much more symbolic can one get – is full of passion and sex ... moreover were the Vampire a man, we would take decidedly more in the way of kissing and caressing' (2009: 356). It is apparent that the lesbian content was considered more objectionable than the frequent nudity. The permissiveness around nudity was thoroughly exploited to the effect that 'a few snippets of extra nudity were smuggled into the film after I had finished it' (Baker cited in Maxford 2019: 826). The lesbian content also seems to have been more offensive to the censors than the decapitation, though Hammer was required to address both: 'shorten the decapitation and remove the scene of Carmilla caressing and kissing Emma' (Examiner's note 1970b) (see Plate 10).

While *The Vampire Lovers* may display more fidelity to the source text than other loose adaptations of Le Fanu's *Carmilla*, the filmmakers tempered the foregrounded lesbianism with 'token heterosexuality' (Powell 2003: 117) and prominent male adversaries. As Anna Powell observes in her reading of the film, Carmilla's 'chief adversary, Baron Hartog [Douglas Wilmer] the vampire-slayer, is given considerable weight, and his voice-over dominates the framing story, replacing Laura's personal recollections' from the novella (2003: 116). Powell identifies several ways in which the film incorporates heterosexuality to offset the lesbian content, including adding a male romantic lead, introducing a heterosexual female vampire in the opening scene, having Carmilla kiss and bite male characters, and getting Emma (Madeline Smith) to enthuse about heterosexual romance (2003: 116–8). Sharon Russell has similarly observed how the heterosexual contact between the female vampires and male heroes that bookend the film works to counter the threat of lesbian relationships at its core: 'The kisses between Renton [Harvey Hall] and Carmilla are more openly passionate as is his fondling of her breast. In the opening, the female vampire's naked nipple touches the Baron's chest, but no such contact between the women is visualized' (1999: para. 7). This opening scene of the first 'Karnstein trilogy' film establishes its recipe of sex and horror (as well as the central conflict wherein male authority figures are both threatened and seduced by the 'lesbian vampire'), particularly in the emblematic moment when the crucifix around Baron Hartog's neck burns the beautiful blonde vampire's breast as she presses up against him, and then he decapitates her.

Emma, the second young female target of Carmilla's lesbian/vampiric seduction, regularly disavows lesbian desire, which works to frame Carmilla both as somewhat of a tragic or pitied figure and also as more predatory. During a bedroom scene with Carmilla, Emma asks: 'Don't you wish some handsome young man would come into your life?' Although Carmilla replies with a smirk, 'No. Neither do you I hope!', Emma's heterosexual leanings set up a tragic outcome for Carmilla; we know it is not going to end well for this possessive lesbian vampire, who then declares to Emma, 'I love you and I don't want anyone taking you away from me'. In a later scene, Emma calls Carmilla a friend, distinguishing their relationship from her new heterosexual romance ('It's not the same thing, it's different') and teasing her for being jealous. At this point in the film, Carmilla's character takes a voracious and violent turn, her role as a monster coming to the fore as she seduces another woman (who is found dead with a bitten neck the next morning) and then invades Emma's dreams and puts her under her sexually seductive spell. Carmilla visits Emma in her bedroom, kisses her, pulls her nightgown down to expose her breasts, lays her down on the bed and kisses her again, as Emma's eyes become wider. Following this scene, Emma wakes up screaming, with a bite mark on her breast (a detail that 'seems like an exploitational masterstroke' yet is also 'discreetly present' in the novella [Rigby 2004: 197]). The predatory aspects of Carmilla developed in this adaptation may partly be attributable to the casting of Ingrid Pitt. In contrast to the 'slender and wonderfully graceful' teenager of Le Fanu's novella, 'she's obviously older and with a much more aggressive physical presence (a "sexual juggernaut" according to one critic)' (Hutchings 1993: 161). There is also a shift in the adaptation due to the influence of the Dracula tradition on *The Vampire Lovers*, according to Russell, who suggests that 'the addition of elements associated with Dracula help demonize Carmilla' and 'reinforce the stereotype of the predatory lesbian' (1999: para. 7). Intertextually, this image is also reinforced by Ingrid Pitt's casting as another voracious killer of young women in *Countess Dracula* (Peter Sasdy 1971), released just four months after *The Vampire Lovers*.

Lust for a Vampire

Lust for a Vampire, the hastily made sequel to *The Vampire Lovers*, has received significantly less critical attention and favour within histories of Hammer horror. For instance, Marcus Hearn and Alan Barnes describe it as 'a cynical and depressing exercise' ([1997] 2007: 142), while Jonathan Rigby calls it 'an embarrassment in almost every way' and an 'unedifying spectacle of Hammer's new sex-and-horror formula descending to witless self-parody' (2004: 202). Although the film has been perceived as 'more humorous than frightening' ('Lust for a Vampire' 1971: 6) and 'significantly inferior' to *The Vampire Lovers* (Barnett 2022: 29), it shares with its predecessor similar elements of sex, horror, topless young women, lesbian vampiric eroticism and heterosexual scenes. Set forty years later, the plot has Carmilla (now played by Yutte Stensgaard), who goes by the name Mircalla, revived through the blood of a sacrificial virgin in Count and Countess Karnstein's satanic ritual. She then joins the student body of an all-girls boarding school, a setting that lends itself to redoubling the amount of female nudity. Author Richard Lestrange (Michael Johnson), who is at first sceptical about the existence of vampires (synonymous with lesbians), cheats his way into a job at the school and falls in love with Mircalla. In addition to various lesbian vampiric liaisons, Mircalla has sex with Lestrange and claims to requite his love. After the body of one of Mircalla's victims is discovered, the villagers burn down Karnstein Castle. Lestrange races to the castle to save Mircalla, who is killed by a fiery stake that falls from the ceiling. Janet (Suzanna Leigh), a junior teacher who was determined both to solve the mystery of the missing girl and to resist Mircalla's vampiric seduction, comes to Lestrange's aid at the film's conclusion, ending the film with the closure of another heterosexual union.

In line with the BBFC's concerns about lesbianism, horror and nudity evident in their treatment of *The Vampire Lovers*, lesbian vampiric seduction was similarly deemed unacceptable in *Lust for a Vampire*: 'A reel five scene wherein Mircalla would be seen to seduce – and then feed on – naked schoolgirl Amanda (Judy Matheson) was entirely removed upon the instruction of the BBFC' (Hearn and Barnes [1997] 2007: 142). Like the other two films in the Karnstein trilogy, *Lust for a Vampire* was granted an X certificate with cuts required. However, while subsequent video, DVD and Blu-ray releases of *The Vampire Lovers* (since 1987) and *Twins of Evil* (since 2002) have been rated 15, *Lust for a Vampire* retains an 18 rating (most recently assessed in 2008). The second Karnstein film further tested the gentlemen's agreement that Trevelyan recalled making with Carreras,

> in which we agreed that his company's horror films would avoid mixing sex with horror and would avoid scenes which people could regard as disgusting and revolting. The second part of this agreement has continued to the present day, but in an increasingly permissive age we modified our attitude to the introduction of sex. Nudity became quite common in these films, and by 1970 we even had lesbian vampires.
>
> (Trevelyan 1973: 165–6)

If sex had become increasingly permissive in the horror film, and nudity was common too, it seems the introduction of *lesbian* sex into horror is what crossed the censorial line.

Accompanying the film's liberal amount of nudity is a self-conscious attitude towards voyeurism. As the topless girls ready for bed at the boarding school, one comments on how schoolmaster Barton is always watching them, tsk-tsking his voyeurism while she and the other girls are on display for the voyeuristic viewer. This is heavily ironic and contributes to the camp nature of the film, as do the close-up shots of Janet's eyes as she resists seduction, and the point-of-view shots that position the viewer as the sexually desiring lesbian vampire character (both of which again emphasize voyeurism).[3] As Jay Daniel Thompson's reading against the grain identifies,

'While *Lust for a Vampire* can of course be read as a voyeuristic film for its viewers, it can also be read less obviously as an exposé and condemnation of voyeurism' or even 'a cultural mirror of patriarchal culture, one that directs the male gaze in upon itself' (2019: 127).

The exploitation levels of nudity were shocking to the actors on set, as Leigh recalled: 'They told me they were making two versions, an English version and a "Swedish" version .... One day I walked on to a set to do a scene and there were all these girls with hardly any clothes on. "Oh, my God!" I said. I froze! At lunch, Jimmy Carreras explained to me, "Oh, it's the *Swedish* version!"' (cited in Maxford 2019: 518). The excessive nudity was understood as unacceptable for the American release so 'an alternative non-topless version of Mircalla's dormitory seduction was shot showing her with a sheet wrapped around herself' (Maxford 2019: 518–9). For the British censors, attitudes to nudity had become significantly liberalized, as Trevelyan traces in his chapter on nudity in *What the Censor Saw* (1973: 93–104). He notes that in the first twenty years, the Board 'was wholly opposed to nudity or the representation of sex on the screen' and even when he joined the Board in 1951, 'there was a clear policy under which nudity was never allowed in a film' (1973: 94). In Trevelyan's latter years, the Board was working to keep 'a tidal wave of sex-obsession ... under reasonable control' and in this context, 'we became less worried about nudity, but we still had reservations about what is called "full frontal nudity" of either sex' (1973: 102). He explains how the Board reconsidered its policy as nudity moved through various genres and test cases to the point where 'Nudity on film is no longer a problem' (1973: 104).

As in *The Vampire Lovers*, lesbian desire is tempered with heterosexual sex and romance. Indeed, as Harry M. Benshoff points out, the very focus of the film is 'a heterosexual male's attraction to Carmilla, and his attempt to draw her away from (and cure her of) her monstrously queer desires' (1997: 192). Lestrange's infatuation with Carmilla/Mircalla drives the narrative, and the sex scene between them is the (cringeworthy) climax of the film. Benshoff's queer reading highlights the issue with this scene:

> Apparently Lestrange thinks that heterosexual intercourse will 'cure' a vampire much as it supposedly will 'cure' a lesbian. But Lestrange's 'love' fails to cure Mircalla, and she is soon back to vamping her fellow-students with renewed sexual vigor: willing maidens continue to fall ecstatically under her kiss ... Queer sexuality, lesbianism, and vampirism exist in the film in an unthinking blur of signification: all are evil forces that the heterosexual male must oppose.
>
> (Benshoff 1997: 195)

Lestrange embodies the way that Hammer's lesbian vampire films express 'a straight man's fear of women's sexuality' more than they express lesbian desire (1997). Nonetheless, the film contains potential for resistant readings and lesbian spectatorial pleasure due to its camp qualities, such as the humour generated by the misjudged choice of 'Strange Love' by Tracy on the soundtrack over the heterosexual sex scene, or Lestrange knocking on the door as Mircalla has sex with another woman and bites her. As Andrea Weiss has noted in her work on the lesbian vampire film, when a horror film falls flat, it leaves itself open to being appreciated as camp (2014: 33). Weiss and Benshoff have both pointed to how the pleasures of camp are available to queer viewers of these films that are underpinned by heterosexist and patriarchal ideologies (Benshoff 1997: 199–200; Weiss 2014: 33–4). The excesses of nudity and heterosexual compensation in *Lust for a Vampire* make the central conflict of male authority figures fighting the threat of the lesbian/vampire all the more explicit and pleasurably camp.

Twins of Evil

The final film in the Karnstein trilogy, *Twins of Evil*, marked something of a return to classic Hammer as it foregrounded a Manichean world view and patriarchal authority and limited the lesbian content. The only explicit lesbian vampiric moment occurs after Frieda (Madeleine Collinson) is turned into a vampire by Count Karnstein (Damien Thomas) and leans into a tied-up peasant girl, moving her lips close to the girl's lips, and then moving down to the girl's breast and biting with her new fangs. This is followed by a close-up of the Count's laughing face, still with blood on his own fangs, and it is in this moment arguably that the diegetic male voyeur gets the last laugh within the trilogy. Frieda is more libertine than lesbian, though lesbianism is suggested by underscoring the trilogy's blurring of lesbianism and narcissism. As Hutchings argues of *The Vampire Lovers* (and we see this again in *Lust for a Vampire*), scenes of 'exploitable female nudity' in which 'female characters look at each other in an erotically charged way' represent the female body as 'the site for an essentially narcissistic female desire which the film insistently equates with lesbianism (this narcissism underlined by the fact that the female characters are often dressed alike, in long white nightgowns)' (1993: 164). Of course the identical twins' matching translucent nightgowns in *Twins of Evil* further underscores the Karnstein trilogy's deployment of 'exploitable female nudity' and the equating of lesbianism with narcissism[4] (see Plates 11 and 12).

In addition to containing limited lesbian content, *Twins of Evil* also features less nudity than the other films in the trilogy (despite the starring roles for Madeleine and Mary Collinson, Playmates of the Month for *Playboy* in October 1970). Douglas Brode suggests that this can be read to mean that 'Hammer, like the world itself, was beginning to consider that sixties-era vision of "liberation" to be passé' (2014: 133). Other aspects of the film required cuts though, including heterosexual sexual content, as a BBFC examiner's report noted:

> Remove shots of Count Karnstein registering extreme sexual pleasure and of Gerta [Luan Peters] entering frame from the left and lying on him.
>
> In the episode in which a woman is prepared for human sacrifice, remove shots of hooded man dipping his thighs in blood, lifting this sheet and moving his hand towards her middle. Further reduction may be needed in this episode.
>
> (Examiner's note 1971)

In the BBFC video reports, '18 is confirmed by the strength of nudity', but another examiner notes that it is 'a safe 18, very mild stuff compared with what passes for horror these days', describing it as 'a good conscientious, straightforward Hammer horror, a genre being appreciated rather more nowadays than in its heyday' (Examiner's note 1987).

Carmilla's Legacy

Compared to the relative restraint of the violence in *Countess Dracula* and *Twins of Evil*, the excesses of Hammer's next film, *Vampire Circus* (Robert Young 1972), saw significant cuts under Stephen Murphy's tenure as BBFC secretary. Prior to production, Carreras anticipated censorship: 'If shot as scripted 50 per cent will end up on the cutting room floor' (cited in Hearn and Barnes [1997] 2007: 154). The decision on *The Vampire Lovers* appears to have been a benchmark for Murphy, as he required a number of cuts related to violence, sex and a decapitation scene: 'Finally we have a splendid decapitation of the Vampire with lots of blood oozing from the neck. Frankly by the time the mayhem had reached such proportions I was reduced to laughter, nevertheless I felt it my censor's duty to ask them to reduce the decapitation to a minimum' (Murphy 1971). Maintaining the taboo on combining eroticism and violence, Murphy instructed Hammer to address several shots of 'blood on breasts' in *The Satanic Rites of Dracula* (Alan Gibson 1974) before an X certificate was issued in April 1973 (Carreras 1973). While violence in Hammer's vampire films, and the combination of sex and violence, continued to raise concerns with the BBFC, lesbian content had been more effectively suppressed.

The way that the 'lesbian vampire' was shaped by the Hammer trilogy within its particular censorship context had a long-lasting influence on how lesbian vampires have been deployed in screen culture ever since.

Shortly after Hammer's cycle, José Ramón Larraz's *Vampyres* (1974) presented an even more explicit X certificate example of the lesbian vampire film that Rigby reads as indicative of how a 'new approach took advantage of the steady collapse of the BBFC's strictures against mixing sex with horror' (2004: 253). In *The Monstrous-Feminine*, Creed argued that '[t]he most persistent threat to the institution of heterosexuality represented in the horror film comes from the female vampire who preys on other women' (1993: 61). Just as the Hammer films (unconvincingly) allayed this threat with a heterosexual union at the end of the film, in *The Hunger* (Tony Scott 1983), 'the final scene re-establishes the vampire as a heterosexual, although the embrace between Sarah and the young blonde girl who looks remarkably like Miriam suggests that the desire to violate that taboo is always at hand' (Creed 1993: 71). The lesbian vampire subgenre has continued to attempt to counter the threat of the lesbian vampire, for example, in the way *Lesbian Vampire Killers* (Phil Claydon 2009) repeats 'the sniggering-schoolboy level of eroticism' (Rigby 2004: 202) of Hammer's productions and presents an awkward display of the heterosexual male characters' anxieties and voyeurism. In an epilogue to her original chapter on lesbian vampires, written twenty-five years later, Weiss comments of contemporary screen examples (such as the *Twilight* films and *True Blood* and *The Vampire Diaries* television series): 'I've found these next-generation vampires to be almost exclusively, even aggressively, heterosexual' (2014: 34). The synergy of Hammer's historical development, the censorship moment (including the timing of the new X certificate) and the broader cultural context worked to define the lesbian vampire in Hammer's early 1970s cycle, immortalizing her exploited yet constrained lesbianism for future cinematic representation.

Notes

1   Indeed, the 'lesbian' content is arguably already limited to performative lesbian elements structured by the male gaze, unrelated to the desires or representation of actual lesbian women. Nonetheless, Hammer's exploitative treatment of lesbianism and the censors' responses to 'lesbian vampire' films are significant in the historical development of lesbianism's cultural image, onscreen representation and censorship.

2   The author is grateful to Sian Barber for sharing her archival research notes from the BBFC files for this chapter (as the BBFC archive was closed during the Covid-19 pandemic). All BBFC file notes, unless otherwise cited, are quoted from Barber's notes. See also Barber (2009, 2011).

3   *The Velvet Vampire* (Stephanie Rothman 1971) presents another self-conscious thematization of voyeurism, as the bisexual vampire Diane LeFanu (Celeste

Yarnall) watches the guests to her home (a heterosexual couple) have sex through a one-way mirror. As Sanjek notes, *The Velvet Vampire* 'remains a rare film both for the genre and motion pictures in general as it was directed by a woman, Stephanie Rothman, and suggestively imports feminist concerns into the exploitation arena' (2019: 216).

4   It also mirrors the type of imagery seen on the covers of erotic occult magazines trending in this period. See 'Naked Witches' (2021).

References

Barber, S. (2009), '"Blue Is the Pervading Shade": Re-examining British Film Censorship in the 1970s', *Journal of British Cinema and Television*, 6 (3): 349–69.

Barber, S. (2011), *Censoring the 1970s: The BBFC and the Decade that Taste Forgot*, Newcastle upon Tyne: Cambridge Scholars.

Barnett, V. L. (2022), '*The Vampire Lovers* and Hammer's Post-1970 Production Strategy', *Journal of British Cinema and Television*, 19 (1): 22–44.

Benshoff, H. M. (1997), *Monsters in the Closet: Homosexuality and the Horror Film*, New York: Manchester University Press.

Brode, D. (2014), 'Heritage of Hammer: Carmilla Karnstein and the Sisterhood of Satan', in D. Brode and L. Deyneka (eds), *Dracula's Daughters: The Female Vampire on Film*, 115–37, Lanham, MD: The Scarecrow Press.

Carreras, M. (1973), Letter to Stephen Murphy, *The Satanic Rites of Dracula* files, 12 April, London: BBFC archive.

'Cineguide' (1970), *Buckinghamshire Examiner*, 3 July.

Cinerama (1969), Letter to BBFC, *The Killing of Sister George* files, 21 February, London: BBFC archive.

Creed, B. (1993), *The Monstrous-Feminine: Film, Feminism, Psychoanalysis*, London: Routledge.

Examiner's note (1969), *The Killing of Sister George* files, 31 January, London: BBFC archive.

Examiner's note (1970a), *The Vampire Lovers* files, 15 June, London: BBFC archive.

Examiner's note (1970b), *The Vampire Lovers* files, 30 June, London: BBFC archive.

Examiner's note (1971), *Twins of Evil* files, 27 July, London: BBFC archive.

Examiner's note (1984), *The Vampire Lovers* files, 8 November, London: BBFC archive.

Examiner's note (1987), *Twins of Evil* files, 9 March, London: BBFC archive.

Eyles, A., R. V. Adkinson and N. Fry ([1973] 1984), *The House of Horror: The Complete Story of Hammer Films*, second edn, London: Lorrimer Publishing.

Forshaw, B. (2013), *British Gothic Cinema*, New York: Palgrave Macmillan.

Hearn, M. and A. Barnes ([1997] 2007), *The Hammer Story: The Authorised History of Hammer Films*, London: Titan.

Holte, J. C. (1999), 'Not All Fangs Are Phallic: Female Film Vampires', *Journal of the Fantastic in the Arts*, 10 (2): 163–73.

Hutchings, P. (1993), *Hammer and Beyond: The British Horror Film*, Manchester: Manchester University Press.

Jennings, R. (2007), *Tomboys and Bachelor Girls: A Lesbian History of Post-war Britain 1945–71*, Manchester: Manchester University Press.

Kermode, M. (2002), 'The British Censors and Horror Cinema', in S. Chibnall and J. Petley (eds), *British Horror Cinema*, 10–22, London: Routledge.

Kinsey, W. (2007), *Hammer Films: The Elstree Studio Years*, Sheffield: Tomahawk Press.

'Lust for a Vampire' (1971), *Variety*, 15 September: 6.

Maxford, H. (2019), *Hammer Complete: The Films, the Personnel, the Company*, Jefferson, NC: McFarland & Company.

Murphy, S. (1971), File note, *Vampire Circus* files, 23 November, London: BBFC archive.

'Naked Witches and Sexy Satanists: The Erotic Occult Magazine Explosion' (2021), *The Reprobate*, 25 February. Available online: https://reprobatepress.com/2021/02/25/naked-witches-and-sexy-satanists-the-erotic-occult-magazine-explosion/ (accessed 7 March 2022).

Petley, J. (2014), 'Horror and the Censors', in H. M. Benshoff (ed.), *A Companion to the Horror Film*, 130–47, Chichester: Wiley Blackwell.

Pirie, D. (1973), *A Heritage of Horror: The English Gothic Cinema 1946–1972*, London: Gordon Fraser.

Pirie, D. (2008), *A New Heritage of Horror: The English Gothic Cinema*, London: I.B. Tauris.

Powell, A. (2003), *Psychoanalysis and Sovereignty in Popular Vampire Fictions*, Lewiston, New York: The Edwin Mellen Press.

Rigby, J. (2004), *English Gothic: A Century of Horror Cinema*, third edn, Richmond: Reynolds & Hearn.

Russell, S. (1999), 'The Influence of Dracula on the Lesbian Vampire Film', *Journal of Dracula Studies*, 1 (1). Available online: https://research.library.kutztown.edu/dracula-studies/vol1/iss1/6 (accessed 2 August 2021).

Sanjek, D. (1991–92), 'Twilight of the Monsters: The English Horror Film 1968–1975', *Film Criticism*, 16 (1–2): 111–26.

Sanjek, D. (2019), *Stories We Could Tell: Putting Words to American Popular Music*, eds. T. Attah, M. Duffett, and B. Halligan, London: Routledge.

Skal, D. J. (1993), *The Monster Show: A Cultural History of Horror*, New York: W.W. Norton.

Springhall, J. (2009), 'Hammer, House of Horror: The Making of a British Film Company, 1934 to 1979', *Historian*, 104: 14–19.

Thompson, J. D. (2019), 'Paranormal women: The "sexual revolution" and female sexuality in Hammer Studios' Karnstein Trilogy', in D. Caterine and J. W. Morehead (eds), *The Paranormal and Popular Culture: A Postmodern Religious Landscape*, 120–32, London: Routledge.

Thorne, T. (1997), *Countess Dracula: The Life and Times of Elisabeth Bathory, the Blood Countess*, London: Bloomsbury.

Trevelyan, J. (1969), Letter to Cinerama, *The Killing of Sister George* files, 24 February, London: BBFC archive.

Trevelyan, J. (1973), *What the Censor Saw*, London: Michael Joseph.

Weeks, J. (2017), *Sex, Politics and Society: The Regulation of Sexuality Since 1800*, fourth edn, London: Routledge.

Weiss, A. (2014), 'The Lesbian Vampire Film: A Subgenre of Horror', in D. Brode and L. Deyneka (eds), *Dracula's Daughters: The Female Vampire on Film*, 21–35, Lanham: The Scarecrow Press.

11

'The Horror Film to End All Horror Films':

10 Rillington Place and the British Board of Film Censors' Shifting Policy on True Crime

Tim Snelson

At the beginning of the 1970s, the British Board of Film Censors (BBFC) changed its long-standing policy on refusing to certify films that portrayed real crimes and court cases that happened within the past fifty years. BBFC secretary John Trevelyan (1958–71) – who was 'widely (though not entirely) regarded as a liberalising force in film censorship' (Hargreaves 2012: 54) – explained in his memoir, *What the Censor Saw* (1973: 161), that the policy was changed for *10 Rillington Place* (Richard Fleischer 1971), a British film based on the crimes and eventual conviction of London serial killer John Christie in the 1940s and 1950s. As this chapter will detail, however, this shift in policy was not reactive but the culmination of ten years of consultation and contention between the BBFC, their legal advisors, the Home Office, the BBC, the Independent Television Authority (ITA) and a variety of British and American filmmakers wishing to make a Christie film. The BBFC files for *10 Rillington Place* are valuable in mapping the gradual shift in policy as they contain correspondence not only for the 1971 film but also for a number of abandoned projects relating to the Christie case that date back to the start of the 1960s.

From 1961, the BBFC blocked numerous Christie projects by filmmakers, who ranged from *Thunderball* producer Kevin McClory to American production company CBS Films to the son of well-known British director Roy Boulting, despite their evolving strategies to sell their productions as explorations of the British justice system, serious psychological studies and indictments of mental health provision in Britain. For the BBFC, a Christie film raised ongoing issues, less of sensationalism and copycat crimes than of balancing their assumed ethical and moral roles in preserving the rights to free comment and criticism while protecting the industry and audiences. This included safeguarding families of victims and perpetrators from further distress, but also defending filmmakers from libel charges or other legal disputes. Trevelyan stressed in a letter to the production company Filmways that a film based on the Christie case might be 'regarded as a contempt of court, and involve film distributors and exhibitors (and possibly the producers) in court proceedings' (Trevelyan 1970b).[1] However, the ongoing pressure to tell the Christie story prompted Trevelyan, only part successfully, to steer the project into the hands of 'a reputable British producer and director', and to instigate a new policy in which each case was considered 'individually and on its own merits' (Trevelyan 1970b). This chapter offers new insights into the policies, processes and practices of the BBFC, contextualizing censorship within historical debates about representations of crime and justice and highlighting the interactions between the BBFC, the film and television industries, and the state.

The BBFC and True Crime in the 1960s

Cinematic depictions of factual murder cases stretch back to the mid-1910s, but Alfred Hitchcock's 1927 silent film *The Lodger: A Story of the London Fog* (based upon Marie Belloc Lowndes's 1913 novel based on Jack the Ripper) was the first narrative focusing on the crimes and detection of a serial killer as its main subject. *The Lodger* was remade four times, including an almost shot-for-shot sound version in 1931, and the Ripper inspired dozens of other, mostly, American, British and German films. This recycling of the Ripper fits the pre-1950s model of literary true crime revisiting the same cases. Jean Murley explains that 'until the 1950s, literary true crime consisted of warmed-over collections of old and tired cases, and murder narration outside of the magazines stagnated' (2008: 51). Murley also highlights this mid-century period as the moment when true crime began to establish the psychological and biographical conventions we identify with it and, largely as a result, its recognition as a serious literary and, to a lesser extent, filmic genre. In shifting towards the individual biographies and psychologies of recent murderers, late 1950s and 1960s true crime writing drew upon and aligned itself with recent psychological developments in trying to understand, even empathize with, the personal histories that led to the psychopathic and sociopathic personality disorders driving these individuals (or, in some cases, pairs of individuals) to kill.

To become a respectable literary genre, therefore, the repetition and seriality of earlier crime writing was eschewed for explorations of highly topical crimes-in-context and the individual psychologies and circumstances that produced them. This shift in approach was also adopted in American cinema. Richard Fleischer – the director of *The Boston Strangler* (1968) and *10 Rillington Place* – arguably instigated this psychological shift in *Compulsion* (1959), based on the 1920s Leopold and Loeb case, taking its name and psychological detail from Meyer Levin's 1956 best-selling book of the same name. Hitchcock's *Psycho* (1960) was pioneering, however, in being based, via Robert Bloch's 1959 novel, upon a very recent and particularly gruesome serial killer, Ed Gein, whose murders were committed from 1954 to 1957, and in establishing the prototype for future cinematic depictions of the pitiable psychopath. Murley sees this mode as becoming 'fully embodied' in Truman Capote's non-fiction novel *In Cold Blood* (1966) and Gerold Frank's *The Boston Strangler* (1966), and reaching its 'full frightening potential in film versions of these books' (154). This cycle of best-selling true crime books depicting recent homicide cases emerged to feed public interest in the phenomenal escalation and shift in the nature of murder in the United States, with far more 'stranger killings' and therefore more unsolved crimes (Lane 1997: 268). The concurrent suspension of the Hollywood Production Code in 1967, and its replacement with an age-based classification system in October 1968, allowed these books to be adapted for the screen (Monaco 2001: 56–66). This cycle of New Hollywood films included: *In Cold Blood* (Richard Brooks 1967) (based upon Capote's book on Dick Hickock and Perry Smith's 1959 Clutter family murders), *The Boston Strangler* (based upon Frank's book claiming that Albert DeSalvo was the strangler of thirteen women from 1962 to 1964), *No Way To Treat a Lady* (Jack Smight 1968) (an adaptation of William Goldman's 1964 novel inspired by the Boston Strangler), *Targets* (Peter Bogdanovich 1968) (based on the 1966 University of Texas sniper Charles Whitman), *Bloody Mama* (Roger Corman 1970) (based on 1930s crime matriarch Kate 'Ma' Baker) and *The Honeymoon Killers* (Leonard Kastle 1970) (based upon the 1940s 'lonely hearts killers' Raymond Fernandez and Martha Beck).

In his memoir, Trevelyan claimed that the BBFC had 'no reservations about reconstruction of actual murder case in other countries' (1973: 161), but these American films did raise issues for the BBFC and all of them were given X certificates. Some were subject to extremely lengthy consultation processes (*Bloody Mama* was refused certification for over a year) and cuts in order to obtain an X certificate. For *The Boston Strangler*, for example, Trevelyan consulted three psychiatrists. Twentieth Century Fox predicted

difficulty in attaining certification in Britain and contacted the BBFC at
script stage to attempt to avert lengthy cuts to the final film. Dr Derek Miller,
a psychiatrist from the Adolescent Department at the Tavistock Clinic, was
consulted at this stage and produced an eight-page report on the script for
Fox producer Stephen Lions suggesting a number of changes that corrected
dangerous representation of sexual perversion and inaccuracy in clinical
details. When the rough cut of the film was submitted, Trevelyan put on a
screening for Miller, the BBFC's go-to psychiatric expert Dr Stephen Black
and Dr Arthur Hyatt Williams, a psychiatrist in the prison service and the
Tavistock Clinic who specialized in violent crime. Trevelyan reported back
to Lions that '[a]ll three of the psychiatrists said that this was a brilliant
film in many ways', but recommended the editing or cutting of a number of
scenes of sexual violence in order to obtain an X certificate. These 'sections
of the film that dealt with sexual perversions, and especially those involving
sadism', were perceived to be 'potentially dangerous to disturbed individuals
who might see the film' (Trevelyan 1968b).

The UK release of the film, in May 1969, prompted a backlash within the
middlebrow press that questioned 'should this film be shown here?' (Davis
1969) and called on Trevelyan to justify his decision to pass the film, even
with an X certificate (Hibbin 1969). He explained that following criticism
for censoring films based on potential libel claims, the BBFC had changed
their policy, instead putting the 'onus on the film company' to obtain court
clearance, as had been done in this case (Davis 1969). However, a number
of British reviews questioned the ethics and even legality of making a film
that made a claim to an individual's guilt when they had not been convicted
of these crimes in court. DeSalvo was arrested and sentenced in 1967 for
a series of rapes in Boston (attributed to the 'Green Man') in 1964, but
was never convicted of the stranglings and sexual assaults attributed to the
Boston Strangler despite confessing to these crimes later while in custody.
As the *Daily Express* explained, 'the remarkable aspect of this movie is that,
although no one has ever been brought to trial for these murders, the killer is
named' (Davis 1969). Derek Malcolm's *Guardian* review expressed extreme
conflict at Fleischer's film, an 'object lesson in how to make a patently
sincere but palpably dishonest film' (1969). Fleischer is commended for
his sociological rather than sensationalizing approach, but the underlying
ethical issue of using an entertainment film to assert the guilt of a multiple-
murder suspect who is yet to be tried in court for those crimes is seen to
completely compromise its purported moral stance: 'if one starts to think,
one ceases to be entertained' (1969).

If, in America, the true crime cycle developed as a response to The Boston
Strangler – as well as the violent media climate of a number of high-profile
political assassinations and the Vietnam War – then in Britain, it must be
understood as emerging in the context of the national trauma of the Moors
murders. The shocking details of child murder and molestation committed

by Ian Brady and Myra Hindley from 1963 to 1965 were revealed and reflected upon across daily newspapers, television news bulletins and books during and following their 1966 trial (Cummins et al 2019: 32). Out of the trial emerged a key critical debate in British media and literary circles: was it ethical, or even possible, to try to understand the motivations and psychology of these killers? Pamela Hansford Johnson, author of *On Iniquity: Some Personal Reflections Arising Out of the Moors Murder Trial* (1967), concluded that 'empathy in this case is impossible. One cannot imagine oneself into the situation of Hindley and Brady, far less into their heads' (Hansford Johnson 1966: 64). It is perhaps unsurprising, therefore, that the announcement that 'controversial young American director' William Friedkin was making a film about the lives of the Moors murderers in 1968 was received unfavourably by the British trade papers and newspapers, politicians and the public.

In June 1968, *Kine Weekly* columnist Derek Todd discussed the cycle of Hollywood true crime films detailed above, but warned that 'we are on the brink of a more disturbing development: a number of semi-documentary features examining recent real life murders of a peculiarly sensational kind' (Todd 1968b). The two films he used to evidence this claim were Friedkin's Moors murder film and CBS's planned *10 Rillington Place* adaptation, stating that this 'new trend' raised ethical questions for filmmakers, censors and audiences. He suggested, 'The time has come, it seems to me, when film-makers must ask themselves: are human tragedies recently retailed in the quiet of a courtroom – and still sounding harmonics of horror – quite the right material to exploit for presentation to a mass audience?' (Todd 1968b). Friedkin challenged Todd's ethical and aesthetic concerns over this 'bombshell' project by responding in a subsequent *Kine Weekly* article that the film would be based upon the factual accounts of Emlyn Williams's best-selling and, mostly, well-received true crime book *Beyond Belief* (1967). Countering medium-specific concerns, he stated that he would avoid a 'Hollywood' approach by filming in colour but '"totally desaturated" to remove from it any unsuitable element of gloss' (Friedkin cited in Todd 1968a).

Controversy over the film did not resonate outside of the trade presses for a further six months, when the *Guardian* reported that Labour MP Robert Sheldon would be raising a question in Parliament the following day 'because of anger in the constituency about the proposed film' (Greenhalgh 1968). Sheldon requested that the Secretary of State refuse permission to the unnamed American director to remain in Britain to make the film because of its effect on relatives of the victims and on the general locality because '[a] film should not be made for commercial gain when it is part of the recent past' (Hansard 1968). In the article, author Williams – now screenwriter and co-producer of the film adaptation of *Beyond Belief* – responded to Sheldon's ethical problems with cinema as a commercial medium by stressing that 'film is an elastic medium in which one can suggest the horror without detailing it' (Greenhalgh 1968). Sheldon's opposition provoked a number of letters to *The Times* supporting his campaign against the film, including from Hansford Johnson, who distanced her book from Friedkin's 'hideous and indecent proposal' and demanded greater film censorship as a necessary antidote to the 'permissive society' (Hansford Johnson 1966: 64).

The conjoined media and political backlashes and threats of legal action from the families of the victims and even, it is claimed, Hindley and Brady were understood to have pushed Palomar Pictures into backing out due to – as Friedkin described it – 'the obvious difficulties, both legal and moral in presenting such a film' (Todd 1968c).[2] Ray Brooks, the actor asked to play Brady in the film, claimed that Palomar dropped out from fear that Brady and Hindley could bring a defamation of character claim in US courts, as De Salvo had attempted to do against Twentieth Century Fox (Brooks 2014). However, Friedkin and Williams were still working on a second draft script in April 1969 – well after the initial controversy and Palomar's withdrawal – as shown in their correspondence: 'It's a very important film, and all the problems connected with making it, of which I'm sure there are many more to come, are more than worth it as far as I'm concerned' (Friedkin 1969). Yet, it appears that it was censorship rather than legal issues that put an end to the project. While there is no correspondence in the BBFC archives relating to the *Beyond Belief* project, Trevelyan spoke in his memoir about his blanket refusal to consider accepting this film, juxtaposing the BBFC's shift in thinking on a Christie film in the late 1960s (discussed below) to being 'firmly opposed to the making of a film based on the "Moors murder" case' (1973: 161). It could be argued that the controversy surrounding Friedkin's 'Moors murders' film produced a favourable climate in which a film based on the *10 Rillington Place* case and book appeared more acceptable through its relative historical distance and lesser emotional resonance for politicians, the press and the public.

The BBFC and the Christie Murders

The examination of failed attempts by filmmakers across the 1960s to get the BBFC to consider certification of a film about recent British serial killer John Christie will situate the issue in relation to contemporary media, political and societal concerns – particularly the shifting debates and consensus on capital punishment provoked, in part, by the resonance of the Christie case.[3] John Reginald Halliday Christie murdered at least eight people, including his wife Ethel, by strangling them in his flat at 10 Rillington Place, Notting Hill, London, in the 1940s and 1950s. Two of Christie's victims were Beryl Evans and her baby daughter Geraldine, who, along with Beryl's husband, Timothy Evans, were tenants at 10 Rillington Place from 1948 to 1949. This case sparked huge controversy after Evans was charged with both murders, found guilty of the murder of his daughter and hanged in 1950. After Christie moved out of Rillington Place in 1953, bodies of three of his other victims were discovered hidden in a wallpaper-covered alcove in the kitchen. Two further bodies were discovered in the garden, and his wife's body was found beneath the floorboards of the front room. Christie was arrested and convicted of his wife's murder, the crime for which he was hanged on 15 July 1953 after an insanity plea was rejected. While awaiting trial he confessed to the murders of the other victims discovered on his property, including Evans's wife but not the child Geraldine.

It is now generally accepted that Christie murdered both of them, and that the police mishandling of the original investigation enabled Christie to escape detection and murder four more women. Evans was posthumously pardoned for the murder of his daughter on 18 October 1966, following a decade of family, political and media pressure (including from Kennedy's best-selling book) and the growing public acceptance of his innocence contributed to the 1965 suspension, and subsequent abolition, of capital punishment in Britain. Therefore, the miscarriage of justice represented by the Evans investigation and trial kept the Christie murders prominent within public culture through the mid-1950s to mid-1960s, until the emerging horrors of the Moors murders were revealed across rolling newspaper headlines and television news reports.

The first correspondence with the BBFC relating to a Christie film was instigated in early 1962 by Irish screenwriter, producer and director Kevin McClory, known most popularly as producer of the James Bond film *Thunderball* (Terence Young 1965). Anticipating the BBFC's response, McClory stated that he 'fully appreciate[d] the controversial nature of the subject matter', but intended to present it in a 'factual and dignified manner', as a 'serious study of a tragic sequence of events unparalleled in the history of criminology' (McClory 1962). Trevelyan consulted with BBFC president Lord Morrison (1960–5) before confirming what he had expressed in his initial phone conversation with McClory: that there was 'no possibility of the project being accepted' (Trevelyan 1962).

The next approach to the BBFC came only a year later from American producer John Clein, who had most recently produced (and passed through the BBFC) the British crime film *Dr Crippen* (Robert Lynn 1963), a revisionist account of the notorious British murder case starring Donald Pleasence in the eponymous role. Dr Hawley Harvey Crippen was convicted and hung for the murder of his wife in 1910, but the film, a combination of courtroom drama and melodrama, portrayed his wife as abusive and questioned his guilt. The film received an X certificate as it met the BBFC's criteria for fifty years distance from the depicted crime. Clein sought to convince the BBFC that his approach to the material would be aesthetically and ethically sensitive, presenting Evans and Christie's trials and the 'events leading there to' as 'semi-documentary fiction', and stressing psychiatric causal factors (Clein 1963). Clein also stressed his track record in producing true crime material (and the precedent of BBFC passing it) with *Dr Crippen*. Trevelyan remained unmoved, restating to the 'most persistent Clein' that the proposed film was 'contrary to our existing policy' and that the BBFC 'saw no reason to alter [... it] in this case' (Trevelyan 1963).

Clein's persistence provoked screenwriter Leigh Vance (who wrote *Dr Crippen*) to contact Trevelyan to distance himself from the controversial project about 'that revolting little pervert', and to stress that Clein's angle was actually to demonstrate that Christie was 'the product of the National Health Act', which clashed with his only interest in being motivated by an anti-capital punishment agenda (Vance 1963). According to Vance, Clein's approach corresponded with that of *Dr Crippen*, in calling into question Christie's culpability while implicating government mental health policy, a post-war shift from a legal to medical model of psychiatric provision that culminated in the 1959 Mental Health Act. The implication is that Clein felt that Christie and Evans (not yet pardoned for murdering his wife and daughter) should have been legally detained in an 'asylum' before their crimes were committed.

Following the Murder (Abolition of Death Penalty) Act 1965 and the 1966 pardoning of Evans, Trevelyan was contacted by Mark Fisher of Aquarius Films on behalf of himself and creative partner Laurence, son of director Roy Boulting. They stated that they were developing a documentary film about the Christie case that would not include 'dramatisations, and therefore impersonations, but having visual material that was factual with overlaid voices. They would not be directly concerned with the murders themselves, but with the psychological and social causes of Christie in particular' (Trevelyan 1966). Trevelyan reiterated the BBFC's fifty-year rule to the filmmakers, but this latest approach prompted him to consult the BBFC president, Lord Morrison, on the BBFC's wider policy which had, until recently, been shared by theatre and television. Trevelyan revisited earlier correspondence on this matter, from 1960, between himself, the Lord Chamberlain (whose Office was responsible for theatre censorship), the Independent Television Authority (ITA), and Sir Charles Cunningham of the Home Office – who had 'strongly advocated the maintenance of this policy' (Trevelyan 1966). This corresponds with Sian Barber's claims of the BBFC and ITA's 'united approach to the issue of censorship', publicly and privately, 'ensuring parity between television and film censorship' (2011: 21,19). However, Trevelyan explained to Lord Morrison that 'as regards to television, it appeared that the position might have altered since the BBC had recently devoted a whole issue of Panorama to the Hanratty case' (Trevelyan 1966).

The *Panorama* episode which Trevelyan was referring to was the 7 November 1966 broadcast 'Hanratty: Case for Enquiry', which revisited the evidence of the 1961 'A6 murder case', for which James Hanratty was convicted and executed in 1962. Here Trevelyan looked to the BBC for censorship advice which Barber suggests was not usually the case for the BBFC as, quoting a 1967 BBC pamphlet, the public sector broadcaster's libel-focused approach was 'more akin to similar process in large newspapers that they are to the machinery of censorship in the theatre and film industry' (Barber 2011: 18). While Fisher and Boulting's documentary never came to fruition, it did set in motion a reconsideration of the fifty-year policy based on recent precedent on television.

The BBC's policy shift for *Panorama*, alongside the recent developments in Hollywood true crime, set up a more favourable climate for discussions with CBS Films in 1968 that would eventually, but not straightforwardly, lead to *10 Rillington Place*. Consultation between CBS and the BBFC started on the wrong foot: a May 1968 press release announcing that CBS had bought the rights to Kennedy's *10 Rillington Place* prompted Trevelyan to contact the studio and assert their long-held policy. The basis in Kennedy's respected and influential book, and the author's involvement in the project, appears to have contributed to the BBFC's decision to revisit their thinking on true crime films. Trevelyan and new BBFC president Lord Harlech (1965–85) met with Kennedy and representatives from CBS in June, and were convinced enough of the honest intentions and sensitive approach of the proposed film to reconsider their policy, immediately contacting their legal advisors, and consulting, once more, with the ITA and BBC. The BBFC's legal advisor, Lord Goodman, was well versed in these converging censorship and legal concerns regarding representing living and recently dead people on stage and screen, having been a member of the 1966 Joint Select Committee on Censorship of the Theatre, whose 1967 report fed into the abolition of State censorship of theatre with the 1968 Theatres Act. One of Goodman's key roles and (failed) interventions within the Joint Committee's deliberations had been in regard to 'fact-based theatre', including his initial proposal of a 'draconian' amendment based upon an untenable distinction between individual's private and public lives (Megson 2011: 141).

Trevelyan's letter to Goodman expresses his and Lord Harlech's conviction that the proposed film focusing on the miscarriage of justice in the Evans case would not 'comment adversely on anyone involved in the case; nor is it their intention to put onscreen details of the revolting murders' (Trevelyan 1968a). He reminded Goodman of the extant fifty-year policy but expressed that some ambiguity and flexibility had creeped in during the 1960s, 'when occasion arose, to the extent of reducing the time lapse to say 30 years'. Trevelyan also cited the recent BBC *Panorama* episode to highlight precedent for greater flexibility in the application of this rule in other media. He asked Goodman, therefore, 'whether such a policy on these lines could not be maintained but that each proposed film should be considered individually in the light of whether there were, or were not, circumstances which made its screening undesirable' (Trevelyan 1968a).

At this stage Trevelyan was seeking to instil some flexibility when 'serious' films such as this were proposed, while seeming to retain a general principle that preserved the status quo. He continued: 'It would clearly be wise to convey our approval in terms which did not establish this as a general precedent which could be used if we had for instance a proposal to make a film of the "Moors" murder case, a film which obviously presents different problems and ones which were likely to cause us much greater concern'. The unrepresentability of the Moors murders was not seen as justification for maintaining a blanket prohibition on recent murder cases but rather as strong dialectical argument for why the Evans-Christie case might actually be acceptable in censorship terms.

Goodman felt this 'rigid rule' was no longer appropriate and that 'each case should be considered individually' (Goodman 1968). Like Trevelyan, Goodman was 'less impressed by arguments that it is wrong to show actual murder cases on film because these may be sensational and sordid', given what was being accepted in regard to scenes of fictional violence, than with legal issues relating to the portrayal of living persons and with issues of libel specifically (Goodman 1968). About 10 Rillington Place he was concerned that 'Kennedy in his book has strong criticisms of the conduct of the prosecution and of two police officers [...] it will be difficult to avoid touching on these points'. His was a measured argument: 'I am not suggesting that the BBFC should provide an alternate remedy to the law of libel. It would be quite wrong to use censorship which prevents freedom of comment or freedom of criticism, but you are, I think, entitled to use it to prevent offensive reference to living people'. He advised, therefore, that both for this film and for a future policy, there should be 'no absolute rule but that each case had to be decided on its merit' based on seeing and approving the script, and that the 'manner of representation of any living person depicted in the film would have to be unobjectionable' (Goodman 1968).

There was no need for the BBFC to contact the Home Office as there was 'no likelihood of any future reopening of the case' (Goodman 1968), and therefore no question of the filmmakers being in contempt of court. Despite this advice, Trevelyan contacted the Home Office to *inform* them (rather than *consult* them) that they had 'approved in principle' a project based on 10 Rillington Place. Francis Graham-Harrison, Deputy Undersecretary of State, replied that the Home Office were unhappy that the film had been 'excepted from the previously agreed policy' given the 'case involved the killing of two people less than twenty years ago', and felt it might create a 'potentially embarrassing precedent' (Graham-Harrison 1968). Trevelyan responded diplomatically that he appreciated Graham-Harrison's 'apprehension' and would keep his points in mind at script approval stage (Trevelyan 1968).

However, when CBS submitted their draft script in May 1969, Trevelyan was 'very disappointed' to see that it 'appeared to consist largely of cheap sensationalism' rather than being 'a serious study' as promised (Trevelyan

1969a). He stated that this 'deplorable' screenplay had no chance of acceptance by the BBFC as it focused far too heavily on Christie's 'horrible murders' and the 'sexual motivations of the crimes', rather than Evans and the miscarriage of justice, and was rife with factual errors and omissions (including the death of the child Geraldine): 'I find it difficult to believe that Ludovic Kennedy who wrote a serious book on this subject, would be happy about this screenplay, and I shall be glad if you will let me know whether or not it has met with his approval?' (Trevelyan 1969a).

CBS immediately dropped the project. Scriptwriter Sean Graham, seeking to save face, contacted Trevelyan to say that there had been a 'monumental failure of communication' between himself, CBS and producer Stan Shpetner, and that if he 'had been made aware of the kind of picture you envisaged and CBS agreed', he would not 'have wasted his time' on this screenplay. Graham felt that a 'good and honest film' could still be made, and agreed with Trevelyan that 'a reputable British producer and director should take on this film' (Graham 1969a). Trevelyan responded to Graham that the BBFC's position had been 'considerably misrepresented to you and Ludovic Kennedy', and felt that the BBFC had 'been used as an excuse to get rid of this project' (Trevelyan 1969b). Kennedy also felt misled by CBS as he was not shown the screenplay; he was relieved that CBS had now withdrawn and hoped to 'reawaken interest in the subject in the film industry in this country' (Kennedy 1969). The collective feeling, therefore, was that Hollywood hadn't been able to bring the sensitivity and seriousness required to produce an ethical Christie film.

The BBFC and *10 Rillington Place*

Within the contexts of the shifting societal, censorship and critical concerns of the late 1960 and early 1970s, the *10 Rillington Place* case highlights how a principle of 'intention' was marshalled by Trevelyan, and the filmmakers, as the key mechanism to give the Board authority, and autonomy from the blanket Home Office rule. However, Trevelyan's decisions on the legitimacy of the filmmaker's intentions continued to be 'bound up with notions of quality and taste which were determined by his own personal preferences and predilections' (Barber 2011: 45). Following CBS's withdrawal from the project, the BBFC helped Graham to relaunch *10 Rillington Place* with 'reputable' British producer Leslie Linder (who had recently produced Tony Richardson's *Hamlet* [1969]). While unable to attach the 'very good British director' they were both looking for, experienced Hollywood director Richard Fleischer, who had directed *Compulsion* and *The Boston Strangler* (both passed as acceptable by the BBFC with A and X certificates, respectively), appeared suitable to the BBFC. Graham, initially at least, persuaded the

BBFC that this new creative team was professionally and personally aligned with the ethical and aesthetic approach they required (Graham 1969b).

Trevelyan met a couple more times with Graham over the subsequent months, during which it was agreed that 'between the two Dicks [Richard Fleischer and Richard Attenborough], yourself, Leslie Linder and myself we can bring out a screenplay that has some stature' (Graham 1970a). Graham thanked Trevelyan for his 'assurance of cooperation' that he said would help seal the financial backing they needed. Trevelyan, therefore, appears to have gone beyond his usual role in brokering with Graham a film of the 'stature, which we have both always wanted' (Trevelyan 1970a). Within a month, however, Graham had withdrawn from the project. He complained to Trevelyan that Fleischer was flouting his 'very sensitive' approach to the screenplay and seeking to 'make "the horror film to end all horror films" [...] He wants to go for it. There is no censorship any more in America' (Graham 1970b). He conceded: 'I am a very small writer fighting two very powerful American corporations: they can be vindictive'. Graham included a letter from Fleischer to the production company Filmways, which set out a plan to switch the narrative focus from Evans to Christie, 'so that it is in fact his story' and the climax is 'the revelation of Christie to the police as being a mass murderer'. Fleischer continued, 'By changing the balance and making Christie the story I think it would then be possible to put much more violence and horror into the screenplay' (cited in Graham 1970b).

This prompted Trevelyan to make a point to Filmways that '[t]he fact that the board is prepared to consider this proposal at all is an important change of policy' (1970b). He explained the ten-year contestation over the project and the Board's gradual shift from a blanket prohibition to the recent decision to consider each project individually. He asserted that this meant 'a film which was created for the purpose of public entertainment would be discouraged, while a film that dealt with a murder case in order to make a valid special point might be considered acceptable'. In addition to issues of intention, Trevelyan explained that his decision would be based upon different factors: the feelings of surviving relatives; the 'possibility that a film of this kind might be regarded as a contempt of court, and involve film distributors and exhibitors (and possibly the producers) in court proceedings'; and possible public reactions – both in regard to the public's opinions of the film industry and in terms of 'stimulative and dangerous effects on others with these kinds of mental disturbances who might see the film'. As the screenplay submitted by CBS in 1969 was not deemed acceptable on these terms, and the studio had betrayed the agreement to make a film that focused on Evans rather than Christie (i.e. legal and capital punishment issues rather than the 'gruesome murders'), he emphasized the importance 'to put the Board's conditions clearly in writing at this stage so that there can be no doubt about them, and no possibility of subsequent dispute'. This letter, dated 12 March 1970, is crucial as it sets out a set of principles emerging from Trevelyan's extended legal and industry consultations that he felt comfortable putting in writing as a working set of guidelines for films based upon recent British murder cases.

Following Graham's departure, Trevelyan struck up a professional dialogue with Ludovic Kennedy, who was subsequently brought on as a script consultant by Filmways. In a letter from Kennedy thanking Trevelyan, the author put his new role down to the BBFC Secretary's influence on the producers (Kennedy 1970). In Kennedy, Trevelyan still had a respected 'friend' on the project with a similar vision for it and, arguably, aligned 'notions of quality and taste' (Barber 2011: 45). Correspondence between the two men suggests that as a result of the alarm raised by Graham, Trevelyan and Kennedy decided to 'meet in private to discuss' a 'few concerns' (Trevelyan 1970c). However, Trevelyan's reading of the second draft script (which Clive Exton wrote and on which Kennedy acted as consultant) raised only two issues – excessive violence in one scene and a point-of-view shot when a body is discovered in the wall – that needed to be changed to be acceptable to the Board. In fact, the final narrative of the film is much as described in Fleischer's letter that was forwarded by Graham to Trevelyan to raise the alarm at the script changes he proposed. These changes included: a new chronological structure around 'Christie's story' and climax in his arrest rather than focusing on Evans and using selective flashbacks and forwards to fill the historical gaps; starting the film with one of Christie's early murders in 1944 and the hiding of the body in the garden, where another body is accidentally exhumed in the process; the 'important' inclusion of the murder of the Evans daughter Geraldine (which Trevelyan had pushed to be added to Graham's earlier draft); and the addition of Christie murdering his wife Ethel following Evans's trial and execution. These changes clearly switched the narrative far more to focus on Christie, rather than the miscarriage of justice with Evans, and as a result the script included far more murders, sexual violence and visual representation of victims' bodies, key censorship issues flagged up as unacceptable in relation to the earlier CBS script.

Aligning with Trevelyan's converging criteria for acceptability regarding intention and tastefulness, critical reception of 10 Rillington Place also focused on these intersecting ethical and aesthetic concerns. In an October 1970 interview with Michael Billington for The Times, the director highlighted the two ethical and aesthetic questions he raised on The Boston Strangler and 10 Rillington Place, showing that his moral convictions had also shaped his aesthetic choices: at what point in history to make the films, and what degree of violence to show? The former question was answered by motivation – does this question need to be asked now? – and the second question was one of balance – 'show too much and you run the risk of gratuitous sensationalism; show too little and you falsify the nature of the murderer. After all, it's easy to feel compassion for Christie or the Boston Strangler if you never see what they actually did'. Fleischer noted concerns relating to surviving relatives' feelings but stressed the political significance of the film in intervening in the capital punishment debate, in Britain and America, as justification for making the film now. Reproducing Trevelyan's distinction between treating true crime cases as entertainment or as evidence to make a 'valid special point' (Trevelyan 1970b), critic Billington concluded that 'Fleischer the crusading campaigner is increasingly taking over from Fleischer the ever-reliable Hollywood professional' (Billington 1970).

Press coverage of the film's production also spoke to Trevelyan's concerns regarding taste and quality, particularly through reference to the highly respected veteran actor Richard Attenborough's casting, and the uncanny authenticity of his performance. A *Daily Mail* news article on the film foregrounded Fleischer's restaging of the mise en scène on location on the original street (though not house) where the crimes were committed, and juxtaposed photographs of Christie and Attenborough on location. The article drew its headline from a former neighbour exclamation: 'It's as if he'd come back from the grave' (Cable 1970). Like Fleischer, Attenborough stressed his moral motivations for making the film, explaining 'this part is so disturbing that I don't really like doing it' (Attenborough cited in Cable 1970). These press reports praised the location filming and claustrophobic staging within the decaying Rillington Place home as a mark of quality rather than tastelessness. Only in the last five minutes do we see Christie outside these drab, deteriorating locations, when he is juxtaposed to a more colourful and multicultural vision of 1950s London (see Plate 13).

10 Rillington Place was released with an X certificate on 29 January 1971 to conflicted reviews. Perhaps surprisingly, a key issue raised by the broadsheet reviewers was that the film was not sensational enough. In his *Sunday Observer* review, Derek Malcolm complained that in its attempt to 'warily tread the old path between fact and fiction', the film was cautious 'to the point of being careworn in the pursuit of the middle path'. The middle (brow) path that Malcolm was critiquing here is the ethical and aesthetic compromise which I have referred to elsewhere as 'Gothic realism' (Snelson 2018: 59) or, as critic Malcolm characterized this dialectic, 'Grand Guignol kitchen sink' (Malcolm 1971). Fleischer's 'methodical reconstruction of one of the most macabre murder cases of the century' (Malcolm 1971) fell short of being either sensational entertainment or serious analysis. Similarly, John Russell Taylor of *The Times* commended Fleischer's 'thoroughly decent' approach, but lamented that in being so cautious to 'meticulously suppress' any of the 'dark and joyless comedy buried beneath' the case, the director had failed to produce 'the far more complex, and in the last analysis, quite a bit more serious' film it should have been (Russell Taylor 1971). Rather than the critics questioning the BBFC's passing of this true crime film, as with *The Boston Strangler*, they complained that it was ineffective precisely because it had strived too hard to appear serious and tasteful in order to see off anticipated objections from censors, critics and the press.

Conclusion

The BBFC's gradual shift in policy on factual murder cases across the period of Trevelyan's tenure broadly attests to the claim of his liberalizing influence on British censorship (Hargreaves 2012: 54). Conversely, however, it also highlights an ongoing nervousness within the BBFC around cinema's role in mediating and commenting on real British criminal cases. The protracted production history of the unmade Christie films and *10 Rilllington Place* must be understood in the context of the political and societal concerns and contentions relating to the death penalty and its abolition, and the shock of the revelation of the Moors murders. The embroilment of these censorship decisions in these post-war watershed moments clearly put additional pressure on Trevelyan and the BBFC to proceed cautiously. The BBFC's nervousness was not triggered by fears about inspiring copycat crimes; they were motivated by concerns about damaging the public perception of the film industry (particularly through bad publicity over distress caused to victims' families) and protecting filmmakers from expensive and contentious libel cases or contempt of court charges. The film of *10 Rillington Place* that eventually emerged in the early 1970s, following ten years of BBFC contention and intervention, was deemed out of sync with critical tastes and with what audiences were experiencing in Hollywood films and on British television. By the time of its release, Stephen Murphy (1970–5) had taken over from Trevelyan and was immediately called upon to make bold decisions on a series of highly controversial crime and horror films, including *Straw Dogs* (Sam Peckinpah 1971), *The Devils* (Ken Russell 1971) and *A Clockwork Orange* (Stanley Kubrick 1971). His decisions to pass these films triggered media panics about their potential to 'inflame people to violence' (*The Sun* 1972), and provoked the *Sunday Mirror* to question, 'How much more violence, sadism and rape is [...] Stephen Murphy going to let movie-makers get away with?' (Simkin 2012: 75). Within just a few months, therefore, the pallid *10 Rillington Place* already appeared a vestige of a Gothic tradition in British cinema subsumed beneath the lurid spectacle of this 'ultra-violence'.

Notes

1   This and all further references to the *10 Rillington Place* files are to the manuscripts held at the BBFC Archive, London.

2   Myra Hindley's biographer Carol Ann Lee claims it was pressure from the victims' families, and even Hindley, that ultimately derailed the film. On receiving a draft contract for the film, Hindley certainly sent a letter instructing her solicitor to try to block the production due to the 'harrowing' effect it would have on her and Brady's families (2011: 289).

3   An important precursor (rather than precedent) to these Christie projects is
     the mid-1950s film *Yield to the Night* (J. Lee Thompson 1956), which raised
     considerable concerns for the BBFC examiners and was given an X certificate.
     The film is often incorrectly characterized as a fictionalized version of the story
     of Ruth Ellis, the last woman in Britain to be hanged. The similarities with
     this case are coincidental, as the script was written two years earlier, but the
     film and its publicity poster that provoked audiences, 'Would you hang Mary
     Hilton?,' were marshalled to tap into the public debate on the death penalty
     (Williams 2002: 8).

References

Barber, S. (2011), *Censoring the 1970s: The BBFC and the Decade that Taste
    Forgot*, Newcastle upon Tyne: Cambridge Scholars.
Billington, M. (1970), 'Richard Fleischer', *The Times*, 10 October.
Brooks, R. (2014), 'Madness', *Random Ray*, 15 September. Available online: http://
    raybrooksactor.blogspot.co.uk/2014/09/madness.html (accessed 7 September
    2015).
Cable, M. (1970), 'As If He'd Come Back from the Grave', *Daily Mail*, 18 May.
Clein, J. (1963), Letter to John Trevelyan, *10 Rillington Place* files, 5 February,
    London: BBFC Archive.
Cummins, I., M. Foley, and M. King (2019), *Serial Killers and the Media: The
    Moors Murders Legacy*, Basingstoke: Palgrave Macmillan.
Davis, V. (1969), 'Should this Film Be Shown Here?', *Daily Express*, 7 May.
Friedkin, W. (1969), Letter to Emlyn Williams, Emlyn Williams Papers (L3/5),
    15 March, Aberystwyth: Llyfrgell Genedlaethol Cymru / National Library of
    Wales.
Goodman, A. (1968), Letter to John Trevelyan, *10 Rillington Place* files, 2 July,
    London: BBFC Archive.
Graham, S. (1969a), Notes to John Trevelyan, *10 Rillington Place* files, 17 and
    25 September, London: BBFC Archive.
Graham, S. (1969b), Letter to John Trevelyan, *10 Rillington Place* files,
    11 December, London: BBFC Archive.
Graham, S. (1970a), Letter to John Trevelyan, *10 Rillington Place* files, 4 February,
    London: BBFC Archive.
Graham, S. (1970b), Letter to John Trevelyan, *10 Rillington Place* files, 9 March,
    London: BBFC Archive.
Graham-Harrison, F. (1968), Letter to John Trevelyan, *10 Rillington Place* files,
    10 August, London: BBFC Archive.
Greenhalgh, A. (1968), 'MP Opposes Film on Moors Murders', *Guardian*,
    6 November.
Hansard (1968), 'Moor Murders (Proposed Film)', 7 November, vol. 772,
    col. 138. Available online: http://hansard.millbanksystems.com/search/
    moors+murders?speaker=mr-robert-sheldon (accessed 7 June 2015).
Hansford Johnson, P. (1966), 'In Ghastly Transcripts, a Test of Our Time', *Life*,
    12 August: 64.

Hargreaves, T. (2012), 'The Trevelyan Years: British Censorship and 1960s Cinema', in E. Lamberti (ed), *Behind the Scenes at the BBFC: Film Classification from the Silver Screen to the Digital Age*, 53–71, London: BFI Publishing.

Hibbin, N. (1969), 'Well-made Strangler Film Raises Censorship Concerns', *Morning Star*, 17 May.

Kennedy, L. (1969), Letter to David (Ormsby-Gore, BBFC President), *10 Rillington Place* files, 28 July, London: BBFC Archive.

Kennedy, L. (1970), Letter to John Trevelyan, *10 Rillington Place* files, 10 March, London: BBFC Archive.

Lane, R. (1997), *Murder In America: A History*, Columbus: Ohio State University.

Lee, C. (2011), *One of Your Own: The Life and Death of Myra Hindley*, Edinburgh: Mainstream Publishing Company.

Malcolm, D. (1969), 'Out of Court', *The Guardian*, 16 May.

Malcolm, D. (1971), 'Hollow at the Heart of the Matter', *Guardian*, 28 January.

McClory, K. (1962), Letter to John Trevelyan, *10 Rillington Place* files, 16 February, London: BBFC Archive.

Megson, C. (2011), 'The Theatres Act (1968), Documentary Theatre and the Actor's Overwhelming Reality', *Studies in Theatre and Performance*, 31 (2): 137–51.

Monaco, J. (2001), *The Sixties: 1960–1969*, Berkeley: University of California Press.

Murley, J. (2008), *The Rise of True Crime: 20th-Century Murder and American Popular Culture*, Westport: Praeger.

Russell Taylor, J. (1971), 'Something Nasty in the Bath House', *The Times*, 29 January.

Simkin, S. (2012), 'Wake of the Flood: Key Issues in UK Censorship, 1970–1975', in E. Lamberti (ed), *Behind the Scenes at the BBFC: Film Classification from the Silver Screen to the Digital Age*, 72–86, London: BFI Publishing.

Snelson, T. (2018), 'Old Horror, New Hollywood and the 1960s True Crime Cycle', *Film Studies*, 19 (1): 58–75.

The Sun (1972), 'The Rising Tide of Violence', 7 January.

Todd, D. (1968a), 'Friedkin to Film Moors Murders', *Kinematograph Weekly*, 4 May: 15.

Todd, D. (1968b), 'Should We Be Exploiting the Harmonics of Horror', *Kinematograph Weekly*, 1 June: 12.

Todd, D. (1968c), 'Director Defends Moors Murder Film Project', *Kinematograph Weekly*, 16 November: 26.

Trevelyan, J. (1962), Letter to Kevin McClory, *10 Rillington Place* files, 22 February, London: BBFC Archive.

Trevelyan, J. (1963), Letter to John Clein, *10 Rillington Place* files, 6 February, London: BBFC Archive.

Trevelyan, J. (1966), Letter to President, *10 Rillington Place* files, 19 November, London: BBFC Archive.

Trevelyan, J. (1968a), Letter to Lord Goodman, *10 Rillington Place* files, 17 June, London: BBFC Archive.

Trevelyan, J. (1968b), Letter to Stephen Lions, *The Boston Strangler* files, 9 October, London: BBFC Archive.

Trevelyan, J. (1968c), Letter to Graham-Harrison, *10 Rillington Place* files, 16 August, London: BBFC Archive.

Trevelyan, J. (1969a), Letter to Richard Cornel (CBS), *10 Rillington Place* files, 13 May, London: BBFC Archive.

Trevelyan, J. (1969b), Letter to Sean Graham, *10 Rillington Place* files, 22 July, London: BBFC Archive.

Trevelyan, J. (1970a), Notes to Sean Graham, *10 Rillington Place* files, 5 February and 10 March, London: BBFC Archive.

Trevelyan, J. (1970b), Notes to Martin Ransohoff 'On proposal from Filmways Productions to film 10 Rillington Place', *10 Rillington Place* files, 12 March, London: BBFC Archive.

Trevelyan, J. (1970c), Letter to Ludovic Kennedy, *10 Rillington Place* files, 12 March, London: BBFC Archive.

Trevelyan, J. (1973), *What the Censor Saw*, London: Michael Joseph.

Vance, L. (1963), Letter to John Trevelyan, *10 Rillington Place* files, 14 February, London: BBFC Archive.

Williams, M. (2002), 'Women in Prison and Women in Dressing Gowns: Rediscovering the 1950s films of J. Lee Thompson', *Journal of Gender Studies*, 11 (1): 5–15.

12

Class and Classification:

The British Board of Film Censors' Reception of Horror at the Time of the Festival of Light

Benjamin Halligan

The New Censor and the New Moralism

With the fortuitous timing of the stuntman, leaping from the window only moments before the building explodes into flames, the secretary of the British Board of Film Censors (BBFC) John Trevelyan OBE (1903–86) retired in the summer of 1971, collecting a CBE (Commander of the Most Excellent Order of the British Empire) that same year. His chatty memoirs of his time with the BBFC, *What the Censor Saw*, followed in 1973. Trevelyan's successor, Stephen Murphy, began work on 1 July 1971 (Walker 1971a).

Within three months of this hand-over, the newly established Festival of Light convened two voluble, Prince Charles-endorsed rallies in central London, which gathered and galvanized a hitherto marginalized and unheard anti-liberal and anti-permissive constituency. For Steve Stevens, the aviator missionary and co-founder of the Festival of Light, these events were in the name of 'a positive stand for the great Christian values of love, purity and family life on which our civilisation is founded' (cited in 'Rallying for Love' 1971). John Capon's official history of this evangelical, ecumenical pressure group identifies their wider concerns: to counter 'the dangers of moral pollution' (1972: 20) with 'Christian moral standards' (20), thereby building a bulwark against the 'systematic corruption of the young' (24).[1] The state of cinema at this precise moment in particular, widely taken as redolent of – even a cheerleader for – the amoral, polluting 'permissive society', was a target.

A combative cadre of Festival-associated and outspoken figures – Mary Whitehouse, Frank Pakenham (Lord Longford) and Malcolm Muggeridge – took to the media to amplify this (in both senses) counteroffensive. At the time, Whitehouse was marshalling her own pro-censorship pressure group, the National Viewers and Listeners Association (NVALA). Longford had initiated a wide-ranging investigation into pornography in Britain, with ample media coverage of his experiences in strip clubs and Soho cinemas. And Muggeridge was often heard declaring – and seemingly living, in public – spiritual warfare on the hegemony of the responsibility-shirking 'liberal humanists' that manage the organs of state (cited in Bakewell and Garnham 1970: 164–5). Behind these three distinctive characters, a phalanx of opinion-formers, sympathetic to (if not formerly associated with) the Festival of Light, added their voices to the debate. The thundering polemicist David Holbrook published four sizeable tomes in 1972 alone, attacking the permissive society, with its ills as manifest everywhere from boarding school cultures of sexual experimentation to the lurid contents of bookshops on railway station platforms (see Holbrook 1972a, 1972b, 1972c, 1972d). The pro-corporal punishment educationalist Elizabeth Manners stepped forward to offer the swift solution to our 'now reaping the bitter harvest of the permissive society ... [i]t has ten letters: D-I-S-C-I-P-L-I-N-E ...' (1971: 205). The like-minded Sir Rhodes Boyson similarly intervened in debates on education, and would later bemoan the loss of school beatings, as resulting in 'a weakening of the close relationship between pupils and staff' (1996: 67). And John Gummer, scourge of liberal Anglicanism, listed books he wanted to see thrown into incinerators: *Sin for Breakfast* (1967) by Mason Hoffenberg, *The Cult of Pain* (1968) by Edmond Dumoulin and *Lesbian Career Woman* (1968), seemingly by Toby Thompson (Gummer 1971: 87). The youthful Festival of Light exemplar was pop singer and film star Cliff Richard, pictured lighting a beacon on the cover of Capon's book, in front of a multi-ethnic, multi-generation crowd, with 'Jesus said "I am the light of the world"' banners aloft, and a jovial policeman. With this intervention into public discourse, Murphy's BBFC came under substantial pressure, and even attack. Within a few years, the BBFC's liberal or progressive phase, as associated with Trevelyan's tenure, and coinciding with the 1960s counterculture, seemed entirely over.[2] The reasons seemed clear; Michael Winner, for example, albeit in the context of complaining about the BBFC X certificate for his film *Scorpio* (1973), would decry Murphy for his capitulation: '... he is the wrong man for the job. He is becoming paranoid about letting the public see films which a year ago would have passed without any problem ... I think he's been completed routed by the Festival of Light' (cited in 'Michael Winner Blasts British' 1973: 19)[3] (see Plate 14).

Trevelyan, profiled before this storm in the *Daily Mirror* in 1970, had clearly felt his time with the BBFC was over in that his task had been completed – and that a bureaucratic process alone remained, around determining boundaries of certificates: 'Already [Trevelyan] knows there's little you can keep from adults in the sexy, swinging Seventies. His principal role is defending children against drugs, violence and sexual brutality that cash-happy producers are longing to put their way' (Malone 1970). A partly devolved, three- or four-tier system of film release was in operation, alleviating the pressure on the BBFC to deliver absolute judgement. Some films that ran the danger of being blocked by the Board for general release, such as sex education films clearly made in bad faith ('white coaters'), could be exhibited locally on the approval of borough councils. Other films, without any hope of BBFC or council certification, such as hardcore pornography, in theory could be screened in private (i.e. membership) film clubs. And celluloid cuts of commercial films for home projection, typically with sound and colour and in Super 8mm, were in circulation with uncertain regulation around their sale and no method of restricting viewing. Sometimes these versions, from companies such as Walton, were comprised of memorable sequences, and sometimes of 'highlights' from films. Finally, films could, even before formal certification, also receive film festival premieres – and so could be on view, garnering press coverage and reactions before the BBFC was asked to consider them. The BBFC could therefore defer a classification judgement in some cases – recommending that distributors initially approach local councils before formally requesting a licence for nation-wide release by the BBFC, as with *Trash* (Paul Morrissey 1970).[4] But council certification, and cinema club screenings, with the right pressures applied, might result in police raids; only a BBFC certificate would seemingly ensure screenings occurred without police interference.[5] It is worth pausing to note what a raid might mean for the film-goer: to be held in a cinema, or even a cinema foyer (even if only passing through – to use the telephone, for example), and asked to provide name and address (for unspecified reasons) before being released, and if they declined, to be formally arrested or body searched. And this was at a time when the names of suspects were allowed to be published in local newspapers (resulting in scandal and job loss), and the police were actively assisting in the illegal blacklisting of suspected 'difficult' characters by private companies, leaving them jobless (Weinfass 2019).

In the event, Trevelyan's belief in a diminished censor's brief turned out to be remarkably ill-founded for a figure who felt (as noted below) informed and justified by a nuanced awareness of – or even ahead of – contemporary mores. Of his replacement's first months in office, Trevelyan recalled what must have seemed to have been the bequeathal of a poisoned chalice rather than a functioning bureaucracy:

> I had left [Murphy] with a problem by having, with Lord Harlech's approval, issued an 'X' certificate for a somewhat modified version of Ken Russell's film *The Devils* ... My successor soon had another serious problem. The film *Straw Dogs*, which the Board passed, was violently attacked ... It was bad luck for Stephen Murphy that very soon after this film the Board had to make a decision on *A Clockwork Orange* ....
> (Trevelyan 1977: 217)[6]

By 11 March 1972 – less than a year after his first day in office – calls were made in the press for Murphy's resignation (Trevelyan 1977: 219–20). Unsurprisingly, these demands emanated from Whitehouse ('Dismiss Censor' 1973). Yet, they also came from film critic Alexander Walker, who complained of a 'dereliction of duty' with respect to certifying the violence and sexual assault in *Straw Dogs* (Sam Peckinpah 1971), and asked therefore whether the censor 'has any further useful role to play in the cinema industry' (1971b: 21).[7] Along with Walker, even nominally progressive film critics such as David Robinson and Dilys Powell, and cultural commentators and figures, such as George Melly, Tony Palmer and John Russell Taylor, were assailing the BBFC. They demanded, in a letter to *The Times*, a statement of explanation from Murphy and Harlech ('even when the continued existence of his [Harlech's] Board was being called into question by several of the signatories to this letter') as to how *Straw Dogs*, then on the cusp of its UK release, could have received a certificate (since it is 'dubious in its intention, excessive in its effect') when *Trash* remained, at this point, in uncertified limbo (Cashin, Coleman et al 1971). 'Is violence a more acceptable part of the scene, in the censor's eyes, than drugs?' they ask. (The letter further laments that film critics have been inadvertently implicated in the BBFC's certification inconsistencies: misleadingly selective quotes from their reviews were being shamelessly used by film distributors to promote films that they instead condemned – so that these film critics would appear to be cheerleading a laissez-faire BBFC attitude around films they reviewed as repellent.)[8] Meanwhile, filmmaker Stanley Kubrick chose to withdraw his 1971 film *A Clockwork Orange* from circulation in the UK – for reasons that remain obscure but are generally understood to have involved threats made to both himself and his family – arising from the continued tabloid coverage of supposedly copycat violence that was attributed to the film (Krämer 2011: 117–9). One could reasonably speculate, then, that such self-censorship may have been a direct result of the vociferous anti-permissive backlash. This time it was the author of the source novel, Anthony Burgess, who found himself unwittingly blamed for, and having to defend, the film's violence: 'It was left to me, while the fulfilled artist Kubrick pared his nails in his house at Borehamwood, to explain to the press what the film, and for that matter the almost forgotten book, was really about, to preach a little sermon about *liberum arbitrium*, and to affirm the Catholic content' (Burgess 1990: 245–6).[9] Meanwhile, Murphy's family were also subject to obscene telephone calls.[10]

These accounts evidence the lively debates circulating around film in the early 1970s, which contributed to the increase in serious journalism and academic writing about film in the UK (on the latter, see Betz 2008), and the burden of trying to accommodate an increasingly provocative, intellectual and therefore adult content. Elsewhere, I have argued for this period as a 'late modernist' phase of European cinema, in part generated with or through the reception of films directed by Ingmar Bergman, Federico Fellini, Michelangelo Antonioni, Andrzej Wajda, Luis Buñuel and Roman Polanski in the UK during the previous decade (Halligan 2016: 37–44). In one profile, Murphy displays an awareness of this sea change in cinema-going culture, as associated with the profound social upheavals of only a few years before: 'The crunch year for the [film] industry was 1968. "It was then", said Mr Murphy, "that the cinema recognised that its audience was largely adult, and that meant of course X certificates ..."' (Mitchell 1974). This was said during what appears to have been a pre-emptive initiative to democratize censorship through wider consultation, via test screenings of *Stardust* (Michael Apted 1974) in the regions, and so away from metropolitan sophisticates.[11] If Murphy's 'crunch' was in relation to the popularity of Dennis Hopper's *Easy Rider*, certified X in June 1969, then it would be understandable that *Stardust* could be read as a pale British equivalent: polyamorous sex and drug use in the hedonistic contemporary counterculture. However, even this initiative seems to have backfired: *Stardust* was eventually modestly certified as AA (barred to those under 14), occasioning further criticism for the BBFC. Despite such attempts to be a forward-looking film censor for the 1970s, Murphy was inexorably caught in the crossfire and seemingly became collateral damage. As per Trevelyan's intimation, Murphy paid the price for Trevelyan's liberalization and stepped down as Board secretary on 3 January 1975. A causal link can be reasonably assumed between Murphy's premature resignation and the controversies, especially considering both his age and his relatively short period as Board secretary. He subsequently returned to work for the Independent Broadcasting Authority ('Murphy Back' 1976: 13).

But an additional comment is warranted in terms of thinking about Murphy's BBFC career. Some of the films passed on Trevelyan's watch may be said to have provoked such intense experiences – in terms of sensuality, hysteria, art and their immersions into unknown worlds, and with such a totality of critique of the institutions of state – that the X certificate had effectively allowed for, particularly in the staid British context, the beginnings of a step forward to a new kind of British cinema altogether. This is particularly true of Ken Russell's work from this period. Anecdotally, few seem to forget the discombobulating impact of seeing *Women in Love* (1969) or, especially, *The Devils* (1972), or specifics of their imagery, upon their initial releases – even now, more than five decades later. That impact is often, in memory, entwined with stories of what it meant to be alive at such moments of upheaval and renewal. In this sense, Trevelyan's X certificate, like Moses' staff, parted the Red Sea to such an extent that a cautious Murphy would invariably prevaricate in his wake – uncertain as to the desirability of the promised land ahead – and became assailed by the latter-day Egyptians (the anti-permissives on one side, and the intellectuals and connoisseurs of this post-1968 cinema culture on the other) in hot pursuit. Alternatively, Murphy's positions of 1971–5 may be read, in retrospect, as part of a wider informal project of rolling back the freedoms of 1968, which included depoliticizing art – a tendency given succour and support by the anti-permissives, who would find their eventual champion in Margaret Thatcher's Conservative Party and their proclaimed establishment of, in Jeffery Weeks's term, a 'new moralism' (1992: 277) or, for Matthew Grimley, paraphrasing Thatcher's advisor Keith Joseph, a 'remoralisation of society' to meet that 'crisis of values' (2012: 78). These were identified, at the time, as 'Victorian values', and this was the context of Boyson's position on the detriment of curtailing the thrashing of schoolchildren, and the kind of straitened solution that the Festival of Light had been looking for.

These liberalizations seem to have been predominantly connected to matters of sex and violence on the screen, so that contentious artistic statements could be afforded a licence for release via the X certificate. The operationalization of this process, now more than half a century ago, is difficult to track. An empirical analysis of the BBFC's files would not reveal substantive information about pre-meeting meetings, informal and advisory, through which films at the point of their conception (i.e. on paper, and before any celluloid had been exposed) were shaped by BBFC advice and warning. For this reason, Trevelyan's memoirs, which do outline stages of this process, are a key source for this chapter. However, a certain set of determining predilections – predicated on class, on collegiality and on a conception of worthy or progressive art – were likely at play. And those predilections coalesced around representations of sex and violence, as the optics for a changing society (for both Trevelyan and the Festival of Light), rather than horror. This chapter therefore considers the paradigms of the differing processes of certification (rather than classification, since almost all films discussed here are X certified) afforded to horror, as different to sex and violence. My argument is one of (historical) institutional critique, looking to the lacuna of the BBFC's liberalization. Beyond that, and looking to star studies approaches, I sketch out what appears to have been the effect on British horror during this regime of certification.

'Horror films were rarely a problem ...'

Trevelyan's twin concerns regarding sex and violence structure *What the Censor Saw*. Chapter 7 is 'Nudity', chapter 8 is 'Sex', and chapter 11 is 'Violence', and the seemingly outlier 'Underground Films' (chapter 9) and 'The American Scene' (chapter 13) are mostly considered in respect to sex and violence. (And studies of film and censorship covering these years from Wistrich, 1978, and Aldgate, 1995, are the same in their twin foci as well.) The majority of critical writing about Trevelyan's and Murphy's BBFC tenures tends to consider the indexical shifts in what may or may not be shown in respect of sex and violence – citing watershed moments of pubic hair (as with Antonioni's *Blow-Up*, 1966) or male genitalia (as with *Women in Love*), or the realistic rendition of violence, as with the torture scenes of *The Devils*, or specifics of sexualized violence (particularly rape, as in *Straw Dogs* and *A Clockwork Orange*). What is missing – and Trevelyan sweeps it into the miscellanea of his chapter 12, 'Odds and Ends' – is the matter of horror. This is all the more striking if we consider that British cinema was arguably in the midst of a 'Golden Age' of horror – and that horror is now remembered as a hallmark of British cinema. Indeed, horror as a genre represented a major element in the prehistory of the X certificate: the H certificate (for 'horrific'), in operation since 1932, was replaced by the X in 1951. Since histories of British censorship of this period turn to matters of these indexical shifts and the arguments around them – thereby taking a lead from Trevelyan – as well as the activism (or echoes of it) of the Festival of Light and NVALA, the question arises as to the BBFC conception of that seemingly marginalized strain of British filmmaking: horror. This does not generate heroic narratives of the artist versus the censor but provides an insight into the nature of the impact of censorship on production more generally.

A consideration of the BBFC's reception of horror needs to be placed with respect to their effective two-track approach, as noted in the Introduction to this volume, and across a number of chapters. On the one hand, there was a preference for the liberal intellectual films, sometimes initiating joint work (between the BBFC and filmmakers) to retain the integrity of the artistic vision of such films. On the other hand, there was an a priori distaste for sexploitation, and those films were subjected to cutting. Before this consideration, however, I wish to speculate as to some of the reasons why horror, which was decidedly heading to the X certificate category, was not a primary point of extended discussion, as with the liberal intellectual films category, in these years. Indeed, to Murphy's seeming chagrin, it was only with the arguments around the certification of *The Exorcist* (William Friedkin 1973) that pure horror (unlike, say, the historical drama *The Devils*) finally caught up as deserving of attention.

First, horror seemed to have become a vehicle for sex and violence, which took an ever-greater prominence in nominal horror films – to the extent of horror offering access to otherwise straightforward sex and violence. But one should preserve nuance, rather than universalize, in any reading of this notion. *Vampyres* (José Ramon Larraz 1974) repeatedly adjusts its balance around the entwining of horror, sex and violence. For horror, there is an old dark house and a holidaying couple unwisely isolated in a caravan on its grounds. For sex, there are prolonged scenes of nudity and sexual activity, with the two titular female vampires (Marianne Morris and Anulka Dziubinska) seducing passers-by. As for violence, the encounters with the vampires invariably lead to blood-letting, on a scale from realistic to spectacular via a particularly stark sequence of projectile bleeding against white bathroom tiles. The impressions of horror are the weakest, even in a film that embraces so entirely the tropes of the genre. The same kind of calculation remains true of innumerable British horrors of the early 1970s: *The Vampire Lovers* (Roy Ward Baker 1970), *Incense for the Damned* (Robert Hartford-Davis 1971), *Lust for a Vampire* (Jimmy Sangster 1971), *Twins of Evil* (John Hough 1971), *Dracula A.D. 1972* (Alan Gibson 1972), *Virgin Witch* (Ray Austin 1972) and *The Satanic Rites of Dracula* (Gibson 1974), to name only a few. One could also note the Lorrimer publication *The House of Horror: The Story of Hammer Films*, with the briefly sketched story itself giving way to a black-and-white soft porn pictorial appendix called 'Brides of Dracula • and Others: Hammer's leading ladies' (Eyles, Adkinson, and Fry [1973] 1975: 94–109). Indeed the studio had flogged its 'Hammer Glamour' selling point in corporate communications (such as Christmas cards) since the mid-1960s (see Hearn 2009: 6–8), and Hammer-affiliated actresses frequently appeared nude in *Titbits* and *Parade* magazines. Barnett notes the split in critical evaluations of *The Vampire Lovers* accordingly: either as heralding Hammer's (and co-production associates) 'qualitative decline' to 'softcore pornography' or as an 'evocative and engaging ... new eroticised approach' (2022: 26). This split looked to a wider question of how Hammer should have transformed on the cusp of the new decade – a question Hammer themselves answered with *Dracula A.D. 1972* (Alan Gibson 1972), which is now cited as an example of their floundering.

Second, the target of choice for anti-permissive activists was sex – mainly in the cinema and on television but also, particularly in the early 1980s, in relation to sex education in schools. This targeting, via the Festival of Light, coincided directly with the change-over from Trevelyan to Murphy, as if an interregnum around July 1971 might allow for a re-alignment of BBFC policy with a censorious morality. And this re-alignment could possibly compensate for, or retrospectively offer correction to, a series of films that seemed to be released without attracting much criticism of the BBFC for their X certifications: *Flesh* (Paul Morrissey 1968), *Witchfinder General*

(Michael Reeves 1968) and *Midnight Cowboy* (John Schlesinger 1969). The next series of films courting outrage were, in contrast, all subsequently decried: *The Devils, Straw Dogs, A Clockwork Orange*, and with the belated additions of *Last Tango in Paris* (Bernardo Bertolucci 1972), *The Exorcist* and *Mera ur Kärlekens språk* (*More About the Language of Love*, Torgny Wickman 1970; first submitted to the BBFC, and declined certification, in 1974). NVALA members would sometimes have to endure these films, as part of waging a media campaign against them – writing letters to regional newspapers and local councillors, crashing town hall meetings, prays-ins outside local authority meetings and talking directly to Members of Parliament, particularly those endangered by their modest electoral majorities.[12] This was no small hardship for NVALA members. Even a seasoned cultural commentator such as John Fraser, for his study *Violence in the Arts*, confessed that he 'could not bring' himself to view *The Devils* (1974: 179). With so much contentious material in circulation, and subject to criticism, the smuggling of sex and violence into horror may have been somewhat effective – removing such nominal horror films (bar the higher profile ones, such as *The Exorcist*) from the direct line of anti-permissive fire.

Third, horror as genre film was seemingly not tied so directly to the changes in the times – in the way I describe as indexical, above. Therefore, defence or mitigation that horror dealt with contemporary mores, and so deserved the expanded freedom of expression that the BBFC afforded to more artistically inclined filmmakers, was not so tenable. Genre, rather, was considered self-contained, with films riffing off preconceived expectations: a form of vernacular entertainment for those with a penchant for their particulars.[13] While horror was 'adult cinema', it was seemingly simply not that 'adult' as an art form.

Finally, in relation to an assumed 'low culture' status of horror and as per Reeves's experience with Trevelyan during the cutting of *Witchfinder General*, horror per se appears not to have been considered a worthy or appropriate ground for battles of freedom of expression, artistic integrity and artistic licence.[14] Questionable interlopers, such as *Witchfinder* producer Tony Tenser (whose milieu was encountered in author Richard Wortley's pseudo-sociological 1969 study of strippers, *Skin Deep in Soho*), meant that discourse with the BBFC was seemingly more around what could reasonably be allowed to be shown to denizens of Tenser's Compton Cinema Club, in a Soho basement, than akin to the Oxford Union debating society (of, say, John Schlesinger's background). Indeed, a distinct divide is recalled in cinemas of the 1960s, which can be read directly in class terms. This can be seen in the starkly contrasting environs of 'thick carpets', 'high ceilings', 'plush' and 'gleaming' foyers and 'sumptuous and elegant lobbies', with 'the local flea-pit' with 'a cheaper ticket price', 'an occasional cat wandering about in the dark', 'lit by gas and ... very cold', and where the films, rather than prestige new releases, 'tend[ed] towards the unsavoury', and 'X-rated, mainly horror films' (Stokes, Jones, and Pett 2022: 25–6).

Liberal debates around enhancing the freedoms for artistic expression were confined to the prestige new releases category, and Trevelyan, writing in 1970, was entirely unapologetic about this bias. This preference could be maintained in the BBFC through a lack of accountability for decisions: 'If there were rules they would have to be applied equally to films of quality and to films of commercial exploitation' (Trevelyan 1970: 25). The avoidance of any set guidance in terms of cutting, irrespective of any resultant 'degree of apparent inconsistency', is then simply 'the price to be paid for having no rules' (Trevelyan 1970: 25). And Trevelyan also adds a measure of obscurantism to the inequities of process, claiming that his censors draw on 'an accumulated knowledge of the films censored over the years' in their advice, and understanding of 'what is, and what is not, technically possible', and with the secretary himself in possession of 'considerable technical knowledge of this kind' (Trevelyan 1970: 25).[15] Simkin's overview of BBFC censorship in 1970–5 suggests that this position on horror remained in operation beyond Trevelyan's time, since Simkin rarely notes horror cutting as something that prompted debate or kickback – beyond *The Devils* (as noted above, arguably not really a horror film). Actual horror films seemed to have been cut for their sexual content alone: *Exposé* (James Kenelm Clarke 1976), *Vampyres*, *Lust for a Vampire* and *Twins of Evil* (Simkin 2012: 83, 84). Nor does horror warrant a case study in Barber's wider study of British cinema in the 1970s (2013), despite her openness to the inclusion of genre and 'low culture' films, such as *Confessions of a Window Cleaner* (Val Guest 1974).

Trevelyan's recollections of dealing with *Hexen bis aufs Blut gequält* (*Mark of the Devil*, Michael Armstrong 1970) – a film often taken to have been made under the influence of *Witchfinder General* – illustrate the BBFC's different approach to horror, as censors rather than classifiers. Trevelyan wrote to the S. F. Films, the distributors who were requesting classification, that the film was 'filthy and disgusting … a clear candidate for total rejection' (cited in Petley 2017), and later recounted that the film represented the way in which 'this kind of violence presented as entertainment is inexcusable' (Trevelyan 1977: 160). In the event, the film was cut by twenty-four minutes to gain an X certificate.[16] Trevelyan recalled that, of problems with American International Pictures (AIP) and Roger Corman films, and lurid Continental horrors from Mario Bava, 'One help to us was that nobody took these films seriously; this included the people who made them as well as the audiences. They were always "X" films of course; indeed the production companies would have been very unhappy if they had not been!' (166). This reading of horror was more than a cynical boast. Trevelyan outlines a gentleman's agreement that seemed aimed at keeping the better-financed horror producers, Hammer Films, reined in rather than generating the bases for polemics:

Horror films were rarely a problem since most of them came to us from Hammer Films, the most successful production company in this field, from whom we always had full co-operation ... I remember a talk that I had with Sir James (Jimmy) Carreras many years ago in which we agreed that his company's horror films would avoid mixing sex with horror and would avoid scenes which people could regard as disgusting and revolting. The second part of this agreement has continued to the present day [1973], but in an increasingly permissive age we modified our attitude to the introduction of sex.

(1977: 165–6)

In terms of reputable credentials then, despite the horror, Hammer received the Queen's Award for Industry in 1968 and Carreras was knighted in 1970.[17] It is telling that, in this, horror can be considered to be an enterprise of industry; it would be unimaginable for the same Royal recognition to be offered to comparable doyens of sexploitation, whose actresses also appeared nude in publicity pictorials, as with Tenser's Tigon British Film Productions and *Cinema X* magazine. Between the BBFC and Buckingham Palace, horror seems to have been kept in its place (see Plate 15).

A Fear of the Working Classes

Any such operative prejudice against horror could reasonably also be taken to contextualize the idiosyncratically conservative nature of British X horror of the mid- to late 1960s. The Anglo-Amalgamated films that preceded Hammer's most profitable years, which David Pirie dubbed 'Sadian movies' (1973: 96–106) – *Horrors of the Black Museum* (Arthur Crabtree 1959), *Circus of Horrors* (Sidney Hayers 1960) and *Peeping Tom* (Michael Powell 1960) – seem an *entrée* into the hedonistic post-war, post-austerity world of the working classes. In Adam Lowenstein's reading, *Peeping Tom* '... exacerbates [the] anxieties of "classlessness" precipitated by an ascendant mass culture in late 1950s and early 1960s Britain' (2000: 221). *Peeping Tom*'s Soho, a rainy, ill-lit, unpoliced inner London enclave of prostitutes and pornography that had remained resistant to (or indeed complimented) the creeping embourgeoisement of post-war British life, suggests a zone of uninhibited working-class pastimes and opportunities. The same seems true for the sensationalist London of *Horrors of the Black Museum* – a semi-criminal underworld of spivs and elderly bachelors preying on readily available younger flesh, and with such women living alone in bedsits and rapidly falling into prostitution (at any rate, the film blurs any distinction). All this is seen as daily fodder for the gloating tabloids. A bloody climax is played out, in public, in *the* locale of raucous working-class entertainment: the fairground. Similarly, the circus of *Circus of Horrors* seems little more than a locus of accidents, animal maulings and sexual assaults – with the open-mouthed nightly audiences (and attendant suspicious detectives) flocking back for more. Such deeply misanthropic visions are unredeemed by the moral lessons or comeuppance that usually underwrite forays into this territory. Leery fascination is not at one remove here, or rendered 'safe' via the kind of period framing that Hammer preferred in the 1960s; Anglo-Amalgamated's mise en scène is one of crude titillation rather than stylized and plush Gothic aestheticism.

By the end of the 1960s, the iconographic male stars of British horror – Christopher Lee, Peter Cushing and Boris Karloff – were rarely presiding over such Anglo-Amalgamated-type 'low culture' carnage. They offered, this time, an *entrée* into the specialist realm of the supernatural rather than an immersion in working-class cultures. In this, the intimation of fissures in polite society, through which the ungodly (often equated with un-English, or non-white) can be glimpsed, and occasionally encountered, now comes to the fore. Thus Charles Gray's smarmy Head Satanist, Mocata, in *The Devil Rides Out* (Terence Fisher 1968) gilds his language and arch delivery with apologetic politeness in the drawing room of the country manor which he is threatening with a demonic onslaught, even at the point of his ejection ('I shall not be back ... but something will'). The arena of battle for this type of horror is positioned in the locale of civilized and well-to-do society, mostly by Hammer: the country cottage or estate, or crumbling ancestral pile, often features – with a mise en scène of libraries with roaring fires, oil paintings in oak-panelled drawing rooms, and drinks, cabinets and smoking jackets. The Satanic arrangements of *The Devil Rides Out* or *Blue Blood* (Andrew Sinclair 1974) turn out to be so effective since they have been easily accommodated within this *Country Life*-type milieu: Lee's Duc de Richleau, in the former, gathers intelligence by breezing through a formal cocktail reception in a country manor. One could contrast this sophistication to the cruder narrative movements to scenes of orgies of non-Hammer films with horror or supernatural themes that attempted to document or recreate non-Christian religious belief systems and rituals: in rural Cornwall (seemingly around Boscastle) for *Legend of the Witches* (Malcolm Leigh 1970); in swinging Kensington for *Secret Rites* (Derek Ford 1971), with the actual occultist, Alex Sanders, presiding; and decamped to Greece, for *Incense for the Damned*.

The affiliations of the iconographic personnel of British horror were uncertain, or changeable, across any number of films: they seemed to move freely from being heroes to villains and back again. Their authority was predicated from a position of knowledge and expertise in arcane matters (Duc de Richleau in *The Devil Rides Out* has made 'a very deep study of these esoteric doctrines') or scientific matters (Andrew Keir's Professor Bernard Quatermass of *Quatermass and the Pit*, Roy Ward Baker 1967);

time spent in libraries and laboratories, in archives and at archaeological sites, and examining ancient tomes, often figure. Such gaining of knowledge and expertise is a prerequisite, and one of the planes of spiritual battle itself. Thus the deus ex machina exorcist mantra that dispels the Angel of Death in *The Devil Rides Out* is lifted from an earlier phase of research ('It is vital that I should go to the British Museum and examine certain occult volumes that are kept under constant lock and key'). The weaponization of the scientific theory that dispels the demon Martian of *Quatermass and the Pit*, towering over the London skyline, seems to need an advanced knowledge of both astrophysics and telekinesis. Or again, in *Incense for the Damned*, the son of the British Foreign Secretary (Patrick Mower) is lured from his Oxford rooms and into the clutches of a jet-setting, LSD-imbibing demonic cult, while on a sabbatical field trip to Greece for his academic research and next monograph.

Conclusion: The Classification of Horror

For such iconographic stars, the authority invested in them is founded on a blind faith: they are those who are the cognizant among us (rather than the formally clerical), and whose warnings against hidden dangers necessarily go unheeded precisely because they cannot or will not provide evidence for the existence of the unseen world. Despite their involvement in or familiarity with the supernatural, the characters played by Lee, Cushing and Karloff are to be found in civilized circles: urbane and sophisticated and rarely ruffled. They retain access to all levels of society – indeed, mediate between them, or use polite society as a cover for their dark deeds or wayward scientific experiments. The male innocent foils, invariably well-groomed and behaved, are colourless (in the sense of being transparent) in comparison. Occultism and spirituality, in this context, seem more like harmless pastimes – interests for the well heeled, as in *Blithe Spirit* (David Lean 1945) – rather than anything more sinister. In the films that resolve with the restoration of the status quo, these iconographic stars suggest a new patriarchy then, within upper-class milieu; the realm of the supernatural is now placed with these envoys of class interest. This makes for horror of a quite different order, and type, to that identified by Pirie as 'Sadian movies' (1973: 96–106). Hammer X films, in this respect, may be read as the conservative antithesis to that transgressive, Sadian thesis: castles over circuses, Transylvania over Soho, eroticism over sexploitation.

The emergence of such a conservative characteristic in horror then may be situated within the wider nexus of cutting, classifying, certifying and censoring: as pre-emptively accommodating anticipated BBFC cautioning, and delivering Queen-approved industrial product. In this, the X certificate would seem to function not so much in relation to debates around excised bits of film, so that some stretches of celluloid may be certified, and other stretches may not be, and what that means for integral artistic visions. Rather, the X certificate represents an anticipatory, corrective régime of permissions that may be granted or denied, and so effectively altered the nature of British horror at the point of, or even prior to, its actual making.

Notes

1   On the constitution of the Festival of Light itself, see Whipple (2011). Charles Windsor would find that his return message to the organizers, acknowledging one rally, was read out to the massed attendees as an endorsement – appropriately or otherwise; see Capon (1972: 70, 73).

2   While Trevelyan is remembered as associated with this phase, Murphy (born 1922) seems forgotten; upon inquiry, the BBFC were unable to provide any biographical information. Enid Wistrich includes an unflattering portrait of Murphy in her memoirs of running the Film Viewing Board of the Greater London Council, including the offer of an encounter with his 'special collection' of 'violent horrors': '[t]he inference was that once the little lady had seen the naughty films, she would be so shocked that she would fall back on the big strong men for protection ... I have never appreciated condescension from men' (1978: 25, 112–3). Newspaper profiles of Murphy note Oxford and previous roles as a teacher, a BBC Education Officer and with the regulatory body, the Independent Broadcasting Authority (Blacklock 1972: 11; Callan 1975: 11).

3   The resultant tussle saw Winner given releases for his film as a BBFC X, and then an A (via the Greater London Council), which prompted the BBFC to downgrade the X to AA. Upton notes that AA had been Trevelyan's 1970 strategy to lessen the number of X certifications (2017: 64–76). On *Scorpio*'s ratings, see Harding (1978: 92). The Festival of Light attempted to directly intervene in the BBFC classification system, making a case for Y and Z ratings for pornography (presumably defined as any element of nudity), as only for those over 25, during a 1972 meeting with the Home Office (Simkin 2012: 73).

4   On this operation, see *Trash* file (n.d.), and for a list of such films, see Wistrich (1978: 147–9). As noted below, the BBFC came under criticism for the amount of time these bureaucratic processes sometimes took.

5   For a selection of correspondence from Whitehouse and her associates in relation to targeted films, see Thompson (2013: 209–35). On, for example, the BBFC's position on the release of Swedish sex education films, see Smith (2018: 34–51). For the Festival of Light's attempts to intervene in film release matters via local councils, see Phelps (1973). 'White coaters' typically claimed a sociological imperative, via documentary-style voice-overs and occasional doctor-type figures, sometimes with both voice-overs and these 'doctors' condemning the very same things that the films showed at length and in

detail. For a discussion of the BBFC's handling of the documentary aspirations of sexploitation, see Hunter (2013: 114). On police raids of cinema clubs, Viscount Norwich (John Julius Cooper) noted concern, in the House of Lords on 24 February 1970, around the thirty-two police constables descending on the Open Space theatre club to seize a print of *Flesh* (Paul Morrissey 1968), and projection equipment, on the grounds of a violation of the Obscene Publications Act of 1959 (and with Trevelyan, telephoned and arriving at the scene by taxi, unable to stop the confiscation). The grounds were then changed to a violation of licensing laws, then to a violation of fire safety regulations, then seemingly to a matter of unspecified fraud, and with the disruptions costing the Open Theatre half of their annual Arts Council grant; see Norwich (1970). The film had not been BBFC certified, but Trevelyan himself had suggested a film club screening release.

6   The 5th Baron Harlech (David Ormsby-Gore, 1918–85) was then president of the BBFC. One rumour as to Murphy's misfortunes concerned his deteriorating eyesight: he would tend to request cuts in respect to what he could hear of a film, rather than what he could actually see of it. The 'somewhat modified' comment is an understatement: certifying *The Devils* prompted considerable discussion and cutting, which did little to temper the condemnations once the film was released, not least after the sensationalist newspaper coverage of its making; see Petley (2015). On releasing *The Devils*, see Crouse (2012). Paul Hoffman's fictionalized account of a BBFC examiner also includes a reflection on the terminal situation Murphy seemingly walked into: 'it is hard to think of a legacy more certain to destroy his successor' (2007: 20).

7   Walker also reproduces an anonymous complaint from 'someone close to the film' that Murphy's maladroit handling of requested cuts had effectively turned a serial vaginal rape into vaginal and anal rape (1971b: 21). Simkin cites an undated internal BBFC note that makes the same claim – that the resultant 'impression' of anal rape 'is a result of the Company's cuts to reduce the sequence to help us' (2012: 83).

8   Writing a letter to *The Times*, a 'newspaper of record', was taken to be the firmest of rejoinders from middle-class individuals – airing their disgruntlement in a forum that was inevitably read by those with political power and sway over policy.

9   One such critic was the associate of Whitehouse and Longford, and serial rapist, the television personality Jimmy Savile, during a radio encounter with Burgess. See Burgess (1990: 256–7) on the encounter with Savile, and Halligan (2022) on Savile's associations with Whitehouse and Longford.

10 The BBFC examiner Ken Penry recalls Murphy telling him this in the BBC *Timeshift* documentary *Dear Censor* (tx 29 September 2011).

11 This outreach strategy of a wider consultation, as recalibrating censorship strategy to that of interested parties and their cultural sensitivities, anticipated the BBFC's position of the last decade or so: the BBFC rebranded as a family service. Of their mobile phone application, for example, the BBFC note: 'Use our app to find out the latest age ratings and ratings info of the content you're

thinking of watching – so you can choose what's right for you and your family ... At the BBFC, our focus is on helping children and families choose well by providing them with the guidance they need ...'; https://www.bbfc.co.uk/about-us/our-app (accessed 21 March 2022). Murphy's innovation, then, was a far-sighted breaking with the more absolute judgement of the Trevelyan era – and censorship sometimes achieved through un-minuted, informal discussions, on the untested basis of what Trevelyan, representing the BBFC, felt should or should not be shown at that point. For an on-the-spot report around such BBFC workings, see Perrott (1968). On *Stardust*, see Barber (2013: 125–41).

12 On such campaigning, from NVALA and as then taken up by as a model of practice, see Egan (2020).

13 The project, in part, of *Movie* journal during these years was to counter such reductive ideas, and the structuralist critique of this moment was well suited to the task. Tellingly, an early history of British 1960s cinema from film journalists and educators Terence Kelly, Graham Norton and George Perry, proposes that two new certificates come into operation once the BBFC, which 'should be abolished', is replaced by the British Film Institute (1966: 188). First, the authors argue for the reintroduction of 'H' for films 'containing horrific scenes' – for this they cite Robert Aldrich's psychological thriller *Hush... Hush, Sweet Charlotte* (1964) and the Amicus horror *Dr. Terror's House of Horrors* (Freddie Francis 1965), both of which contain elements of comedy or camp. Second, they suggest a 'XH' for 'adult films with horrific scenes', for which they indicatively cite *Psycho* (Alfred Hitchcock 1960) and *Repulsion* (Polanski 1965). X films, 'likely to appeal to mature minds', are then seemingly redeemed by being the esteemed category of Schlesinger, Jean-Luc Godard and Antonioni (Kelly, Norton, and Perry 1966: 188). Their proposal implies that horror would remain somewhat quarantined: away from, since effectively not a part of, worthy filmmaking. Their suggestion was not taken up but it highlights that the BBFC, the Institute for Economic Affairs (the publishers of Kelly, Norton and Perry) and the Festival of Light – regulatory, free market and moralistic entities – held the same position in common, which was their essential disregard for horror.

14 For a detailed discussion of this process around *Witchfinder General*, see Halligan (2003: 120–4, 152–62).

15 Simkin also cites an internal BBFC note evidencing the persistence of this mindset among the censors: '... for the past decade at least the board has not been so ready to treat arthouse movies like Fiona Cooper tapes [i.e. softcore stripping VHS videos, of the late 1980s and mid-1990s] and to cut, mechanically, when a certain level of genital exposure is noted ...' (cited in Simkin 2012: 214 n. 90).

16 Petley (2017) details the particulars of this process of cutting.

17 Hammer had also made non-adult films – see Frith (2020) – but the acceptance of the prize by Hammer's horror icons underscores how this recognition was understood.

References

Aldgate, A. (1995), *Censorship and the Permissive Society: British Cinema & Theatre, 1955–1965*, Oxford: Clarendon Press.

Bakewell, J. and N. Garnham (1970), *The New Priesthood: British Television Today*, London: Allen Lane.

Barber, S. (2013), *The British Film Industry in the 1970s: Capital, Culture and Creativity*, Houndsmills, Basingstroke: Palgrave Macmillan.

Barnett, V. L. (2022), '*The Vampire Lovers* and Hammer's Post-1970 Production Strategy', *Journal of British Cinema and Television*, 19 (1): 22–44.

Betz, M. (2008), 'Little Books', in L. Grieveson and H. Wasson (eds), *Inventing Film Studies*, 319–49, Durham, NC: Duke University Press.

Blacklock, P. (1972), 'How the Film Censor Sees His Own Role', *Country Times and Gazette*, 28 January: 11.

Boyson, R. (1996), *Boyson on Education*, London: Peter Owen Publishers.

Burgess, A. (1990), *You've Had Your Time: Being the Second Part of the Confessions of Anthony Burgess*, London: Heinemann.

Callan, P. (1975), 'Censor Murphy Seeks New Role', *Daily Mirror*, 21 July.

Capon, J. (1972), *... And There Was Light: The Story of the Nationwide Festival of Light*, London: Lutterworth Press.

Cashin, F., J. Coleman, N. Hibbin, M. Hinxman, D. Malcolm, G. Melly, T. Palmer, M. Plowright, D. Powell, D. Robinson, J. R. Taylor, A. Thirkell, and A. Walker (1971), 'Film Censorship', *The Times*, 17 December.

Crouse, R. (2012), *Raising Hell: Ken Russell and the Unmaking of The Devils*, Toronto: ECW Press.

'"Dismiss Censor" call as *Last Tango* Gets an X' (1973), *The Birmingham Post*, 17 February.

Dumoulin, E. (1968), *The Cult of Pain*, North Hollywood: Brandon House.

Egan, K. (2020), '"The Film That's Banned in Harrogate": *Monty Python's Life of Brian* (1979), Local Censorship, Comedy and Local Resistance', *Historical Journal of Film, Radio and Television*, 41 (1): 152–71.

Eyles, A., R. Adkinson, and N. Fry ([1973] 1975), *The House of Horror: The Story of Hammer Films*, London: Lorrimer Publishing.

Fraser, J. (1974), *Violence in the Arts*, London: Cambridge University Press.

Frith, P. (2020), '"Wholesome Rough Stuff": Hammer Films and the "A" and "U" Certificate, 1959–1965', in D. Petrie, M. Williams, and L. Mayne (eds), *Sixties British Cinema Reconsidered*, 151–64, Edinburgh: Edinburgh University Press.

Grimley, M. (2012), 'Thatcherism, Morality and Religion', in B. Jackson and R. Saunders (eds), *Making Thatcher's Britain*, 78–94, Cambridge: Cambridge University Press.

Gummer, J. (1971), *The Permissive Society: Fact or Fantasy?*, London: Cassell.

Halligan, B. (2003), *Michael Reeves*, Manchester: Manchester University Press.

Halligan, B. (2016), *Desires for Reality: Radicalism and Revolution in Western European Film*, London: Berghahn Books.

Halligan, B. (2022), *Hotbeds of Licentiousness: The British Glamour Film and the Permissive Society*, London: Berghahn Books.

Harding, B. (1978), *The Films of Michael Winner*, London: Frederick Muller Ltd.

Hearn, M. (2009), *Hammer Glamour*, London: Titan Books.

Hoffenberg, M. (1967), *Sin for Breakfast*, New York: The Traveller's Companion.

Hoffman, P. (2007), *The Golden Age of Censorship: A Novel*, London: Doubleday.

Holbrook, D. (1972a), *The Case Against Pornography*, London: Tom Stacey.

Holbrook, D. (1972b), *The Masks of Hate: The Problem of False Solutions in the Culture of an Acquisitive Society*, Oxford: Pergamon Press.

Holbrook, D. (1972c), *The Pseudo-Revolution: A Critical Study of Extremist 'Liberation' in Sex*, London: Tom Stacey.

Holbrook, D. (1972d), *Sex and Dehumanization: In Art, Thought and Life in Our Times*, London: Pitman.

Hunter, I. Q. (2013), *British Trash Cinema*, London: Palgrave Macmillan.

Kelly, T. with G. Norton and G. Perry (1966), *A Competitive Cinema*, London: Institute of Economic Affairs.

Krämer, P. (2011), *A Clockwork Orange*, Hampshire: Palgrave Macmillan.

Lowenstein, A. (2000), '"Under-the-Skin Horrors": Social Realism and Classlessness in *Peeping Tom* and the British New Wave"', in J. Ashby and A. Higson (eds), *British Cinema, Past and Present*, 221–32, London: Routledge.

Malone, M. (1970), '"Some People Think I Am Entirely Responsible for the Permissive Society": John Trevelyan, Britain's Film Censor, Talks to Mary Malone', *Daily Mirror*, 17 September.

Manners, E. (1971), *The Vulnerable Generation*, London: Cassell.

'Michael Winner Blasts British Censor Murphy for X-rating *Scorpio*' (1973), *Variety*, 15 August: 19.

Mitchell, L. (1974), 'Public Gets the Films It Deserves – says the Censor', *Evening Express*, 18 October.

'Murphy Back to the IBA' (1976), *The Stage and Television Today*, 23 September: 13.

Norwich, Viscount (1970), 'Open Space Theatre and Film Seizure by Police', House of Lords debates, 24 February, *Hansard*, volume 308: columns 38–40.

Perrott, R. (1986), 'Behind the Scenes with John Trevelyan', *Observer Colour Magazine*, 15 September: 41–4.

Petley, J. (2015), 'Witch-hunt: The Word, the Press and *The Devils*', *Journal of British Cinema and Television*, 12 (4): 515–38.

Petley, J. (2017), 'Witchfinding in General and the Censors', *Cine-Excess*, no. 3. Available online: https://www.cine-excess.co.uk/witchfinding-in-general-and-the-censors.html (accessed 20 September 2021).

Phelps, G. (1973), 'Censorship and the Press', *Sight and Sound*, 42 (3): 138–40.

Pirie, D. (1973), *A Heritage of Horror: The English Gothic Cinema*, London: Gordon Fraser.

'Rallying for Love and Family Life' (1971), *The Glasgow Herald*, 12 July.

Simkin, S. (2012), 'Wake of the Flood: Key Issues in UK Censorship, 1970–75', in E. Lamberti with J. Green, D. Hyman, C. Lapper and K. Myers, *Behind the Scenes at the BBFC: Film Classification from the Silver Screen to the Digital Age*, 72–86, London: Palgrave Macmillan, British Film Institute.

Smith, A. (2018), '*The Language of Love*: Swedish Sex Education in 1970s London', *Film Studies*, 18 (1): 34–51.

Stokes, M., M. Jones, and E. Pett (2022), *Cinema Memories: A People's History of Cinema-going in 1960s Britain*, London: BFI Publishing.

Thompson, B. (2013), *Ban This Filth! Mary Whitehouse and the Battle to Keep Britain Innocent*, London: Faber and Faber.

Thompson, T. [pseud.] (1968), *Lesbian Career Woman*, North Hollywood: Brandon House.

Trash file (1970), BBFC case study, n.d. Available online: https://www.bbfc.co.uk/education/case-studies/trash (accessed 10 September 2021).

Trevelyan, J. (1970), 'Film Censorship in Great Britain', *Screen*, 11 (3): 19–30.

Trevelyan, J. (1977), *What the Censor Saw*, London: Michael Joseph.

Upton, J. (2017), 'Innocence Unprotected? Permissiveness and the AA Certificate 1970–1982', *Journal of British Cinema and Television*, 1 (14): 64–76.

Walker, A. (1971a), 'The Thing That Worries the New Film Censor … It's Not Sex', *Evening Chronicle*, 21 June.

Walker, A. (1971b), 'After This, Anything Goes', *Evening Standard*, 25 November.

Weeks, J. ([1981] 1992), *Sex, Politics and Society: The Regulation of Sexuality Since 1800*, second edn, New York: Longman Group Ltd.

Weinfass, I. (2019), 'Settlement Agreed in Blacklisted Workers Case', *Construction News*, 14 May. Available online: https://www.constructionnews.co.uk/contractors/balfour-beatty/settlement-agreed-blacklisted-workers-case-14-05-2019/ (accessed 10 March 2022).

Whipple, A. C. (2011), 'Speaking for Whom? The 1971 Festival of Light and the Search for the "Silent Majority"', *Contemporary British History*, 24 (3): 319–39.

Wistrich, E. (1978), '*I Don't Mind the Sex, It's the Violence*': Film Censorship Explored, London: Marion Boyars.

Wortley, R. (1969), *Skin Deep in Soho*, London: Jarrolds Publishers.

CONTRIBUTORS

Lucy Bolton is Reader in Film Studies at Queen Mary University of London. She is the author of *Contemporary Cinema and the Philosophy of Iris Murdoch* (2019) and *Film and Female Consciousness: Irigaray, Cinema and Thinking Women* (2009), and the co-editor of *Lasting Screen Stars: Images that Fade and Personas that Endure* (2016: winner of BAFTSS best edited collection). She publishes widely on film philosophy and film stardom, and is the co-editor of the book series *Visionaries* on the work of women filmmakers.

Anne Etienne is Lecturer in Modern and Contemporary Drama at University College Cork. Her research focuses on theatre censorship and Arnold Wesker. Her publications include *Theatre Censorship: From Walpole to Wilson* (2007); a special issue of *Coup de théâtre* on Wesker's *Shylock* (2014); *Populating the Stage: Contemporary Irish Theatre* (2017), co-edited with Thierry Dubost; *Arnold Wesker: Fragments and Visions* (2021), co-edited with Graham Saunders. She is currently co-editing two volumes on theatre censorship (forthcoming 2023, 2024).

James Fenwick is Senior Lecturer in the Department of Media Arts and Communication at Sheffield Hallam University, UK. He is the author of *Stanley Kubrick Produces* (2020) and *Unproduction Studies and the American Film Industry* (2021), editor of *Understanding Kubrick's 2001: A Space Odyssey* (2018) and co-editor of *Shadow Cinema: The Historical and Production Contexts of Unmade Films* (2021). His research on the films of Stanley Kubrick has also been published in *Cinergie, Feminist Media Studies*, the *Historical Journal of Film, Radio and Television, Screening the Past* and *Senses of Cinema*.

Kevin M. Flanagan is Term Assistant Professor of English at George Mason University, USA, where he teaches courses on film, literature, Hollywood, composition and rhetoric, and the Cold War. He is author of *War Representation in British Cinema and Television: From Suez to Thatcher, and Beyond* (2019) and the editor of *Ken Russell: Re-Viewing England's Last Mannerist* (2009). He has published essays on post-war British cinema and culture in *Critical Quarterly, Framework, Screen* and the *Journal of British Cinema and Television*.

Benjamin Halligan is Director of the Doctoral College of the University of Wolverhampton, UK. His publications include *Hotbeds of Licentiousness: The British Glamour Film and the Permissive Society* (2022), *Desires for Reality: Radicalism and Revolution in Western European Film* (2016) and *Michael Reeves* (2003), and his co-edited collections are *Diva* (2023), *Politics of the Many* (2021), *Stories We Could Tell* (2018), *The Arena Concert* (2015), *The Music Documentary* (2013), *Resonances* (2013), *Reverberations* (2012) and *Mark E. Smith and The Fall* (2010).

Claire Henry is Senior Lecturer in Digital Media Production at Massey University, Aotearoa New Zealand. Her publications include a forthcoming BFI Film Classics volume on *Eraserhead* (2023), *Screening the Posthuman* (co-authored with Missy Molloy and Pansy Duncan, forthcoming 2023), *Revisionist Rape-Revenge: Redefining a Film Genre* (2014), and journal articles in *Journal of Digital Media & Policy*, *Senses of Cinema*, *Porn Studies*, *Open Cultural Studies*, *Studies in European Cinema*, *Cine-Excess* and *Frames Cinema Journal*.

Simon Lee is Assistant Professor of English at Texas State University, USA, where he researches and teaches post-war British literature with a particular focus on working-class writing and culture. He is the author of *The Intersection of Class and Space in British Postwar Writing: Kitchen Sink Aesthetics* (2023) and the editor of *Locating Classed Subjectivities: Intersections of Space and Working-Class Life in Nineteenth-, Twentieth-, and Twenty-First-Century British Writing* (2022). He has published a wide range of scholarship on British writing, specifically work from authors like Pat Barker, Shelagh Delaney, Colin MacInnes, Douglas Stuart, Nell Dunn and John Osborne.

Moya Luckett teaches at New York University's Gallatin School of Individualized Study. She is the author of *Cinema and Community: Progressivism, Exhibition and Film Culture in Chicago, 1907–1917* (2014) and co-editor of *Swinging Single: Representing Sexuality in the 1960s* (1999). Her current research explores how celebrity culture masks restricted social mobility in recessionary cultures, shaping concepts of work and discourses of failure. She has published essays on 1960s film, TV and popular culture, British cinema, femininity in mass media, celebrity culture, early cinema and fashion.

Kim Newman is a movie critic, author and broadcaster. He is a contributing editor to *Sight & Sound* and *Empire* magazines. His books include *Nightmare Movies*, *Millennium Movies*, *Kim Newman's Video Dungeon*, and BFI Classics studies of *Cat People*, *Doctor Who* and *Quatermass and the Pit*. He has also authored fiction and comics, written for television (*Mark Kermode's Secrets of Cinema*), radio (*Afternoon Theatre: Cry-Babies*) and the theatre (*The Hallowe'en Sessions*), and directed a tiny film (*Missing Girl*).

Adrian Smith is an independent researcher with interests in British and European popular cinema of the 1960s and 1970s. Recent publications include the articles 'The Language of Love: Swedish Sex Education in 1970s London' in *Film Studies* (2018) and 'International Sexpionage! European Popular Film on Sixties British Cinema Screens' in *Contemporary British History* (2021), as well as the chapter 'The Yellow Teddybears: Exploitation as Education' in *Researching Historical Screen Audiences* (2022).

Tim Snelson is Associate Professor in Media History at the University of East Anglia, UK. His research addressing the relationship between media and social history has been published in journals including *The History of Human Sciences*, *Cultural Studies* and *The Historical Journal of Film, Radio and Television*. He has a monograph titled *Phantom Ladies: Hollywood Horror and the Home Front* (2015) and is leading the AHRC-funded 'Demons of the Mind: the "Psy" Sciences and Cinema in the Long-1960s' project: www.psychologyandcinema.com

Sarah Street is Professor of Film at the University of Bristol, UK. Publications on British cinema include *British National Cinema* (1997) and *Transatlantic Crossings: British Feature Films in the USA* (2002). Publications on colour include *Colour Films in Britain: The Negotiation of Innovation, 1900–55* (2012). Her latest books are *Deborah Kerr* (2018), *Chromatic Modernity: Color, Cinema, and Media of the 1920s* (2019, with Joshua Yumibe) and *Colour Films in Britain: The Eastmancolor Revolution* (2021, with Keith M. Johnston, Paul Frith and Carolyn Rickards). She is Principal Investigator on the ERC Advanced Grant: Film Studios in Britain, France, Germany and Italy, 1930–60.

Christopher Weedman is Assistant Professor of English at Middle Tennessee State University, USA, where he serves as both Director of General Education English and advisor of the interdisciplinary Film Studies Minor. His scholarship has appeared in *Film International*, *Jewish Film and New Media*, *Journal of Cinema and Media Studies*, and the edited collections *Fifty Hollywood Directors* (2015) and *David Fincher's* Zodiac: *Cinema of Investigation and (Mis)Interpretation* (2022). He is co-editor of the collection *Liminal Noir in Classical World Cinema* (2023, with Elyce Rae Helford). Currently, he is writing a biography of Anne Heywood, the groundbreaking British film star of *The Fox* and *I Want What I Want*.

INDEX